Lincroft Academy
Station Road, Oakley, Bedford MK43 7RE
School No. 8225404 Tel: 01234 822147
e-mail: administration@lincroft.academy
www.lincroft.beds.sch.uk

HEALTH AND SOCIAL CARE

SECOND EDITION

J835

Judith Adams, Mary Riley & Maria Ferreiro Peteiro

The teaching content of this resource is endorsed by OCR for use with specification OCR Level 1/Level 2 Cambridge National in Health and Social Care (J835).

All references to assessment, including assessment preparation and practice questions of any format/style are the publisher's interpretation of the specification and are not endorsed by OCR.

This resource was designed for use with the version of the specification available at the time of publication. However, as specifications are updated over time, there may be contradictions between the resource and the specification, therefore please use the information on the latest specification and Sample Assessment Materials at all times when ensuring students are fully prepared for their assessments.

Endorsement indicates that a resource is suitable to support delivery of an OCR specification, but it does not mean that the endorsed resource is the only suitable resource to support delivery, or that it is required or necessary to achieve the qualification.

OCR recommends that teachers consider using a range of teaching and learning resources based on their own professional judgement for their students' needs. OCR has not paid for the production of this resource, nor does OCR receive any royalties from its sale. For more information about the endorsement process, please visit the OCR website.

Every effort has been made to trace all copyright holders, but if any have been inadvertently overlooked, the Publishers will be pleased to make the necessary arrangements at the first opportunity.

Although every effort has been made to ensure that website addresses are correct at time of going to press, Hodder Education cannot be held responsible for the content of any website mentioned in this book. It is sometimes possible to find a relocated web page by typing in the address of the home page for a website in the URL window of your browser.

Hachette UK's policy is to use papers that are natural, renewable and recyclable products and made from wood grown in well-managed forests and other controlled sources. The logging and manufacturing processes are expected to conform to the environmental regulations of the country of origin.

Orders: please contact Hachette UK Distribution, Hely Hutchinson Centre, Milton Road, Didcot, Oxfordshire, OX11 7HH. Email education@hachette.co.uk Telephone: +44 (0)1235 827827. Lines are open from 9 a.m. to 5 p.m., Monday to Friday. You can also order through our website: www.hoddereducation.co.uk

ISBN: 978 1 3983 5123 3

© Judith Adams, Maria Ferreiro Peteiro, Mary Riley 2022

First edition published in 2017
This edition published in 2022 by Hodder Education,
An Hachette UK Company
Carmelite House
50 Victoria Embankment
London EC4Y 0DZ
www.hoddereducation.co.uk

Impression number   10 9 8 7 6 5 4 3

Year   2026 2025 2024 2023 2022

All rights reserved. Apart from any use permitted under UK copyright law, no part of this publication may be reproduced or transmitted in any form or by any means, electronic or mechanical, including photocopying and recording, or held within any information storage and retrieval system, without permission in writing from the publisher or under licence from the Copyright Licensing Agency Limited. Further details of such licences (for reprographic reproduction) may be obtained from the Copyright Licensing Agency Limited, www.cla.co.uk

Cover photo © Jose Luis Pelaez Inc/Digital Vision/Getty Images
Illustrations by Integra Software Ltd.
Typeset by Integra Software Ltd.
Printed and bound by CPI Group (UK) Ltd, Croydon CR0 4YY
A catalogue record for this title is available from the British Library.

Contents

Acknowledgements — iv

Introduction — v

How to use this book — vii

R032 Principles of care in health and social care settings — 1

Topic area 1 The rights of service users in health and social care settings — 2
Topic area 2 Person-centred values — 13
Topic area 3 Effective communication in health and social care settings — 27
Topic area 4 Protecting service users and service providers in health and social care settings — 47

R033 Supporting individuals through life events — 69

Topic area 1 Life stages — 70
Topic area 2 Impacts of life events — 96
Topic area 3 Sources of support — 110

R034 Creative and therapeutic activities — 125

Topic area 1 Therapies and their benefits — 127
Topic area 2 Creative activities and their benefits — 142
Topic area 3 Plan a creative activity for individuals or groups in a health or social care setting — 147
Topic area 4 Deliver a creative activity and evaluate your own performance — 166

R035 Health promotion campaigns — 187

Topic area 1 Current public health issues and the impact on society — 189
Topic area 2 Factors influencing health and well-being — 209
Topic area 3 Plan and create a health promotion campaign — 221
Topic area 4 Deliver and evaluate a health promotion campaign — 225

Glossary — 232

Index — 236

Acknowledgements

Huge thanks to Liz Cartmell and Rosie Stewart, my patient, insightful and supportive editors. Also, thanks to Ruth Murphy for the welcome guidance and to all of the other editors involved in the production of this book.
My husband Tony, for your never-ending support (and the mugs of coffee).
Judith Adams, author of R032

I wish to thank Ruth Murphy and the whole Hodder team for all their hard work, and a very special thank you must go to all the encouraging and helpful editors involved. To my husband Chris – your huge understanding and support are always appreciated. To my forever loyal, canine friend Simba – you just keep on obliging with timely, distracting plays and walks.
I couldn't have done it without you all!
Maria Ferreiro Peteiro, author of R034

Much gratitude is owed to the Hodder staff who directed me throughout this book, but especially Ruth Murphy and Liz Cartmell for their good humour and forbearance. Thanks to my husband, Ian and my dogs who kept me sane and dragged me out on walks!
Mary Riley, author of R033 and R035

Photo credits

p.1 © LIGHTFIELD STUDIOS/stock.adobe.com; **p.5** © amazing studio/stock.adobe.com; **p.6** © marilyn barbone/stock.adobe.com; **p.7** © DC Studio/stock.adobe.com; **p.9** © Barry Barnes/123RF; **p.14** © Андрей Журавлев/stock.adobe.com; **p.20** © SpeedKingz/Shutterstock.com; **p.22** © didesign/stock.adobe.com; **p.29** © radub85/123RF; **p.32** © chajamp/stock.adobe.com; **p.36** © Monkey Business/Fotolia.com; **p.38** © JuanCi Studio/stock.adobe.com; **p.39** © pamela_d_mcadams/stock.adobe.com; **p.41** adapted from https://makaton.org © The Makaton Charity, 2019; **p.51** © WavebreakmediaMicro/stock.adobe.com; **p.54** © sebra/stock.adobe.com; **p.56** © Monkey Business/stock.adobe.com; **p.59** © Tyler Olson/stock.adobe.com; **p.62** © Counter Terrorism Policing HQ/Metropolitan Police; **p.63** © Andriy Popov/123RF; **p.69** © jovannig/stock.adobe.com; **p.72** © Africa Studio/stock.adobe.com; **p.76** © Rawpixel.com/stock.adobe.com; **p.79** © mavoimages/stock.adobe.com; **p.83** © Pixel-Shot/stock.adobe.com; **p.87** © Vladimir Voronin/stock.adobe.com; **p.89** © Monkey Business/stock.adobe.com; **p.94** © olando/stock.adobe.com; **p.99** © laurenpretorius/stock.adobe.com; **p.101** © Monkey Business/stock.adobe.com; **p.113** © Yakobchuk Olena/stock.adobe.com; **p.114** © LIGHTFIELD STUDIOS/stock.adobe.com; **p.118** © highwaystarz/stock.adobe.com; **p.125** © zinkevych/stock.adobe.com; **p.128** © Ingram Publishing Limited/Ultimate Lifestyle 06; **p.132** © Monkey Business/stock.adobe.com; **p.134** © 2B/stock.adobe.com; **p.139** © fizkes/stock.adobe.com; **p.143** © Monkey Business Images/Shutterstock; **p.145** © Jacob Lund/stock.adobe.com; **p.151** © Jules Selmes; **p.151** © Ian Allenden/123RF; **p.153** © belahoche/stock.adobe.com; **p.154** © Diego Cervo/Shutterstock.com; **p.157** © fizkes/stock.adobe.com; **p.164** © Robert Kneschke/stock.adobe.com; **p.170** © Rido/stock.adobe.com; **p.180** © chachamal /stock.adobe.com; **p. 187** © Jacob Lund/stock.adobe.com; **p.194** © Public Health England in association with the Welsh Government, Food Standards Scotland and the Food Standards Agency in Northern Ireland – Crown Copyright; **p.199** © Yulia Furman/stock.adobe.com; **p.202** Mary Riley; **p.211** © WavebreakMediaMicro/stock.adobe.com; **p.219** © oneinchpunch/123RF.com

Introduction

Lincroft Academy
Station Road, Oakley, Bedford MK43 7RE
School No. 8225404 Tel: 01234 822147
e-mail: administration@lincroft.academy
www.lincroft.beds.sch.uk

This book will help you to develop the knowledge, understanding and practical skills you need to complete your Level 1/Level 2 Cambridge National in Health and Social Care course. As well as preparing you for your final exam and set assignments, the book will introduce you to the health and social care sector. You will learn specialist health and social care knowledge and skills and will have the opportunity to interview an individual about their life events as well as planning and delivering a creative activity or produce a health promotion campaign.

Each of the chapters in this book closely follows all the topics required for each unit in the course specification, which you can find on the OCR website. To help with your learning, the book covers the key content in detail and includes a range of real-world examples. There are also lots of activities and learning features; you can find out more about these and how to use them on the next page.

Note for teachers: You can find out more about how we have designed the textbook to support you at: www.hoddereducation.co.uk/health-social-care

Mandatory and optional units

The Cambridge National in Health and Social Care qualification is made up of four different subject units. All students need to complete Units R032 (Principles of care in health and social care) and R033 (Supporting individuals through life events); these are the mandatory/compulsory units.

In addition, students will complete one of the following optional units:

- R034: Creative and therapeutic activities
- R035: Health promotion campaigns

The book covers each of these units in equal depth and detail.

Assessment: Examined unit and final set assignments

- Unit R032 is an examined unit where you will sit a one hour 15-minute examination paper, which is set and marked by OCR.
- Units R033, R034 and R035 are assessed through a series of tasks for a set assignment that you will be given. The assignments are set by OCR, marked by your tutor and then moderated by OCR.

All the examination questions contain 'command' words. These tell you what you have to do to answer a question or complete the

OCR Cambridge National in Health and Social Care

task. A full list of common command words is available on the OCR website. Always check the command word before starting a task or answering a question. For example, if you describe something when an explanation is required, you will not be able to gain full marks; this is because an explanation requires more detail than a description. There are a range of practice questions in this book in Unit R032 to help you get to grips with the command words.

Once you have learned all the required parts of the moderated units, you will complete an assignment that will be used to assess your knowledge and skills of the subject. It will be set in a vocational context, which means that it will simulate what it would be like to be given a project by a client or employer in a work situation. You will use the OCR set assignment for the assessment. This assignment will include a series of tasks that follow the same process and sequence of the units for R033 (Supporting individuals through life events), R034 (Creative and therapeutic activities) and R035 (Health promotion campaigns). The assignment practice features in this book in Units R033-R035 will help you get used to working using a health and social care context.

Note: The practice questions and accompanying marks and mark schemes included in this resource are an opportunity to practice exam skills, but they do not replicate examination papers and are not endorsed by OCR.

Plagiarism and referencing

Your work for the OCR set assignments in Units R033-R035 must be in your own words. You must not plagiarise. Plagiarism is the submission of another's work as one's own and/or failure to acknowledge the source correctly.

Sometimes you might need to use a diagram or include a quotation from someone else or a website. If you do this it is very important that you always provide a reference for any information you use that is not your own work. Quotation marks should be placed around any quoted text. You should put the source reference next to the information used. In addition to referencing the picture, diagram, table or quotation, you should explain in your own words why you have used it, what it tells you, how it relates to your work, or summarise what it means. Providing a reference means that you will include details of the source, which is where you found the information. You should include the full website address (URL) and date that you found it or, for a textbook, the page number, title, author's name, date it was published and the name of the publisher. For newspaper or magazine articles you should give the date of publication, title of the paper or magazine and the name of the author. When producing your work for the assessment, you should never use any templates or writing frames. You must always decide yourself how to present your information.

How to use this book

This textbook contains all four units for the Cambridge National Level 1/2 in Health and Social Care.

These are:

- Unit R032 Principles of care in health and social care settings
- Unit R033 Supporting individuals through life events
- Unit R034 Creative and therapeutic activities
- Unit R035 Health promotion campaigns

Each unit is then divided into topic areas. All of the assessment criteria for each learning outcome are covered in the book.

Key features of the book

The book is organised by the units in the qualification. Each unit is broken down into the topic areas from the specification. Each unit opener will help you to understand what is covered in the unit, the list of topic areas covered, and what you will be assessed on, fully matched to the requirements of the specification.

Topic areas

The topic areas are clearly stated so you know exactly what is covered.

How will I be assessed?

Assessment criteria are clearly listed and fully mapped to the specification.

Getting started

Short activities to introduce you to the topic.

Key term

Definitions to help you understand important terms.

Case study

See how concepts are applied in settings and learn about real-life scenarios.

Stretch activity

Take your understanding and knowledge of a topic a step further with these stretch activities, designed to test you and provide you with a more in-depth understanding of the topic.

Test your knowledge

Questions and quick tasks to test your knowledge and understanding at the end of each learning outcome. Answers are provided online at: **hoddereducation.co.uk/cambridge-nationals-2022/answers**

Activity

A short task to help you understand an idea or assessment criteria.

OCR Cambridge National in Health and Social Care

Research
Activities that draw on the content covered in the book and help you to research more about the subject to reinforce your understanding.

Synoptic links
Links to relevant details in other parts of the book so you can see how topics link together.

Read about it
Includes references to books, websites and other sources for further reading and research.

Practice question
This feature appears in Unit R032 where you will be assessed via an exam. Mark schemes and example answers are provided online at: **hoddereducation.co.uk/cambridge-nationals-2022/answers**

Assignment practice
This feature appears in Units R033 to R035 and will help you prepare for non-examined assessment with model assignments. Mark schemes and example answers are provided online at: **hoddereducation.co.uk/cambridge-nationals-2022/answers**

Unit R032

Principles of care in health and social care settings

About this unit

The focus of this unit is to examine key aspects of working in health and social care settings.

You will learn about the ways of supporting service users' rights and using effective communication skills so that you can provide person-centred care. You will also learn about ways of valuing diversity and providing equal opportunities in order to meet the needs of service users who are using care settings.

It is essential that care environments are safe, healthy, hygienic and secure. This unit explores the measures and procedures that are needed to protect service users who use health and social care services.

Topic areas

In this unit you will learn about:

1. The rights of service users in health and social care settings
2. Person-centred values
3. Effective communication in health and social care settings
4. Protecting service users and service providers in health and social care settings.

OCR Cambridge National in Health and Social Care

How will I be assessed?

You will complete a written examination lasting **1 hour and 15 minutes** that is set and marked by the OCR examination board. The examination paper is worth 70 marks.

The examination paper will include:

- a range of short and medium-length questions, worth a total of 50 marks
- one extended response question, worth 8 marks
- two extended response questions, worth 6 marks each.

Some questions will be context-based. This means that the questions are based on care setting scenarios, for example, in a hospital or a care home. You have to apply your knowledge to produce a response that is relevant to the care setting.

Some questions will be fact- and knowledge-based. The questions will not be based on any particular care setting.

Unit R032 covers three Performance Objectives (POs):

- PO1 Recall knowledge and show understanding
- PO2 Apply knowledge and understanding
- PO3 Analyse and evaluate knowledge and understanding.

Topic area 1 The rights of service users in health and social care settings

Getting started

In small groups, produce a list of six different examples of care settings that you know of in your local area.

Classify each setting as either a healthcare or social care setting.

Share your examples with the rest of your class and check you have classified them correctly using Figures 1.1 and 1.2.

Unit R032 Principles of care in health and social care settings

1.1 Types of care settings

A care setting is anywhere where care is provided. Examples of the two main different types of care settings, health and social care, are shown in Figures 1.1 and 1.2.

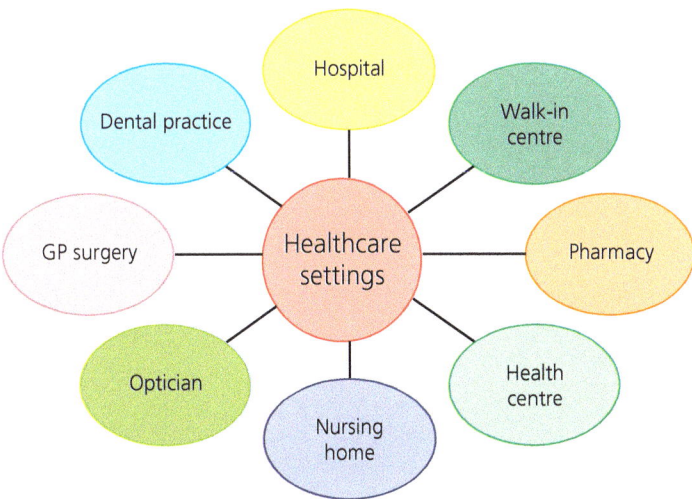

Figure 1.1 Examples of healthcare settings

Healthcare settings provide medical care, preventative screening and treatment for illness, disease, disability or injury.

Figure 1.2 Examples of social care settings

Social care settings offer a wide range of different types of care. The main areas of social care are:

- domiciliary care in service users' homes
- providing protection or support services for adults and children in need or at risk.

This type of care also provides practical support with personal and daily living tasks, as well as emotional and mental health support in coping, for example, with illness or injury.

> **Test your knowledge**
> 1. What are two examples each of health and social care settings?
> 2. Write down two examples each of the type of care provided by healthcare settings and social care settings.

OCR Cambridge National in Health and Social Care

1.2 The rights of service users

Everyone is legally entitled to rights. Rights are set out and supported by **law**, such as the **Equality Act 2010**.

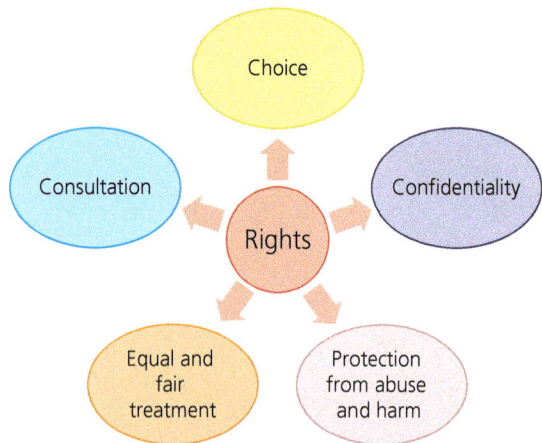

Figure 1.3 The rights of service users

Choice

Choice gives service users control over their lives and promotes independence. It also ensures that they receive care and treatments that meet their needs.

Examples of providing choice in residential social care settings:

- offering a range of different activities so that residents can choose whether or not to take part
- ensuring that residents have access to both a television lounge and a quiet room
- supporting residents in making their own decisions about, for example:
  - which clothes to wear
  - when to get up and go to bed
  - whether they have a bath or shower.

Examples of providing choice in residential healthcare settings:

- where to receive care (e.g. support at home or in a residential setting)
- choice of male or female doctor to meet cultural requirements
- whether or not to receive treatment
- offered food options that take account of special dietary needs or religious or cultural requirements.

Additional information about providing choice can be found later in this unit, Topic area 2, section 2.2, Benefits of applying the values of care.

> **Key terms**
>
> **Law** These are passed by Parliament, and state the rights and entitlements of service users. If someone breaks the law, they can be prosecuted by being taken to court.
>
> **Equality Act 2010** A law intended to prevent discriminatory practice, to ensure service users are treated fairly.

> **Activity**
>
> **How are your rights supported?**
>
> In small groups, discuss how your school or college supports your rights.
>
> - Think about ways that confidentiality, choice, consultation and protection from harm are provided.
> - Discuss your examples with the rest of your class.

Unit R032 Principles of care in health and social care settings

Confidentiality

Confidentiality is an important right for all service users.

- Personal information and medical records must be kept secure. Service providers may have access to a lot of personal information about the people they are caring for, and should always ask if it is all right to pass on any information to another service provider.
- Information should only be shared on a **'need-to-know' basis**, with people who are directly involved with a service user's care.
- Meetings about service users should take place in private where information cannot be overheard by people who do not need to know about that service user. A social worker, for example, should not share details of a service user's finances, bank accounts and property in public as this could put their safety at risk.

If private information is not kept private, the service user will lose trust in the care provider as they will not feel valued and respected.

Protection from abuse and harm

All care settings should have policies and procedures in place to help protect both the service providers and service users who use the services provided. Some health and social care settings provide care for service users who are more at risk of abuse and harm, such as:

- service users with dementia
- service users with a learning disability
- children.

These service users may not know what abuse is or understand their rights. They may not realise they are being abused or receiving poor treatment and many may not be able to remember what has happened or tell anyone clearly. So, it is essential that all staff are aware of and follow **safeguarding** procedures to protect the children and adults using the care setting.

Health and safety policies and procedures should be implemented, such as staff training in safeguarding, first aid and regular fire drills. For example, staff involved in providing physical care in nursing homes and hospitals must be trained in **manual handling**. This is to avoid injuring themselves or the service user they are moving, such as from a bed into a chair. Risk assessments must be carried out for situations such as visits, outings and activities to minimise the risk of harm.

See Topic area 4, Protecting service users in health and social care settings, for additional detailed health and safety information.

Key terms

Confidentiality Limits access or places restrictions on sharing certain types of sensitive information, such as medical records, so that it is kept private and available only to those who need to be aware of it.

'Need-to-know' basis Information is only shared with those directly involved with the care and support of the service user.

Safeguarding Actions taken to protect service users by ensuring a safe and healthy environment where the risks of danger, harm or abuse are reduced.

Manual handling Using the correct procedures when physically moving any load by lifting, putting down, pushing or pulling; for example, transferring a client from a chair to a bed.

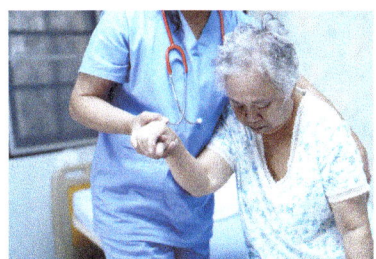

Figure 1.4 Manual handling requires training to avoid injuries for both the service user and service provider

Equal and fair treatment

Equal treatment means being given the same opportunities and choices as everyone else.

Fair treatment means being able to have full access to those opportunities and choices, as well as receiving the correct type of care that meets service user needs.

Service users should be treated fairly and so that their own needs are met. Everyone should be able to access education, health and social care in the same way.

It is important to realise that providing the same treatment does not always guarantee equality, because different service users are in different situations and have different needs. The care provided should meet a service user's specific needs.

Examples of equal and fair treatment in care settings:

1 A secondary school child with special educational needs or disability should be enabled to take part in the same lessons as the rest of their class. This may mean that they need:
    - extra support such as simpler worksheets and tasks
    - one-to-one support from a teaching assistant who could, for example, act as an interpreter or use sign language.

    In this way, being treated differently ensures the child has equal opportunities.

2 Staff at a residential home for older adults have arranged a day trip to the coast for all of the residents who want to go. The coach that is taking them on the trip must have a wheelchair ramp, otherwise those residents who are wheelchair users will be unable to go because they would be unable to access the coach.

See Topic area 2: Person-centred values, for more information about how to provide equal and fair treatment.

Figure 1.5 Equal and fair treatment means ensuring all individuals have access to the same opportunities

Unit R032 Principles of care in health and social care settings

Consultation

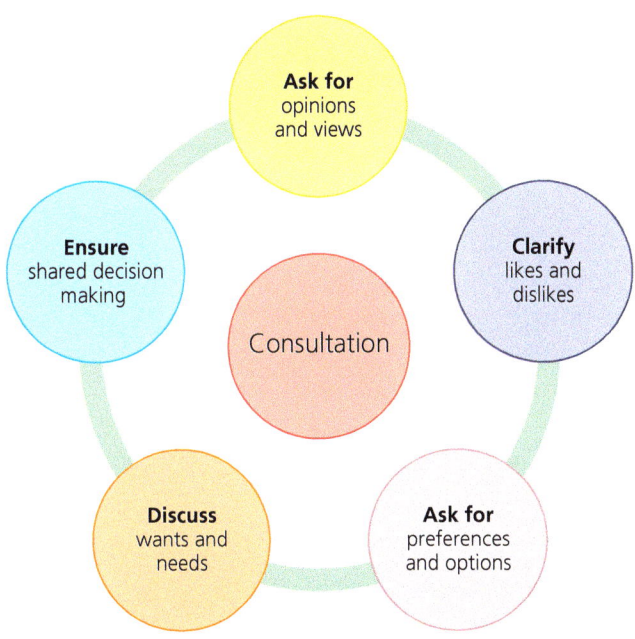

Figure 1.6 Aspects of consultation

Service users in health or social care environments should be asked for their opinions and views about the type of care they would like. Their views and opinions should be taken account of as much as possible when planning and providing their care.

It is very important that service users are involved in the **consultation** and decision-making process for their own care and support. This requires service providers and service users to work in partnership so that care provided is appropriate and meets the service user's needs.

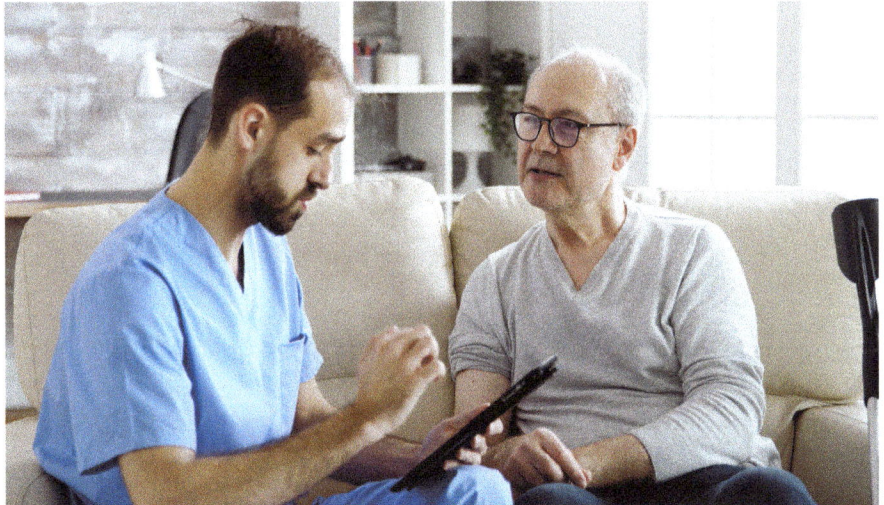

Figure 1.7 Getting to know a service user to support their rights

Key term

Consultation The process of discussing an issue with another person in order to receive their thoughts, advice or opinion, so that a decision can be made that is acceptable and appropriate for all involved.

Stretch activity

Supporting consultation

Figure 1.7 shows a service provider having a conversation with a retirement home resident.

1. Make a short list of questions that the service provider could ask to support the resident's right to consultation.
2. Share your questions with a partner and explain how each question supports the right of consultation.

OCR Cambridge National in Health and Social Care

> **Test your knowledge**
> 1. What is the meaning of the term 'consultation'?
> 2. A nurse shares patient information with other staff on a 'need-to-know' basis. What does 'need-to-know basis' mean?
> 3. Why is confidentiality important in a GP surgery?
> 4. Which of the following means equal and fair treatment?
>   - giving everyone the same opportunities
>   - treating everyone the same
>   - providing the same treatment for everyone
> 5. Write about procedures that would help to reduce the risk of harm in a care setting.

1.3 The benefits to service users' health and well-being when their rights are maintained

> **Activity**
> **Maintaining service users' rights**
> 1. In groups, discuss the following question:
>   What is the most important piece of information a service provider should remember about the person they are caring for?
>   - their email address / phone number
>   - whether they are Muslim, Jewish or Christian
>   - that they are an individual
>   - their age
> 2. Share your conclusions with the rest of your class.

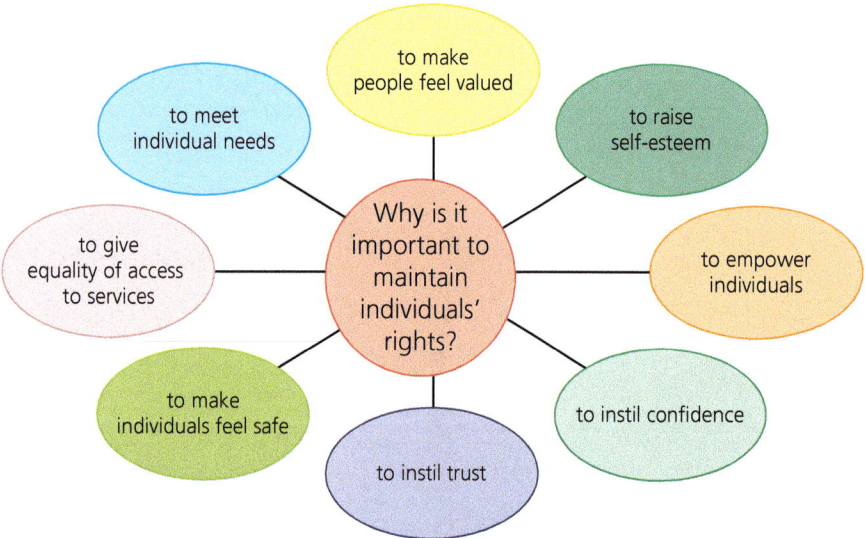

Figure 1.8 Why is it important to maintain service users' rights?

Unit R032 Principles of care in health and social care settings

Empowerment

Having choices and being consulted about care preferences gives service users control over their lives and promotes their independence. This increases their self-esteem and makes them feel valued.

Empowerment:

- encourages independence and being self-reliant
- makes service users feel in control of their lives
- gives service users choice, control and independence
- ensures equality of access to care services.

High self-esteem

A person with high **self-esteem** feels valued and respected. If someone is treated fairly and receives appropriate care that meets their needs, and which enables them to live a better life, they will benefit emotionally and feel more positive.

Having high self-esteem improves mental health and leads to feeling:

- valued
- respected
- confident.

Service users' needs are met

Service users who receive appropriate care and treatment will be helped to recover from injury or illness, or learn to manage a disability or health condition, and still enjoy and achieve in life. Examples of meeting needs are: a child having a support worker in class, being provided with mobility aids, being helped with personal care or daily living tasks, appropriate medication, and provision of meal planning for a special dietary need.

Meeting a service user's needs:

- means giving appropriate care or treatment so that service users' requirements are met
- results in good and improving physical health
- results in good and improving mental health.

Key terms

Empowerment Giving someone the authority or control to do something. The way a health or social care service provider encourages a service user to make decisions and to take control of their own life.

Self-esteem How much a person values themselves and the life they live. High self-esteem is associated with people who are happy and confident. A service user with low self-esteem experiences feelings of unhappiness and worthlessness.

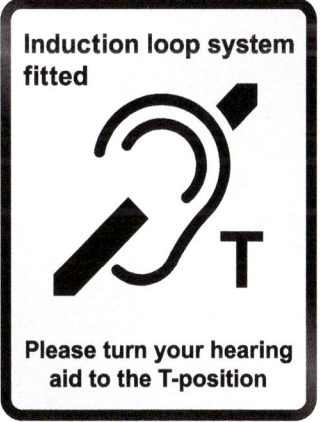

Figure 1.9 Hearing loop symbol at a GP surgery

Activity

Meeting service users' needs

1. With a partner, discuss how installing a hearing loop system in a GP's surgery, the symbol for which is shown in Figure 1.9, maintains a service user's rights.
2. Consider how adapting the environment improves access to services.
3. Share your ideas with the rest of your class.

OCR Cambridge National in Health and Social Care

Trust

It is important that service users receiving care feel able to trust their care providers. Service users must be able to feel that service providers are trustworthy, that they will not harm them and that they have their best interests at heart.

It is likely that service users who lack trust may not continue with the care they should be receiving. This could have negative effects on their physical and mental health and well-being.

Service users who can trust their care providers will feel:

- reassured that service providers will not harm them
- confident that service providers have their best interests in mind
- confident in the care they receive
- confident that staff will be able to provide a safe environment for care, following health and safety policies and procedures.

Research

1 Use the internet to find a website for a local care setting, such as a GP surgery, a dental practice or a nursery.
2 Make a list of information provided by the care setting that shows the setting is supporting the rights of service users.
3 For each way of supporting rights that you have found, write an explanation of how it benefits the service users.

Test your knowledge

1 What are the five rights to which service users are entitled?
2 What are three benefits for service users of having their rights maintained?

Synoptic links

Unit R032	Links with other units
Topic area 1: The rights of service users in health and social care settings	**R033 Supporting individuals through life events** **Topic area 2:** Impacts of life events
	R034 Creative and therapeutic activities **Topic area 3:** Plan a creative activity for service users or groups in a healthcare or social care setting **Topic area 4:** Deliver a creative activity and evaluate your own performance

Unit R032 Principles of care in health and social care settings

Practice questions

Question 1

Faiza works for social services. Every day she visits Anna, who lives in her own home and has had a stroke. While Anna recovers, she receives help from Faiza with bathing, dressing and preparing meals.

Anna has rights. For each right in the table below, identify an example of how it could be maintained by Faiza. The first example has been done for you.

[3 marks]

Right	How the right could be maintained
Equal and fair treatment	Faiza should carry out an assessment of Anna's needs so that she can have appropriate care.
Choice	
Confidentiality	
Consultation	

Question 2

A community centre for young adults with learning disabilities is an example of a social care setting. Identify two other, different, examples of social care settings.

[2 marks]

Question 3

Read the information below about a local GP surgery.

- The surgery tries to arrange appointments as soon as possible. If you wish to see a doctor of your own choice, the appointment may be in three to four days.
- The surgery is accessible to all; we have wheelchair ramps and accessible toilet facilities and parking. If you think we could improve access in any way, please let the surgery manager know.
- We are introducing telephone, Skype or Facetime appointments where appropriate. You can also make a 'normal' appointment if you prefer. We would like your feedback and opinions about this new system and if it is working for you.
- Prescriptions are available by post, in person or online.

Explain ways that the GP surgery is supporting the rights of its patients to **choice** and **consultation**.

[6 marks]

OCR Cambridge National in Health and Social Care

Question 4

The health and well-being benefits of supporting individuals' rights in health and social care settings are:

- trust
- empowerment
- individual needs are met
- high self-esteem.

Complete the table below by matching the benefit with its example. Each benefit can be used once only.

Example of supporting rights	Benefit to individuals
Providing different worksheets for children of different abilities.	
A doctor and a patient having a discussion about different treatments before making a decision.	
A social worker sharing information on a 'need-to know' basis.	
A primary school teacher praising a child's achievement.	

[4 marks]

Unit R032 Principles of care in health and social care settings

Topic area 2 Person-centred values

Getting started
Read the following statement:

Equality means treating everyone the same.

Do you agree or not?

- In small groups, discuss what you think.
- Share your thoughts and have a class discussion guided by your teacher.

> **Key term**
> **Equality** This means treating people fairly and valuing them for who they are. Everyone should be provided with the same rights and opportunities, and this should not be affected by their age, ability, gender, culture or religion.

2.1 Person-centred values and how they are applied by service providers

Person-centred values of care are key principles that underpin the work of those providing care and support in health and social care services.

- They are a set of guidelines that provide ways of working for care settings and their staff.
- Person-centred practice enables service users to receive person-centred care that meets their own unique needs.

Person-centred values
Person-centred values of care include:

- individuality
- choice
- rights
- independence
- privacy
- dignity
- respect
- partnership
- encouraging decision making of service user.

Let's look at each of these values below.

Individuality
This value means recognising that each person has their own identity, needs, wishes, beliefs and values. These individual differences must be considered and taken account of when providing care and support.

Choice

All service users are entitled to make their own choices. Choice is empowering and this is a feature of person-centred care. For example, service users should be offered a range of different care options and given enough information about them to make an informed choice.

Ensuring each service user is supported to make choices and in control of their care is important, and their individual needs and preferences should always be used to inform their care.

Rights

Everyone is entitled to rights. Rights are set out by legislation (see Topic area 1, section 1.2 The rights of service users).

Service providers who support service users' rights will be working within the law and providing a high standard of personalised care.

Independence

Having independence means that a service user:

- does not have to rely on others
- has the opportunity and freedom to make their own decisions.

A service provider should support service users to have as much control over their lives as possible, as this enables person-centred care.

Privacy

Many procedures in healthcare and social care require privacy, such as showering and dressing someone, or carrying out intimate procedures. It is vital to respect and protect the service user's privacy. An example of good practice is to knock on the service user's door before entering.

This value also includes not talking about a service user's personal details with anyone who is not involved in providing their care.

Figure 1.10 The service user's privacy must be respected

Dignity

This value involves having regard for the feelings, opinions and wishes of others. By respecting and valuing the service user's rights, views and needs, the service provider supports their self-esteem and makes them feel valued.

Unit R032 Principles of care in health and social care settings

Respect

Having respect means treating someone in a way that shows they have importance as an individual, and their opinions and feelings have value.

Service providers should respect service users'

- diversity
- sexuality
- faith, cultural needs and preferences
- rights
- confidentiality.

The people using healthcare and social care services will be from a range of different backgrounds. The Equality Act 2010 identifies nine protected characteristics, and it is illegal to discriminate against any of these characteristics:

- age
- disability
- gender reassignment
- marriage and civil partnership
- pregnancy and maternity
- race
- religion or belief
- sex/gender
- sexual orientation.

Any unfair treatment, exclusion or discrimination against service users is against the law.

Partnership

This involves different professionals, services and agencies working together to provide the most effective care for a service user requiring treatment or support. This could involve, for example, the hospital, a social worker and a care home working together to provide care to meet the needs of an older adult being discharged from hospital after a fall.

Encouraging decision making of service user

It is important to ensure that service users are supported to make choices, and to be involved and in control of their care. Care decisions should be based on the service user's needs and should focus on their strengths and abilities.

For example, a service user may be recommended to use a walking aid to help with mobility:

- The suggestion is to use a walking frame rather than a walking stick to help the service user walk short distances, but they do not want to use a frame.
- The service user should be encouraged to make their own decision by discussing the advantages and disadvantages of each aid.
- The service user is more likely to use a walking aid if it has been their own choice.

OCR Cambridge National in Health and Social Care

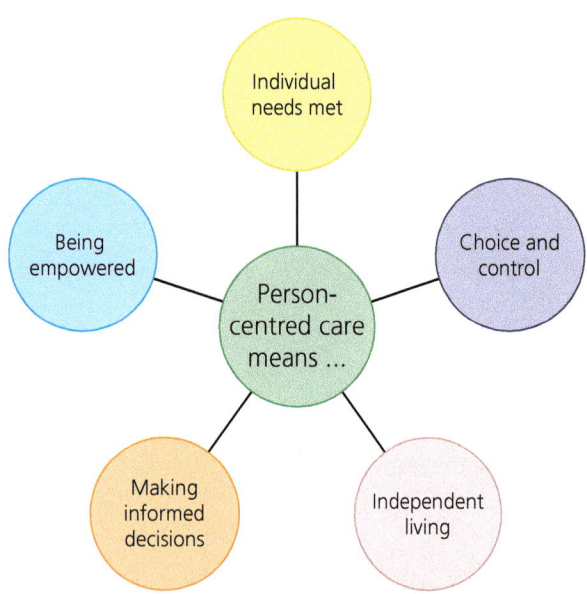

Figure 1.11 The features of person-centred care

Qualities of a service provider: the 6Cs

The 6Cs are:

1 care
2 compassion
3 competence
4 communication
5 courage
6 commitment.

The 6Cs are key principles which should inform every health and social care service provider's practice and enable them to provide person-centred care.

- **Care** means a service provider will do all they can to provide appropriate treatment or support that will maintain or improve a service user's health and well-being.
- **Compassion** is being able to provide care and support with kindness, consideration, respect and empathy. It is also having consideration for the service user receiving care or treatment, as well as being able to put yourself in the patient's situation and show understanding.
- **Competence** refers to the ability of a service provider to provide high-quality, effective care through applying their knowledge, skills, understanding and expertise to meet a service user's care needs.
- **Communication** is essential to developing good relationships with service users, their families and also with colleagues. It is important to be able to listen carefully and speak in a way that service users receiving care and support can understand.

- **Courage** is being brave: being able to speak up when having concerns, doing the right thing and also trying something new such as a new way of working.
- **Commitment** is when a service provider is dedicated to providing care and support to meet the service user's needs.

The Care Certificate sets out the standards that should be covered by induction training before members of the health and social care support workforce are allowed to work without direct supervision. The 6Cs form an important part of the Care Certificate standards.

Examples of how person-centred values can be applied in health and social care settings

Individuality, rights, choice and decision making

- Care environments such as hospitals and residential care homes could provide access to a prayer room or transport to a place of worship, to support service users' religious beliefs.
- In healthcare, the right to choose for a pregnant woman could be supported by consulting with her about the choice of birth she would like, whether at the hospital or a home birth, for example.
- By providing a menu with vegetarian or vegan, gluten-free, halal and kosher options, you are catering for different types of dietary needs and providing choice for service users.

Respect

Service providers should always use non-discriminatory language and avoid patronising the service users they are caring for.

They should challenge discrimination if they see or hear it happening, whether it is a staff member or another service user using the care setting. The discrimination can be challenged by:

- explaining to the service user how they are being discriminatory, to raise their awareness
- reporting it to senior staff.

Privacy and dignity

- Staff working in care settings who have access to confidential information should not gossip about the service users in their care or discuss them with friends and family.
- Privacy and dignity are very important when helping someone with personal care, for example, having a shower and helping them to get dressed if they have mobility difficulties. It is essential for privacy, and dignity of the service user, that a curtain/screen is used or the bathroom door is closed.

> **Research**
> Use this link at the skillsforcare.org.uk website to find out more about the Care Certificate Workbook and see how the 6Cs are a part of each of the 15 Care Certificate standards:
>
> www.skillsforcare.org.uk/Learning-development/inducting-staff/care-certificate/Care-Certificate-workbook.aspx

dence

An important way to promote independence is to provide care that meets a service user's specific needs. For example:

- If a theatre trip is arranged for residents of a care home, it should be to somewhere that has wheelchair access and a hearing loop system for those who need them.

Partnership, individuality, decision making and rights

Producing a plan for the care of a service user should be done in partnership between them and health and social care services; other family members may be involved if appropriate. The service user's needs, strengths and wishes should be the focus.

- Everyone should meet together.
- The service user should be fully involved in any discussions.
- They should be given a copy of the plan that has been decided.

2.2 Benefits of applying person-centred values

When service providers apply person-centred values of care in their day-to-day work, they ensure that service users using health and social care services:

- receive appropriate care that meets their needs
- do not experience discriminatory attitudes
- have their **diversity valued** and their rights supported.

Benefits for service providers of applying person-centred values

There are many benefits for service providers when they apply person-centred values. These are outlined below.

Provides clear guidelines of the standards of care that should be given

Service providers will know how to do their job effectively. Service users will receive appropriate care, attention and treatment to meet their individual needs. All of the staff in a care setting will be working to the same high standards.

Improves job satisfaction

The service provider's role is clearly defined and they are aware of how to apply 'best practice'; this provides job satisfaction for service providers.

Test your knowledge

1. What are the 6Cs?
2. What does 'person-centred' care mean?
3. What is one way of supporting 'individuality' in a residential care home?
4. Write down the meaning of the term 'compassion'.
5. What are two service providers that could work in partnership when producing a plan for care of a service user?

Key term

Valuing diversity
Accepting and respecting individual differences such as faith, diet, sexuality, ethnicity and customs.

Unit R032 Principles of care in health and social care settings

Maintains or improves quality of life

People who use services will have their individual needs met. For example, by:

- providing hospital patients with appropriate nutritional meals
- providing help to eat and drink
- discussing their treatment with them
- consulting with them about alternative types of treatment potentially available to them.

Supports rights to choice and consultation

Choice is empowering and this is a feature of person-centred care as service providers will be involved in helping to construct a plan of care with a service user that fully takes account of their care needs and preferences.

Supports service providers to develop their skills; enables the sharing of good practice

Partnership working enables collaboration between colleagues to develop best practice which, along with involvement of the service user receiving care, can only ensure the best possible outcomes as individual needs will be met.

Benefits for service users of having person-centred values applied

When a service provider applies person-centred values, the service user will reap the benefits.

Figure 1.12 Service users are empowered by person-centred practice

Ensures standardisation of care being given; improves the quality of care being given to the service user

The person-centred values provide clear guidelines of the standards of care that should be given, and this maintains quality of care.

When service providers apply the person-centred values of care in their day-to-day work, they ensure that service users using health and social care services:

- always receive appropriate care that meets their needs
- do not experience discriminatory attitudes
- have their diversity valued and their rights supported.

Figure 1.13 Kitchen aids can enable a service user to prepare their own meals independently

Maintains or improves quality of life for the service user

Service users' rights, beliefs and preferences will be respected and their individual needs will be met. This ensures that the care they receive is beneficial in every way. For example, an occupational therapist carries out a home assessment of an older person with arthritis. As a result of the visit, various kitchen aids such as an easy grip knife and a special 'bottle and jar opener' are provided. These will enable the service user to continue preparing their own meals independently.

Supports service users to develop their strengths

Person-centred care ensures the service user is involved in decision making by discussing their care needs and then being given, for example, information about the different options that will meet their needs. The service user can then choose the care that they prefer.

This is enabling and empowering, ensuring the service user is at the centre of their care and has choice and control. Their rights to choice and consultation are supported.

Stretch activity

Understanding person-centred practice

You can carry out this activity individually or in pairs.

- Read the information in this section (Person-centred values, The 6Cs and The benefits for service users of having person-centred values applied).
- Write a short case study of a service user who has care or support needs, for example, a service user with hearing or sight loss, dementia or mobility difficulties.
- List the service user's needs.
- List examples of person-centred practice that would help to meet the service user's needs.

2.3 Effects on service users' health and well-being if person-centred values are not applied

Effects on service users can be:

- **p**hysical
- **i**ntellectual
- **e**motional
- **s**ocial.

It can help to remember them as '**PIES**' effects.

Physical effects

These relate to a service user's body. Here are some examples of possible physical effects when the service user doesn't receive appropriate care:

- A nursing home resident suffers with coeliac disease – this causes unpleasant symptoms if gluten is consumed. If they are not given gluten-free food, it will lead to a deterioration of their digestive health.
- If a hospital patient is not given regular drinks, they will become dehydrated and their condition will get worse.

Intellectual effects

These relate to a service user's thought processes such as thinking skills, understanding, learning, reasoning, comprehension and knowledge. Here are some examples of possible intellectual effects on service users if they don't receive appropriate care:

- If a young adult who has learning difficulties is not given support and learning activities matched to their special needs, their learning will not progress and they will not reach their potential.
- If staff at a retirement home expect residents to sit and watch television for most of the day and do not provide a range of activities to engage their interest, the residents will lack mental stimulation and suffer loss in concentration. This can have negative effects on their mental health and well-being.

OCR Cambridge National in Health and Social Care

Figure 1.14 Social and intellectual activities are important for mental health and well-being

Emotional effects

These relate to a service user's feelings. Below are some examples of possible emotional effects of service users not receiving appropriate care:

- An elderly woman attends a day centre. She is a vegetarian but at lunch is expected to eat the same meal as the others, just without the meat. This is unfair treatment, and is likely to upset her as she is not being treated as well as the others. She might develop low self-esteem as she feels she is not important enough to be given a proper vegetarian meal. She could also feel embarrassed that she is being a nuisance, expecting a 'special' meal.
- An expectant mum would be upset, angry and frustrated if her midwife told her that she cannot have a home birth, without explaining the reasons why or giving her the chance to ask questions.

Social effects

These relate to a service user's relationship with others. Here are some examples of possible social effects of service users not receiving appropriate care:

- If staff at a day centre do nothing about other young adults laughing at a girl who has a birthmark on her face, the girl may lack friends, become isolated and withdrawn, and refuse to attend.
- An elderly resident at a retirement home has an undiagnosed hearing problem. The staff do not bother to talk to him much because they think he just doesn't like socialising and prefers to be by himself. He avoids spending time with other residents, he can't hear properly and has to keep asking for things to be repeated. He doesn't want to bother people so he keeps to himself.

Some more examples of effects on service users of the values of care not being applied in care settings are shown in Table 1.1.

Table 1.1 Effects on service users if person-centred values of care are not applied

Physical effects	Intellectual effects
• pain • existing illness gets worse • bruising • cuts and grazes • broken bones • dehydration • malnutrition • injury	• lack of skills development • lack of knowledge • lack of progress • loss of concentration • losing interest • lack of stimulation • will not achieve potential
Emotional effects	**Social effects**
• low self-esteem • low self-confidence • disempowered • upset • loss of trust • angry • depressed • stress • frustrated • humiliated • self-harm • frightened • feeling unsafe	• withdrawn • isolated • lonely • excluded • become anti-social • unco-operative • lack of friends • develop behavioural problems • refusal to use the service

It is important to realise that these effects do not occur in isolation but are 'interrelated' (they affect each other). For example:

- A teenage boy who is being bullied at college may suffer physical harm such as bruises.
- This could lead to him feeling frightened and unsafe, causing him to not attend college so as to avoid the bullies.
- Not attending college will affect his learning and development of skills in the course he is taking.
- This will also negatively affect his social skills, as he will not be mixing with other students.

OCR Cambridge National in Health and Social Care

> **Stretch activity**
>
> **Demonstrating a person-centred approach**
>
> Read the conversation between Mrs Talbot and Adrianne shown below.
>
> Write an alternative script for the same conversation between Adrianne and Mrs Talbot. The script should demonstrate ways that Adrianne could value Mrs Talbot with a person-centred approach when providing care.

Case study: Mrs Talbot's cup of coffee

Two volunteers perform a role play of the following conversation to the rest of your group. The conversation is between Mrs Talbot (a retired grandmother living in a residential home) and Adrianne (a care assistant).

Adrianne	Hurray up, Mrs T! Your coffee is going cold and we need to get you into your nightie before I go off duty.
Mrs Talbot	It's too hot to drink – you have only just given it to me.
Adrianne	Oh, you are imagining things again, Mrs T! I gave it to you ten minutes ago. Now come on.
Mrs Talbot	I do wish you wouldn't call me 'Mrs T', Adrianne. My name is Mrs Talbot.
Adrianne	Oh, don't be so formal – Mrs T is nice. Anyway, let's get this coffee finished and then you can get into your nightie and watch the news; it starts in 15 minutes.
Mrs Talbot	(*Sips her coffee.*) Ugh – you've not put any sugar in it.
Adrianne	Sorry, I forgot. Now come on, I have to get you into that nightie right now.
Mrs Talbot	It's far too early.
Adrianne	No, it's not. We always start getting people ready for bed at around 5 o'clock after teatime.
Mrs Talbot	Oh well, I suppose so then, if I must.
Adrianne	That's my girl.

These questions could be discussed by the whole group and then answered as a piece of written work.

1 Explain the ways in which Adrianne has not supported Mrs Talbot's rights.
2 Analyse the effects on Mrs Talbot of Adrianne not applying person-centred values in this way.

Unit R032 Principles of care in health and social care settings

Test your knowledge

1. Write about how person-centred values can improve the quality of care provided.
2. How is providing choice empowering for care service users?
3. What is an example of how providing person-centred care can improve quality of life for service users?
4. Write down four examples of effects on service users when person-centred values are not applied – one example each of physical, intellectual, emotional and social effects.

Synoptic links

Unit R032	Links with other units
Topic area 2: Person-centred values	**R033 Supporting individuals through life events** **Topic area 2:** Impact of life events **Topic area 3:** Sources of support
	R034 Creative and therapeutic activities **Topic area 3:** Plan a creative activity for individuals or groups in a health or social care setting **Topic area 4:** Deliver a creative activity and evaluate your own performance
	R035 Health promotion campaigns **Topic area 2:** Factors influencing health and well-being **Topic area 4:** Deliver and evaluate a health promotion campaign

Practice questions

Question 1

Linda is a nurse working on a busy hospital ward.

Identify **four** of the 6Cs that Linda should apply when caring for her patients.

[4 marks]

Question 2

Explain the possible **social** effects on a young adult if the person-centred values 'choice' and 'independence' are not applied when they attend a day centre.

[6 marks]

OCR Cambridge National in Health and Social Care

Question 3

Listed below are four benefits of the person-centred values of care being applied:

- Care provided meets service users' needs as their rights, beliefs and preferences will be respected.
- Care improves the servicer user's quality of life.
- The service user is involved in decision making, which promotes independence.
- Appropriate care demonstrating best practice will be provided.

Choose the correct benefit from this list to match each example in the table below. An example has been done for you.

Each benefit can be used once only.

Applying person-centred values of care	Benefit to service users of the value of care being applied
Applying person-centred care guidelines ensures standardisation of care.	Appropriate care demonstrating best practice will be provided.
An occupational therapist arranges for mobility aids to be provided for a service user.	
A doctor and a patient have a discussion about different treatments before making a decision.	
Service users do not experience discriminatory attitudes, and their diversity is valued.	

[3 marks]

Question 4

In your own words, write a definition that explains the meaning of 'person-centred care'.

[3 marks]

Unit R032 Principles of care in health and social care settings

Topic area 3 Effective communication in health and social care settings

Getting started

In pairs, list as many different ways of communicating with others that you can think of.

- Compare your list with the rest of the class.
- Have a class discussion about the types of information or situations that each different method of communicating would be most suitable for. An example is giving a presentation – what would that be useful for?

3.1 The importance of verbal communication skills in health and social care settings

Verbal communication is the exchange of information between people using speech – what we say to each other. Using verbal communication and having good interpersonal skills are both necessary for interacting successfully with other people.

If service providers use communication and interpersonal skills effectively, this will enable service users who use care services to feel respected, supported and valued, and to feel that their needs are being met. Good communication means service users can:

- be actively involved in their care
- let their changing needs be known
- make informed choices, as they will have the information they need in order to develop a clear understanding of procedures, treatments or plans of their care.

A service provider has to use their communication skills when they:

- give or receive information about the care that is being provided for a service user
- provide emotional support for a service user or a member of their family
- carry out an assessment of a service user's care needs
- participate in continuing professional development
- receive or deliver training.

Adapting type/method of communicating to meet the needs of the service user or the situation

There are many ways to adapt your type or method of communication to meet the needs of individual service users. Some examples are given below.

- Use vocabulary that can be understood – avoid **jargon** or specialist medical terminology, and give age-appropriate explanations.
- Use specialist methods if needed, such as sign language, hearing loop, interpreter or Braille. (See also Topic area 3, section 3.4.)
- Adapt communication to meet the needs of service users; for example, by using repetition, gestures and body language, flash cards.
- Adapt the environment in order to aid communication; for example, by moving a meeting to a quiet room away from noise and distractions, or providing chairs so people feel more relaxed and comfortable when having a discussion.

Key term
Jargon Specialist or technical language, or terms and abbreviations, that are difficult for non-specialists to understand.

Clarity

Clarity involves service providers being able to share information with other staff or with service users in a clear and accurate way that can be easily understood.

- Spoken words must be clear – a service provider must not mumble and must pronounce words carefully.
- When speaking with service users, a service provider should always use straightforward terminology where possible and explain any technical terms clearly to help understanding. Short sentences can help with understanding.

Empathy

This is the ability to:

- understand and share the feelings of another person
- understand another person's way of thinking
- imagine what it would be like to be in that person's situation.

This can help a service provider to gain a better understanding of other people's viewpoints, and shows the service user that their feelings have been acknowledged.

Patience

Patience involves:

- giving a service user the time to say or do what they need to
- being supportive
- not rushing them
- not making them feel pressured.

For example, an older person with arthritis may take a little longer to move than others because their condition makes mobility difficult or an individual may find it difficult to get their words out because of a stroke.

Using appropriate vocabulary

'Vocabulary' refers to the collection of words used. In order to communicate effectively and with understanding, you must use words which are appropriate. For example:

- If a nurse was explaining treatment to a child, they would use simple words that are easily understood.
- Adults understand more advanced vocabulary than a child, but they might not understand some technical, medical terminology.

It is therefore very important to explain information using vocabulary that is appropriate for the situation.

Avoid abbreviations, as it is likely that service users may not know the meaning. For example:

- CCU (Critical care unit)
- CNS (Clinical nurse specialist).

Appropriate vocabulary also includes using the appropriate language. Information should be available in a range of different languages. A 'Welcome' sign in a variety of different languages will send a positive message that everyone is welcome to use the service.

Figure 1.15 A warm welcome – 'Hello' in 13 languages

Tone

Tone is how your voice is heard.

- The tone of your voice should be calm and not rushed. A varied tone of voice will come across to others as friendly and interested.
- It is important not to use a tone of voice that may come across as aggressive. Also, a slow and steady monotone voice may be boring to listen to and might suggest or cause a lack of interest.

Volume

How loudly (although not shouting) or quietly you need to speak depends on the situation. For example:

- Raising your voice may be appropriate in a noisy environment such as in the Accident and Emergency department in a hospital, to attract someone's attention, but it would not be appropriate when discussing a patient.

You need to speak loudly enough to be heard but not so loud that everyone else can hear. This is particularly important when service users' personal information is being discussed. Moving to a quiet area or into an office would be more appropriate, so that confidentiality is not breached.

Some service users have hearing difficulties, so these conversations will have to be a little louder than usual to meet the person's needs.

Pace

It is important to have the correct pace when speaking.

- If a service provider speaks too quickly, the service user may miss important information.
- If the service provider speaks too slowly, the service user may become bored and stop listening.

Willingness to contribute to team working

Team working is when a group work together to achieve a common (shared) goal. When working as a part of a team, each individual should:

- share information as appropriate for the scenario, and as needed by the team to provide care
- communicate effectively
- work to meet the team's shared goals in the best interests of the service users.

Team workers need to be reliable and contribute fully to any task. If they do not do this, resentment and bad feelings can develop which results in the service users' best interests not being met. For example, a team of care assistants working in pairs to bathe residents before bedtime would develop problems if every night one team bathed two residents and another team bathed four residents.

- The whole team would need to look at why this is happening – does one team need more help to bathe certain residents because they require more assistance, or are they simply taking longer than they should and not working hard enough?
- Problems like this have to be discussed and resolved in order to achieve the whole team's goals.

Unit R032 Principles of care in health and social care settings

Teams do not always work together face to face – they can communicate with each other through:

- conference calls
- patient records – these are usually electronic and must be updated regularly so that up-to-date information, for example, about care and treatment, is available to the whole team
- emails
- telephone calls.

This enables necessary information to be shared.

Examples of team working include:

- A GP, midwife, **sonographer**, **obstetrician**, **anaesthetist** and health visitor all work together to achieve the safe development and delivery of a baby.
- A social worker, care assistants, **podiatrist**, GP and occupational therapist work together to enable an 89-year-old person to remain living at home because she does not want to go into residential care.

Key terms

Sonographer A health professional who is specially trained to carry out ultrasound scans.

Obstetrician A doctor specialising in the care of pregnant women, who assists with births if there are complications.

Anaesthetist A doctor who specialises in pain relief and anaesthetics during surgery.

Podiatrist A health professional who provides foot care such as removing corns, hard skin and ingrowing toe nails.

Test your knowledge

1. Write down the meaning of 'verbal communication'.
2. What is the meaning of 'empathy' when dealing with a patient?
3. Give an example of adapting communication to meet the needs of a service user.
4. Why is the use of jargon discouraged?
5. Write about why being patient is an important skill for service providers.

3.2 The importance of non-verbal communication skills in health and social care settings

Non-verbal communication involves the transfer of information through the use of body language such as gestures, eye contact and facial expressions. It does not include speech, as that is verbal communication.

Figure 1.16 You can communicate without words

Adapting type/method of communicating to meet the needs of the service user or the situation

Eye contact

Service providers must always be sensitive to the service user's views and cultural differences, as shown in these examples:

- In some cultures, such as East Asian including Japanese and Middle Eastern cultures, eye contact is considered disrespectful.
- Western Europeans, however, have a different view and will maintain eye contact, seeing it as positive and reassuring.

Unit R032 Principles of care in health and social care settings

- In America and Latin America, not looking the other person in the eye is a sign of disrespect. It might even look suspicious, or be interpreted as 'They don't dare to look me in the eye, so they are hiding something'.

Direct eye contact is recognised in Western culture as a way of showing interest in a conversation. It shows the listener that they are the central focus of the communication. When service providers make eye contact, it should be positive but avoid staring for too long or it may be interpreted as aggressive.

Facial expressions

These can act as positive and negative responses to a situation. Examples are:

- raising eyebrows
- frowning
- moving your mouth.

A service user could use facial expressions to show a service provider they have a question.

Facial expressions should match the message. For example, when giving bad news, you would use a sympathetic expression – smiling would not be appropriate.

Gestures

Gestures involve hand movements. Examples include:

- drumming fingers on a surface or twiddling thumbs (these signal impatience)
- thumbs up signal (this means OK, all good)
- thumbs down (this is a negative sign)
- waving goodbye
- beckoning someone with your hand
- pointing something out
- using British Sign Language (see Figure 1.16).

Activity

Understanding the effect of facial expressions

Look at Figure 1.16.

- Make a list of the meaning of each facial expression shown.
- Compare your answers with a partner.
- In pairs, try out some facial expressions that might occur in health and social care situations. Examples could be receiving a diagnosis, or getting test results, or feeling pain.
- Then role play one of the situations, with the facial expression, to the whole group. Can they guess the situation?

Positioning

Height

It is better for effective communication if people are at the same level as the service provider speaking with them. This reduces the risk of feeling dominated by someone 'talking down' to them. This is particularly important when speaking to service users with learning difficulties, or someone who uses a wheelchair.

Space and personal space

Personal space differs between cultures and between service users. Some people feel uncomfortable if others are close, whereas other people find it acceptable.

Many spaces in health and social care settings are not suitable for meetings or consultations: they may be too small, so service users invade each other's personal space or cannot sit facing each other in the position they would like.

Often in offices a large desk is placed between those attending a meeting. This makes it rather formal, which might not be appropriate for what is going to be discussed, for example, between a patient and a doctor. This may have a negative impact on service users attending the meeting.

For communication to be effective, it is important that service users are made to feel comfortable and at ease during conversations or consultations.

The room layout will be affected by whether it is a group, one-to-one, formal or informal situation:

- A confidential discussion will require a private area where there are no disturbances or noise.
- A group training activity with the staff will require space and an area where noise doesn't matter.

Positive body language, no crossed arms/legs

Health and social care staff need to be approachable by service users and so it is important that they use open body language.

- It makes service providers appear more welcoming and trustworthy.
- It will also make the service users feel more comfortable and relaxed in any situation.

Below is a list of do's and don'ts to achieve open and positive body language.

DO:

- maintain eye contact at all times during your conversation
- smile if appropriate for the situation
- keep your hands on the sides of your body
- keep a friendly, upright and open posture
- lean forward to show interest.

DON'T:

- fold your arms or clench your fists
- cover your body with your arms
- hide your hands in your pockets.

Unit R032 Principles of care in health and social care settings

Sense of humour

This is the ability to see the funny side of things. Careful use of humour can lighten the mood and remove tension, making people feel more at ease and relaxed.

However, it is important that service users and their families feel that they are being taken seriously, and so humour should be used with care and not inappropriately.

> **Test your knowledge**
> 1 What is the meaning of the term 'non-verbal communication'?
> 2 How can eye contact help when talking to a service user?
> 3 Why is personal space important to consider when arranging a meeting?
> 4 What are features of open and positive body language?

3.3 The importance of active listening in health and social care settings

Active listening is an effective method of listening to build rapport, trust and understanding between those involved.

Active listening by a service provider involves demonstrating an interest in and responding to what a person is saying, by fully concentrating on what is being said rather than just passively 'hearing'.

Active listening can involve non-verbal cues which show understanding, such as nodding, eye contact and briefly saying 'I see' or 'Sure', for example, to build trust and confidence.

Active listening skills

Active listening skills include:

- having an open, relaxed posture
- making eye contact, looking interested (observing facial expression, gestures, body language)
- nodding agreement
- showing empathy, reflecting feelings
- clarifying (by asking questions that cannot be answered with a one word response)
- summarising to show understanding of key points (paraphrasing).

See the photo in the Case study for an example of active listening in practice.

OCR Cambridge National in Health and Social Care

Case study

Naz is a service provider. She enjoys working with older adults in a residential care home. She likes to get to know them well and uses good communication skills to help achieve this.

Naz likes to plan activities that the residents will enjoy. She thinks it is very important to build up good relationships with the older residents, so that they feel safe and secure in the care setting and will want to take part in all the activities.

1. Consider the picture of Naz working in the residential home.
2. Identify and explain the ways that Naz is using effective communication with the residents. Think about body language, facial expression, gestures, positioning and active listening.
3. How is Naz's effective use of communication benefitting the residents?
4. Share your thoughts with the rest of your class.

3.4 The importance of special methods of communication in health and social care settings

Communication difficulties may be as a result of:

- physical disability – an individual could be unable to speak due to the effects of a stroke
- sensory impairment – an individual could be deaf or blind
- language impairment – an individual could be unable to speak a certain language
- learning difficulty – this could lead to a lack of understanding.

Unit R032 Principles of care in health and social care settings

There are many different ways to communicate and there are many strategies that can help. These are explored below.

Advocate

An advocate is someone who speaks on behalf of a service user who is unable to speak up for themselves. For example, this could be:

- a young child
- a service user with learning disabilities
- someone who has been assessed as lacking mental capacity
- an older person with **dementia**.

An advocate for a child could be a parent; an advocate for an adult could be a friend or carer. A professional advocate could be provided by, for example, a charity organisation such as Age UK to represent an older adult.

An advocate could represent the service user at a care review meeting, for example, and act in their best interests.

An advocate is independent. They will represent the views, needs and interests of service users who are unable to represent themselves, without judging them or giving their own personal opinions.

> **Key term**
> **Dementia** A group of symptoms that affect how a person thinks, remembers, solves problems, uses language, communicates and carries out tasks and activities. They occur when brain cells stop working properly and the brain is damaged by injury, or by disease such as Alzheimer's.

Figure 1.17 The benefits of advocacy

An advocate can:

- go with a service user to meetings or attend for them
- help a service user to find and access information
- write letters on the service user's behalf
- speak for someone at a case conference to express their wishes.

> **Research**
> **Finding out about advocacy**
> Three organisations that provide advocacy services are:
> - SEAP (Support, Empower, Advocate, Promote)
>
> www.theadvocacypeople.org.uk
>
> - Mencap
>
> www.mencap.org.uk
>
> - Mind
>
> www.mind.org.uk
>
> 1 Choose one of these organisations and access their website.
> 2 Find out about the advocacy services that they provide.

37

OCR Cambridge National in Health and Social Care

An advocate will:

- be completely independent and represent the service user's views, not their own personal opinions
- ensure a service user's rights and needs are recognised
- represent the service user's wishes and views
- speak for someone who is unable to do so for themselves
- act in the best interests of the person they are representing.

An advocate will not:

- judge the service user
- give their own personal opinion
- make decisions for the service user.

Braille

This is a method of communication used by visually impaired or blind people. It was devised by Louis Braille in 1829, who became blind from an accident when he was three years old. He developed the Braille system to help teach blind children to read and write.

Braille consists of a series of dots which are read by touch. Each character is made up of raised dots; the raised dots may be in any of six positions within a rectangle. There are sixty-four possible combinations of dots.

Figure 1.18 Using Braille

Unit R032 Principles of care in health and social care settings

British Sign Language

British Sign Language (BSL) involves using the hands and fingers to make visual signs. This is used by people who have impaired hearing, and by other people to communicate with them.

Figure 1.19 British Sign Language alphabet

Voice-activated software

Speech-activated programs allow users to:

- write text
- use the internet
- send emails
- use applications by using their voice rather than a mouse or keyboard.

These programs can be very helpful to people who do not have full use of their hands and therefore have difficulty using a keyboard and mouse.

For example, someone with cerebral palsy may have difficulties with fine motor skills, which makes handwriting and using a keyboard challenging. They would benefit from using voice-activated software to help with communication.

Below are some examples of software:

- Dynavox is speech-generating software. The service user touches a screen that contains text, pictures and symbols, which the software then converts into speech.
- Lightwriter is a text-to-speech device. A message is typed on a keyboard, displayed on a screen and then converted into speech.

More communication strategies

Communication with service users can also be achieved by using:

- an interpreter – who will convert a spoken or signed message from one language to another, and speak it
- a translator – who will convert a written message from one language to another, and write it
- Makaton – a system that uses a combination of speech, gestures and pictures to communicate
- PECS – this stands for 'Picture Exchange Communication System'. It is a method of communicating where pictures are used to indicate what is needed, and can be useful for individuals with communication difficulties such as dementia or autism.

Unit R032 Principles of care in health and social care settings

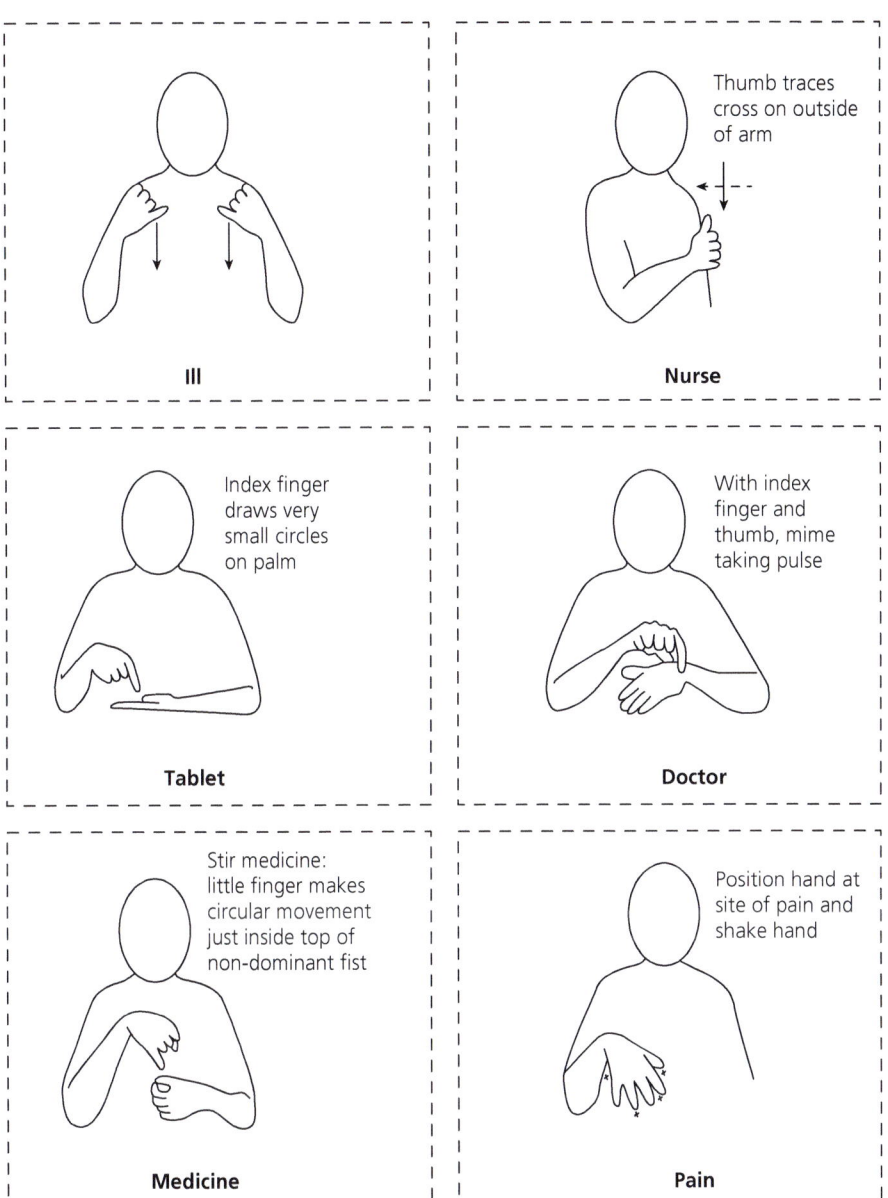

Figure 1.20 Using Makaton could help a service user to communicate in a care setting (adapted from The Makaton Charity)

Test your knowledge
1. What is Braille and how is it used?
2. Write about two ways of communicating effectively with a service user who has dementia.
3. What are the benefits of using 'active listening'?
4. Write down two examples of ways in which a health centre could make information accessible to service users with visual and hearing impairments.
5. What is meant by the term 'advocate'?

3.5 The importance of effective communication in health and social care settings

Effective communication supports the person-centred values of care

The person-centred values of care are:

- individuality
- choice
- rights
- independence
- privacy
- dignity
- respect
- partnership
- encouraging decision making of service user.

See Topic area 2 for more on person-centred values.

Good communication empowers service users, giving them choice and control over their care. This reassures them that they are at the centre of their care and fully involved in the decision-making process. If service users have been provided with all of the necessary information in an understandable format, they will feel valued and respected, and will develop trust in their service providers. See page 10 for further information about developing trust.

Helps to meet service users' needs and protects their rights

Successful and effective communication depends on:

- how well the service user can hear and see
- how comfortable they feel
- how attentive they are
- how well they understand what is happening
- how well they can express themselves
- whether they are motivated to communicate.

Communication profiles, sometimes called 'communication passports', are often created to inform staff about how a service user communicates with others and how they wish to be communicated with.

The communication profile/passport:

- helps service providers to understand the communication and other needs of a person who has difficulties communicating information, due to illness or a mental or physical disability
- includes information about the service user such as their likes, dislikes and communication skills
- will be updated regularly
- enables consistency between staff – this benefits the service user, as all staff will be communicating with them in the same way.

Unit R032 Principles of care in health and social care settings

Communication profile	
Name:	
Name of person completing this profile:	
I like to be called:	
I communicate by:	
I initiate communication by:	
I can speak	Yes / No
I can read	Yes / No
I can write	Yes / No
I can sign my name	Yes / No
I can use the phone to make a call	Yes / No
I can answer the phone and say hello	Yes / No
I can use / understand Makaton	Yes / No / A little
I can use / understand BSL	Yes / No / A little
I can use photographs / pictures to communicate	Yes / No
I can tell the time	Yes / No
I can understand what is on the television	Yes / No
I can tell you if I am unhappy. I do this by:	
I will not communicate with you when:	
I do / do not need to use communication tools. If I do, these are:	
When I am happy or like something, I will show you by:	
I have / have not had a hearing assessment in the last two years.	
I have / have not had a speech assessment in the last two years.	
The date of my last communication assessment:	
I do / do not wear glasses.	
If I wear glasses I need to wear them all the time / just for reading.	
Date profile completed / updated:	

Figure 1.21 An example of a communication profile

This communication tool can be used with many service users, such as those people who:

- have a learning disability
- have a physical disability
- have had a stroke
- are deaf or blind
- do not speak English as their preferred language
- are shy and introverted, and may not enjoy communicating information with new staff.

The communication profile/passport will have all the details needed to ensure that a service user's needs and rights are met.

OCR Cambridge National in Health and Social Care

The impact of good communication skills

- Well-informed service users will know what to expect, why they are receiving care or treatment, and the effect on their health and well-being. They will feel able to ask questions if they are not sure about something that is worrying them.
- Actively listening to service users' needs, concerns and opinions enables them to feel valued and respected. They will be reassured that they are being supported and that their questions and concerns are being taken seriously.
- Using appropriate vocabulary, and avoiding jargon, helps understanding. Service users feel reassured as they will understand the straightforward language that will be used by the service providers.

The impact of poor communication skills

- If information is not clearly explained, it can lead to misunderstandings. Service users need information to be clearly explained to them, or there is a danger they will not understand complicated medical procedures, treatments or conditions, for example. This could impact on the success of their care, because anxiety and stress about what is happening does not help recovery.
- Poor communication can lead to errors or danger to health due to inaccurate record keeping. For example, if medication has been given but not noted on the medication record, or the wrong amount is recorded, there could be serious health consequences for a patient.
- If a service user feels patronised or stupid, it can make them feel upset or distressed. A service provider's role is to help a service user with their care needs, and different service users have different needs. Service users with learning disabilities or who have poor hearing, for example, may need information to be repeated. It is important that service providers do not do this in a patronising and disrespectful way.
- If speech is too fast, the listener will not have time to understand it. Service providers should not cause information overload. For example, being in hospital is stressful in itself, without being bombarded by lots of new information that the service user cannot understand. Service providers should always be aware of, and be sensitive to, service users' need for information, but not overload them with it.

It is important that health and social care service providers do not create communication barriers. They should ensure that they use their communication skills effectively to avoid creating barriers to care. Table 1.2 gives a summary of how they can achieve this.

Unit R032 Principles of care in health and social care settings

Table 1.2 Ways service providers can avoid creating communication barriers

How to avoid creating communication barriers	Explanation
Using vocabulary that can be understood	<ul><li>no jargon</li><li>specialist terminology must be explained</li><li>age-appropriate vocabulary</li><li>simplified language, for example, with young children, individuals with learning disabilities or patients with dementia</li><li>using interpreters or translators</li></ul>
Not being patronising	<ul><li>no sarcasm or talking down to the person</li><li>not ignoring their views or beliefs because they are different to yours</li><li>use of positive body language, e.g. nodding agreement, appearing relaxed</li><li>being polite</li><li>make them feel that they are being taken seriously</li><li>being patient and listening to repetitions</li></ul>
Adapting communication to meet service users' needs or the situation	<ul><li>emphasising important words</li><li>slowing the pace if necessary</li><li>increasing the tone of voice, but not shouting</li><li>repetition where appropriate</li><li>using gestures or flash cards/pictures</li><li>making use of aids to communication, e.g. loop system</li><li>using specialist methods, e.g. Braille, signing</li><li>technological aids, such as Dynavox, Lightwriter</li></ul>
Listening to service users' needs	<ul><li>active listening – demonstrating interest in response to what a person is saying, using body language to show a positive reaction</li><li>ask the person – do not assume you know what they want, need or prefer</li><li>concentrate on what the person is saying, which can encourage them to communicate their needs</li></ul>

Test your knowledge

1. What is the purpose of a communication profile/passport?
2. How do staff with good communication skills empower service users?
3. Write down three impacts on service users of staff with poor communication skills.
4. Write about ways in which communication can be adapted to meet service user needs.

OCR Cambridge National in Health and Social Care

Practice questions

Question 1

Stephen works for the social services department as a family support worker with children who are at risk of being taken into care. When Stephen meets the children he has to use effective communication skills to help put them at ease.

Explain three examples of how Stephen could use effective communication when he meets the children.

[8 marks]

Question 2

Parkes Day Centre provides activity sessions for young adults. The young people attending are culturally diverse and some do not speak English.

Identify three ways that staff at the day centre could communicate effectively with the young people.

[3 marks]

Question 3

Describe two examples of the possible impact of a hospital healthcare service provider having poor communication skills.

[4 marks]

Question 4

There are situations when service users need the help of an advocate.

Give two examples of service users who might need an advocate and explain the role of an advocate.

[8 marks]

Unit R032 Principles of care in health and social care settings

Topic area 4 Protecting service users and service providers in health and social care settings

Getting started

In groups, create a spider diagram to show as many ways as you can think of that your school or college keeps you safe.

Share and discuss your spider diagram with the rest of the class and your teacher.

As a class, organise the ways under the following headings:
- safeguarding
- general hygiene
- safety procedures
- security measures.

A volunteer could use a flipchart for recording the lists.

4.1 Safeguarding

Safeguarding refers to the actions taken to protect a service user's health and well-being to ensure they are not at risk of harm, danger or abuse.

It also refers to the actions taken to protect service users by creating a safe and healthy environment in care settings.

All care environments must have safeguarding procedures in place:
- They must have a specific person with responsibility for safeguarding.
- All staff and service users should be aware of the procedures to follow to report safeguarding issues.
- Staff should know how to deal with **disclosures** of abuse.

Service users who need safeguarding

Some service users may be more **vulnerable** to abuse or harm than others because of their individual needs or circumstances. However, it must not be forgotten that anyone can potentially be at risk of abuse or harm.

Vulnerable groups include:
- homeless people
- children
- people with physical disabilities
- people with learning disabilities
- people with mental health conditions
- older adults in residential care settings
- people who have a sensory impairment – sight loss, hearing loss
- people in residential care dependent on carers – children, older adults.

Key terms

Disclosure This is when a service user tells you directly, or indirectly through their behaviour, that they have been, or are being, abused.

Vulnerable A word to describe someone who is less able to protect themselves from harm or exploitation due to, for example, mental health problems, a learning disability or physical impairment such as mobility problems, loss of hearing or sight.

OCR Cambridge National in Health and Social Care

Figure 1.22 Service users who are most at harm of risk or abuse

Abuse and harm are more likely to occur in situations where people are dependent on others. For example:

- If the service user depends on others to provide personal care and money management, this makes them vulnerable.
- Some service users are very challenging and may be aggressive. This can lead to carers being verbally or physically abusive in response, especially if they have not been trained properly.
- The service user is vulnerable where there is an invasion of privacy, such as doors or curtains deliberately not being closed when they are receiving help to get dressed or undressed.
- Lack of staff could cause carers to rush as there is so much to do. They could handle a service user roughly when giving personal care, causing bruising.
  Although not intentional, it is still abuse.
- Lack of staff training can lead to abuse. Staff may not know how to bathe someone safely or how to use hoists to move a service user from bed to a chair. They could unintentionally cause injury.

Unit R032 Principles of care in health and social care settings

Impacts for service users of a lack of safeguarding

Impacts on service users can be **P**hysical, **I**ntellectual, **E**motional and **S**ocial. It can help to remember them as '**PIES**' impacts.

Physical impacts

These relate to a service user's body. Some examples of possible physical impacts of a lack of safeguarding include:

- anxiety
- broken bones
- bruising
- depression
- illness
- injury
- lack of sleep
- pain
- poor health / health deterioration
- self-harm injuries.

Intellectual impacts

These relate to a service user's thought processes such as thinking skills, understanding, learning, reasoning, comprehension and knowledge. Some examples of possible intellectual impacts of a lack of safeguarding include:

- confusion
- cannot think straight
- denial
- lack of skills development
- lack of interest
- lack of motivation
- lack of understanding
- loss of concentration
- not asking questions.

Emotional impacts

These relate to a service user's feelings. Some examples of possible emotional impacts of a lack of safeguarding include:

- feeling betrayed
- feeling disempowered
- feeling excluded
- feeling unsafe
- feeling afraid
- feeling upset
- feeling unhappy
- loss of self-confidence
- loss of self-esteem
- poor mental health
- self-harm
- being withdrawn.

Social impacts

These relate to a service user's relationship with others. Some examples of possible social impacts of a lack of safeguarding include:

- becoming anti-social
- aggression
- behaviour problems
- being isolated
- lack of trust in others
- refusal to use the service
- unco-operative
- withdrawal from other people.

See also some further detailed examples in Topic area 2, section 2.3: Effects on service users' health and well-being if person-centred values are not applied.

Safeguarding procedures in care settings

Safeguarding policy
All organisations must have a safeguarding policy that states their ways of working and procedures to follow regarding safeguarding.

All staff must be trained so that they are aware of the policy.

Designated Safeguarding Lead
The Designated Safeguarding Lead (DSL) is the person in an organisation or service that has responsibility for safeguarding.

Common safeguarding issues in adult care environments
These include:

- maladministration of medication – incorrect, late, inappropriate (such as sedatives)
- pressure sores – service users who are frail or who have restricted mobility are at risk of developing sores on the points of their body which receive the most pressure. These are known as pressure sores and are sometimes called bed sores or ulcers. People need to be moved often so that these don't develop. If left untreated, they can become very deep and infected
- falls – residents not being assessed on their risk of falls; walking aids not provided
- rough treatment – being rushed, shouted at, ignored
- poor nutritional care – appropriate food not provided for chewing and swallowing problems, of for religious or dietary needs; this could result in malnutrition
- lack of social inclusion – no stimulation, activity, opportunities for social interaction
- physical abuse between residents or staff and residents
- financial abuse – e.g. theft of personal money or possessions; staff inappropriately accepting gifts
- institutional abuse occurs when the routines and systems of an organisation result in poor or inadequate standards of care and poor practice. This affects the whole setting and denies, restricts or ignores the dignity, privacy, choice and independence of service users. Examples would be forcing people to eat or go to bed at a particular time.

Unit R032 Principles of care in health and social care settings

Safeguarding children

This involves:

- protecting children from maltreatment – e.g. physical, emotional, psychological abuse
- preventing damage to children's health and development, such as their physical health, well-being and education
- ensuring children grow up in a stable home with the provision of safe and effective care – in extreme cases when other interventions have failed, removing them from neglectful, unstable and chaotic family life
- taking action to enable all children to have the best outcomes – providing support for the family, fostering or adoption.

Safeguarding training for all staff

All staff, service providers and other staff, regardless of their job role, must be trained in safeguarding. They should receive regular refresher training to stay up to date in safeguarding procedures. It is compulsory for all those who come into contact with children and vulnerable adults in their work.

Figure 1.23 All staff must be trained in safeguarding

The training will ensure that all service providers working at a care setting:

- are aware of their duty to report a serious concern
- know the care setting's procedures for reporting a disclosure of abuse or serious concern
- can recognise possible signs of abuse or harm
- know who to report to.

OCR Cambridge National in Health and Social Care

Some organisations use the 'five Rs' to help staff develop awareness of their responsibilities regarding safeguarding. These are explained below.

The five Rs

The five Rs are:

1. Recognise
2. Respond
3. Report
4. Record
5. Refer.

Recognise (all staff)

All staff should be able recognise the signs and symptoms of abuse or harm. However, sometimes it may be a direct disclosure about harm or abuse from a service user.

Respond (all staff)

The issue must be reported, whether it is a specific concern raised by a service user or just a suspicion.

- Do not ask questions – just listen, then write it down as soon as possible, in the person's own words.
- Reassure them that they have done the right thing.
- Inform the person sharing with you that the concerns they have raised must be recorded and passed on so that possible abuse can be dealt with, and that this will be done on a limited 'need-to-know' basis.

Report (all staff)

Report your concerns, urgently, to the DSL member of staff. It is then their responsibility to take further action.

Record (DSL)

The DSL will record the member of staff's concern, including direct quotes. If appropriate for the situation, they might include notes about the person's physical and emotional state that they have observed.

Refer (DSL)

The DSL will carry out an investigation into complaints, allegations or suspicions of abuse. If a crime is suspected, the DSL will contact the police.

Disclosure and Barring Service

The Disclosure and Barring Service (DBS) works closely with the police and helps prevent unsuitable people from working with vulnerable service users.

DBS checks are a requirement for anyone aged over 16 for roles that involve working or volunteering with children or vulnerable adults. This also applies to anyone applying to foster or adopt a child. DBS checks ensure that people are safe to work or volunteer with vulnerable adults and children.

Research

Look online for a safeguarding policy. An example can be found at:

https://ptp-training.co.uk/wp-content/uploads/2017/07/Safeguarding-Policy-1.pdf

Using information from the policy, create a 'Factsheet' that could be used to train staff in their safeguarding responsibilities. In this example, pages 15 to 21 are particularly useful.

Your Factsheet should include:

- identifying abuse – signs and symptoms
- the five Rs
- how to react to suspicions of abuse.

Unit R032 Principles of care in health and social care settings

There are three types of DBS checks:

1 **standard** – checks for criminal convictions, cautions, reprimands and final warnings
2 **enhanced** – an additional check of any information held by police that is relevant to the role being applied for
3 **enhanced with barred list checks** – additionally checks the barred list, which is a list of individuals who are on record as being unsuitable for working with children or vulnerable adults. Therefore, they are 'barred', that is not allowed, to do this kind of work.

Research
Use the internet to find out more detail about the role of the DBS.

Test your knowledge
1 Write down the meaning of 'safeguarding'.
2 What are two groups of service users who are most at risk of harm or abuse?
3 Write down a common safeguarding issue in an adult care environment.
4 What does the '5Rs' mean?
5 What is the role of the DBS?

4.2 Infection prevention

Activity
Understanding the importance of hygiene measures
Think about what you have done so far today.

- Make a list of everything you have touched since you got out of bed this morning.
- On your list, highlight or underline all the things that someone else could have touched as well.
- List any hygiene measures you have used today.
- Share and discuss with the rest of your class **hygiene** measures that could be taken to reduce the spread of germs and **infections** between service users in care settings.

Key terms
Hygiene Practices that keep yourself and your surroundings clean in order to prevent illness and the spread of disease.

Infection What happens when germs (pathogens), for example bacteria, viral, fungal or parasitic, invade the body and cause a disease or illness.

Different care settings have different types of furniture and equipment. The methods of maintaining general cleanliness will vary depending on the setting. However, there are standard ways to maintain a clean and hygienic environment, as shown here.

OCR Cambridge National in Health and Social Care

General cleanliness

Germs will grow very easily in most environments that are warm, light and moist. In order to prevent the spread of infection, general cleaning should take place regularly in all care settings:

- Use anti-bacterial sprays on surfaces.
- Clean toys and play equipment regularly.
- Mop floors and vacuum carpets daily.
- Clean and disinfect toilets frequently.
- Dispose of hazardous waste in health and social care settings correctly. For example:
  - hard yellow **sharps** box for used syringes
  - red bags for soiled bedlinen
  - yellow bags for clinical waste such as used dressings, disposable gloves.

Figure 1.24 Regular cleaning helps to prevent the spread of infection

Personal hygiene measures

There are lots of opportunities for germs to grow and spread in health and social care settings. This is because settings are accessed by many service users and service providers over the course of a day – many different activities take place, such as meals being prepared and served, physical examinations or treatments. So, it is important that everyone working in a care setting has high standards of personal hygiene to prevent the spread of infection.

> **Key term**
>
> **Sharps** Examples include used needles and cannulas (thin tubes that surround a flexible needle that is inserted into a vein to administer medication from a drip). These can cause injury by a needle or sharp edge pricking or cutting the skin.

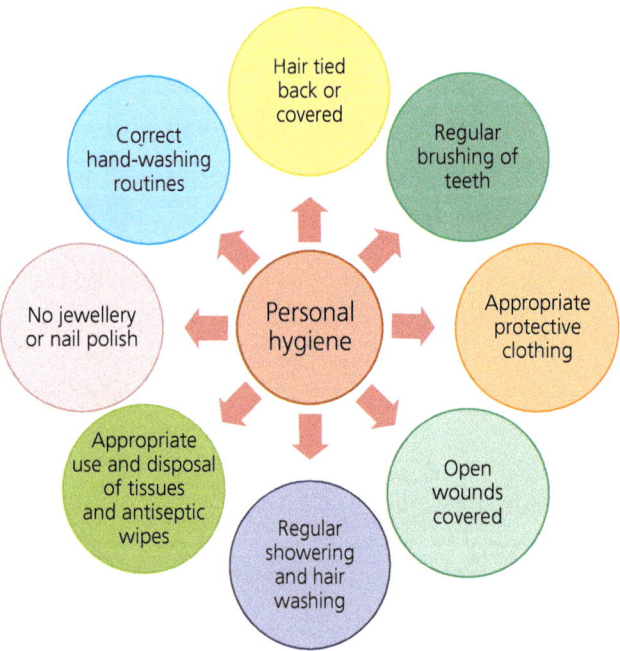

Figure 1.25 Personal hygiene measures

Unit R032 Principles of care in health and social care settings

Hand washing

It is important to wash your hands:

- before and after touching raw food or meat
- after visiting the toilet
- after emptying rubbish bins
- after exposure to cleaning materials
- after dealing with soiled bedding or continence pads
- before and after undertaking clinical procedures
- before and after providing personal care for a service user, such as feeding them or helping them get dressed
- after coughing or sneezing.

How personal hygiene measures protect service users

Personal hygiene measures can protect service users in the following ways:

- Correct hand washing routines can destroy germs and stop them from being transferred.
- The service user carries fewer germs, which reduces opportunity for spreading infection.
- Barrier methods reduce and prevent the transfer of germs and spread of infection. Examples include wearing disposable gloves, wearing a disposable apron or covering open wounds.
- Not wearing jewellery removes places for germs to be trapped.
- Not wearing nail polish removes the risk of it flaking off and contaminating food or a wound.
- If hair is tied back or covered, it can't drop into food and contaminate it with any germs that may be present.

Activity

Finding out about correct hand washing procedures

1. Find a YouTube clip (or information in a textbook) which shows the correct technique for washing hands. An example of a detailed clip is:

    www.youtube.com/watch?v=mWe51EKbewk

    This is a short film showing how to wash your hands correctly with both alcohol rub and soap and water within a medical environment. This clip was originally used when training medical students at the University of Leicester.

2. Write a set of illustrated step-by-step instructions for the correct method of handwashing.

Personal protective equipment

Wearing personal protective equipment (PPE) is a barrier method of preventing the spread of infection. The clothing or equipment can prevent the transfer of germs from one person to another.

Examples of PPE include:

- disposable aprons, disposable gloves and rubber gloves – a fresh pair of disposable or rubber gloves/apron should be used for each new task, to prevent cross-contamination
- face masks provide a barrier that retains droplets released when talking, sneezing or coughing
- hairnets or hygiene hats – for example, these are important when serving food to prevent hair contaminating the food, and when changing dressings
- overalls, overshoes – these provide a barrier covering the service provider's clothes and so reduce the likelihood of transferring germs
- surgical garments/scrubs – when carrying out operations and other surgical procedures and dental work, they can protect the service provider and the patient from infection.

> **Test your knowledge**
> 1. Write three examples of ways to ensure general cleanliness in a care setting.
> 2. How does good personal hygiene protect service users in care settings?
> 3. Write about three examples of when a service provider wears disposable gloves.
> 4. Write down three pieces of advice for correct hand washing.
> 5. Why is it important for service providers to wear PPE?

Figure 1.26 It is very important to use protective clothing in healthcare

Unit R032 Principles of care in health and social care settings

4.3 Safety procedures and measures

The importance of safety procedures and measures

The difference between a 'procedure' and a 'measure'

It is important that you understand the difference between safety procedures and safety measures:

- **Safety procedures** are a set of actions or instructions that are carried out in a particular order. They will tell service providers what they have to do and how to do it. Examples of safety procedures are how to deal with emergency situations such as a fire, or how to arrange a safe trip out for elderly residents of a care home by carrying out a risk assessment.
- **Safety measures** are specific actions, such as putting out a 'Wet floor' sign or placing a fire extinguisher by each exit.

Procedures to prevent accidents and promote good practice

Care settings should have the following procedures in place to prevent accidents and promote good practice:

- emergency fire procedures
- emergency evacuation procedures
- equipment considerations (e.g. appropriate training)
- specialist training for the use of manual handling equipment
- regular risk assessments
- regular fire drills
- **first aid** procedures
- food safety procedures
- supervision – children at all times / adults as necessary
- adequate staff to children/patient/resident ratio.

How safety procedures protect service users and service providers

Safety procedures provide guidance for staff so they know what to do to keep service users and themselves safe at all times. Knowledge of safety procedures enable staff to take quick, efficient action in emergencies.

Staff will know how to treat service users with first aid and how to reduce the risks of cross-contamination to avoid the spread of infection. Training staff how to use equipment prevents accidents, which helps to provide a safe environment.

> **Key terms**
>
> **Safety procedure** A set process that is followed, such as a fire drill or carrying out risk assessments.
>
> **Safety measure** A particular action, such as putting up a 'Wet floor' sign.
>
> **First aid** The immediate treatment provided for a service user who has an accident or is suddenly taken ill.

Safety procedures for reducing risk/danger and promoting good practice

First aid policy

According to the Health and Safety (First Aid) Regulations 1981, it is a legal requirement that all care settings and service providers must have enough trained first aiders available for the number of staff and service users in case of health emergencies.

Numbers of service users with specific health needs or conditions have to be noted, as this may impact on the number of first aiders that should be available.

Staff trained in using **adrenaline auto-injectors**, **e.g. EpiPens**, should be available, based on an assessment of the number of service users in a care setting who are at risk of **anaphylactic shock**.

Risk assessments

Risk assessments need to be carried out for any activities or visits and trips that care settings organise. They are needed to check that equipment is safe and that the care setting building itself is safe. Risk assessments identify dangers such as:

- potential accidents
- trip hazards
- risky activities that require more than the usual amount of staff supervision.

The five risk assessment steps

Carrying out a risk assessment involves the following five steps:

1. Look for hazards.
2. Decide who might be harmed and how.
3. Consider the level of risk – decide on the precautions needed to reduce the risk.
4. Make a written record of the findings.
5. Review the risk assessment from time to time and improve precautions if necessary.

> **Key terms**
>
> **Adrenaline auto-injector (e.g. EpiPen)** An emergency treatment for use if someone has a severe anaphylactic reaction. It is an automatic injector device which contains a dose of adrenaline which is injected into the thigh.
>
> **Anaphylactic shock** An extreme allergic reaction. Common causes and triggers can be nuts, celery, seafood, and wasp or bee stings.

Unit R032 Principles of care in health and social care settings

Why carry out a risk assessment?

There are many reasons for carrying out risk assessments:

- It is a legal requirement under the Health and Safety at Work Act. The written record provides evidence that the risk assessments have been carried out.
- Staff, service users and visitors have a right to be protected and kept safe from harm.
- An assessment will check what could cause harm to people using the care setting.
- A risk assessment should help prevent accidents, illness and danger.
- Staff, service users and visitors will feel confident using the service, knowing that risk assessments are carried out.

Staff training programmes

Equipment use

Service providers in health and social care settings will use a wide range of equipment with service users, from mobility aids and manual handling equipment to household appliances.

Staff should be appropriately trained to use specialist equipment such as:

- hoists
- transfer boards
- slings
- slide sheets
- leg-lifters
- fire evacuation chairs.

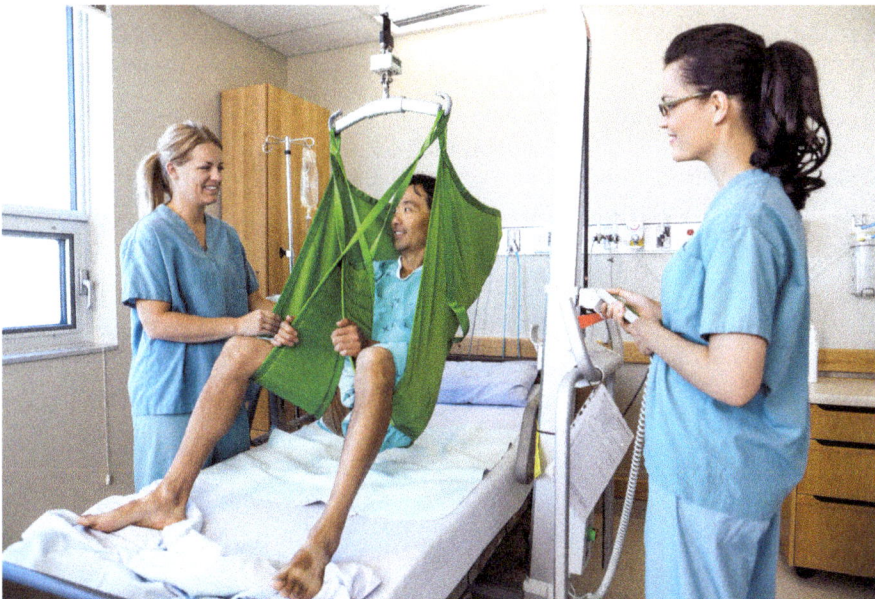

Figure 1.27 A hoist can be used to move a patient safely into or out of bed

OCR Cambridge National in Health and Social Care

Moving and handling techniques

Service providers in health and social care settings will often need to move items of equipment such as tables and chairs. In social and healthcare, service providers may have to assist service users to move. Scenarios include:

- assisting an older person or a service user with a physical disability to get out of a bed/chair/shower/bath
- transfer from bed to chair
- moving and handling objects, such as shopping bags
- use of hoists, when bathing or getting out of bed.

It is essential to have staff who are trained in moving and handling techniques if this is part of their job role. The training helps to protect service providers as well as the person receiving care and support, as shown in Table 1.3.

Table 1.3 The benefits of using correct moving and handling techniques

Who benefits?	The benefits of being trained in moving and handling techniques
Service providers	• Staff are given guidance on good practice – they will be aware of the correct posture and position to be in when using equipment for lifting or moving. • The environment, equipment and load will always be risk assessed. • The risk assessment identifies if a second person is needed to assist with the lift. • It prevents injury to service providers. • It helps service providers to do their job correctly; this results in a safer environment as it reduces risk. • Improved knowledge of moving and handling develops the service provider's confidence when moving and handling service users. • The training provides protection from accusations of abuse as correct procedures will have been followed.
Service users	• Training of staff prevents injury to service users. • It improves the comfort and dignity of service users. • It shows respect. • It instils confidence, trust and a feeling of safety as the service user knows that the service provider is trained and qualified to carry out manual handling. • It results in a safer environment and reduces risk to service users. • Service users will not feel disempowered by being handled incorrectly.

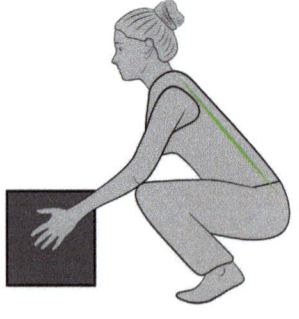
correct posture

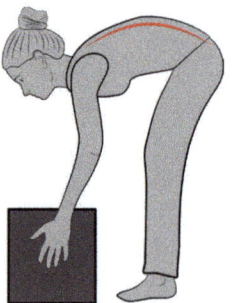
incorrect posture

Figure 1.28 Using the safe lifting position to avoid injury

Guidance for safe lifting:
- Stand with feet apart.
- Bend the knees.
- Keep the back straight.
- Lean slightly forward to get a grip of the item.
- Lift smoothly.

Unit R032 Principles of care in health and social care settings

Case study: Willowfield residential home

Serena is the new manager at Willowfield, a residential home which has 25 residents aged between 75 and 96 years. Serena has been checking the accident book and has discovered that over the last 12 months there have been numerous occasions when residents have had falls, including one when a resident had to spend six weeks in hospital because of their injuries. Two staff have had back injuries due to lifting and handling residents.

Serena urgently wants to do something to address the problem and asks the staff for volunteers to be part of an 'accident reduction team'. You are part of the team and have been tasked with producing an action plan to reduce the number of accidents.

Create an action plan of what needs to be done to help protect residents and staff, making Willowfield a safer place. Consider the following factors when creating the action plan:

1 The residents' bedrooms are personalised with their own furniture and belongings including ornaments, rugs, lamps and televisions. How can the risk of falls be reduced in the residents' bedrooms?
2 Suggest what could be done at Willowfield to reduce the risk of staff getting injured when moving and handling the residents.

First aid

First aid is an important part of training in social care. It includes basic life support as part of inductions for new staff. First aiders must be trained and must attend regular refresher training every three years to ensure they have up-to-date knowledge.

The Health and Safety (First Aid) Regulations 1981 require employers to provide:

- suitable and appropriate equipment
- facilities such as a first aid room.

This will ensure that staff and service users can receive immediate help if they are injured or taken ill at the care setting.

Emergency procedures

All care settings should have emergency procedures in place for situations such as fire, bomb scares and intruders.

- Service providers should be made aware of the procedures and their role in an emergency.
- Service users also need to be made aware of fire evacuation procedures.

OCR Cambridge National in Health and Social Care

There should be regular evacuation practices and fire drills so that everyone is familiar with what to do and where to go, and can do it quickly in an emergency. Figure 1.29 shows a fire evacuation procedure for a nursing home.

> **Checkleigh Nursing Home**
> **Fire evacuation procedure**
> - If you discover a fire, raise the alarm – alert people in the immediate area, activate alarm system, call 999.
> - All staff to remove people from their immediate area – direct them to the fire assembly point, use designated fire exits, never use lifts.
> - Designated staff assist residents with:
>   – mobility difficulties (use of evac chairs/wheelchairs)
>   – hearing difficulties (may not hear alarm)
>   – dementia patients (may be confused/unaware of what is happening).
> - Staff to close doors and windows, switch off lights as they leave.
> - Staff evacuating the building must check their locality is clear.
> - Everyone to assemble at designated external assembly point to await further instructions.
> - Do not re-enter the building until told it is safe to do so.
> - Carry out head count to ensure everyone is accounted for.
> - Senior staff to inform fire brigade if anyone is left in the building.

Figure 1.29 An example of a fire evacuation procedure

Emergency events such as:

- gas leak
- flood
- bomb threat

will all require a setting to be evacuated quickly and efficiently to keep people safe.

In the very rare event of a firearms or weapons attack, the Government provides advice on how service users can keep themselves safe. Leaflets, posters and YouTube films are available.

Care settings are encouraged to ensure that they raise awareness of this advice sensitively, particularly with children.

- **Run –** if you can
- **Hide –** if you can't run away
- **Tell –** the police when it is safe to do so.

Figure 1.30 Stay safe advice

Unit R032 Principles of care in health and social care settings

Equipment considerations

When using equipment in care settings, the staff need to be aware of several considerations around safety.

Table 1.4 Equipment considerations

Equipment considerations	How it improves safety
Appropriate training of staff for specialist equipment (e.g. hoists, transfer boards)	Staff will know how to use it correctly.
Is equipment fit for purpose, appropriate for the task? Is specialist equipment available?	Correct equipment provided for the task, which reduces risk of injury to staff and service users.
Regular safety checks for damage – items repaired or disposed of if necessary (e.g. wheelchairs)	No worn-out, damaged or potentially dangerous equipment will be used.
Is equipment risk assessed to ensure it is safe? Is special training required?	Only equipment deemed safe is used. Staff will receive training if required.
A reporting system for damaged or faulty equipment	Action can be taken immediately to take equipment out of use. This reduces the risk of accidents.
Replacement programme for older or worn-out equipment	A good standard of safe equipment is maintained.
Regular PAT testing of electrical equipment	Testing ensures safe electrical equipment.

Safety measures

Fire safety measures include:

- fire safety notices that are displayed and visible throughout the setting
- signs indicating fire doors and assembly points
- keeping fire doors clear
- a fire extinguisher available by each exit
- a fire blanket in kitchen areas.

General safety measures include using warning signs such as:

- a 'Wet floor' sign after mopping the floor
- a 'No entry' sign to prevent unauthorised access.

Figure 1.31 Putting out a 'Wet floor' sign after cleaning is a safety measure

4.4 How security measures protect service users and staff

Security measures

An important part of maintaining the safety of a care setting is keeping it secure from strangers and intruders entering the building. Security measures also prevent service users leaving the care setting on their own, for example, children from a breakfast club or service users with dementia leaving a residential home.

Figure 1.32 shows a whole range of security measures, and Table 1.5 shows how security measures benefit service users and service providers.

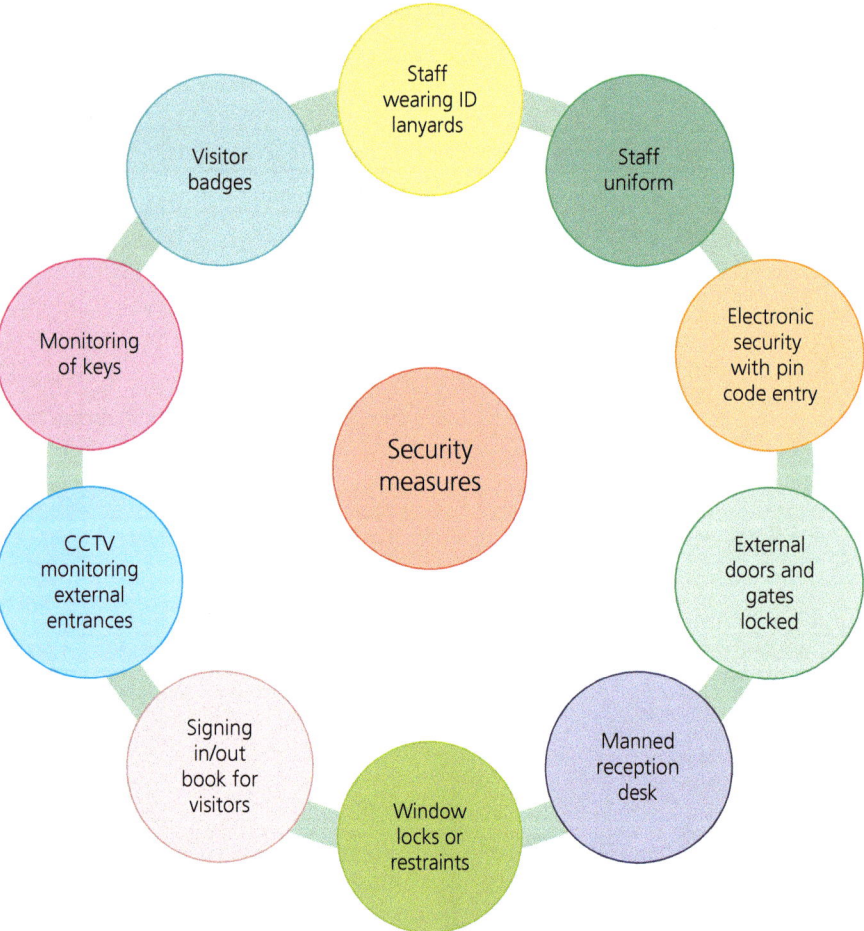

Figure 1.32 Security measures in a care setting

Unit R032 Principles of care in health and social care settings

Table 1.5 How security measures keep service users and service providers safe

Security measure	How it helps to keep service users and service providers safe
Identifying staff	Wearing ID lanyards and staff uniform makes it easy to spot unauthorised people, as lanyards and uniforms quickly identify who is a member of staff.
Monitoring keys	This will limit the number of people with access to keys and there will be a list of authorised key holders. This means that the location of each set of keys is known.
Receiving and monitoring visitors	<ul><li>If there are staff on duty at the entrance, access can be monitored.</li><li>A receptionist can monitor external CCTV to ensure there are no intruders around, and report any incidents to the manager.</li><li>A signing in and signing out book for visitors ensures that reception knows who is there and who has left the building.</li><li>Some settings have staff signing in and out, or swiping their ID card.</li><li>Issuing visitor badges identifies visitors quickly and clearly.</li></ul>
Reporting concerns to line managers	It is important to report concerns to the manager so that they are aware of security breaches. Senior staff can take appropriate action to address security issues.
External doors, restricting access	<ul><li>An electronic swipe card entry system or a security pad with a pin code will prevent unauthorised people from gaining entry into the setting, as only those with the correct card or pin will be able to enter.</li><li>A buzzer entry system allows reception staff to control who enters.</li></ul>
Window locks and restraints	These are important in care settings, particularly in settings such as residential homes, where service users may have dementia and can wander out of the building without realising. These aids:<ul><li>keep vulnerable service users safe – for example, window locks and restraints prevent service users falling out of or leaving through open windows</li><li>prevent intruders from entering.</li></ul>

Test your knowledge

1. What should a first aid policy cover?
2. Write an example of a safety procedure and one example of a safety measure.
3. What are the five stages of carrying out a risk assessment?
4. Write about what should happen during a fire evacuation procedure.
5. What are procedures a residential home should have in place for visitors?

Activity

Create a quiz

1. In small groups, create a quiz about health and safety in care settings. Each group could be allocated a different health and safety topic.
2. Each group should write ten questions and produce an answer sheet.
3. Have a quiz session with the whole class. Which group will score the most points?

OCR Cambridge National in Health and Social Care

Synoptic links

Unit R032	Links with other units
Topic area 4: Protecting service users and service providers in health and social care settings	**R033 Supporting individuals through life events** **Topic area 2:** Impacts of life events **Topic area 3:** Sources of support
	R034 Creative and therapeutic activities **Topic area 3:** Plan a creative activity for individuals or groups in a healthcare or social care setting **Topic area 4:** Deliver a creative activity and evaluate your own performance
	R035 Health promotion campaigns **Topic area 2:** Factors influencing health and well-being **Topic area 3:** Plan and evaluate a health promotion campaign

Practice questions

Question 1

Maintaining security is very important in all health and social care settings.

Identify **three** different security measures. Describe how each security measure could protect service users.

[6 marks]

Question 2

Explain reasons for staff applying to work in a residential care home for young adults with learning disabilities having Disclosure and Barring Service (DBS) checks before being employed.

[8 marks]

Question 3

One safety procedure that could be used at a day centre, which provides sports activities for young boys with learning disabilities, is 'equipment considerations'.

Explain how two examples of equipment considerations would help to improve safety at the day centre.

[4 marks]

Question 4

Describe how personal hygiene measures can protect service users in care settings.

In your answer you must include:

- some examples of personal hygiene measures
- details of how these personal hygiene measures protect service users in care settings.

[6 marks]

Read about it

Reference books

Ayling, P. (2009) *Knowledge Set: Infection Prevention and Control*. Heinemann. For Topic area 4.

Collins, S. (2009) *Effective Communication: A Workbook for Social Care Workers*. Jessica Kingsley Publishers. For Topic areas 2 and 3.

Morris, C. (2009) *Knowledge Set: Safeguarding Vulnerable Adults*. Heinemann.

Stretch, B. (2007) *Core Themes in Health and Social Care*. Heinemann. All topic areas. For Topic area 1, see especially Chapter 2, 'Promoting equality of opportunity in health and social care settings'. For Topic area 3, see especially Chapter 1, 'Interpersonal skills in Health and Social Care'. For Topic area 4, see especially Chapter 5, 'Health and Safety at Work'.

Weblinks

www.equalityhumanrights.com/en

Equality and Human Rights Commission – this website provides comprehensive information on all aspects of equality, diversity and rights.

www.skillsforcare.org.uk/Home.aspx

Skills for Care – an organisation that provides resources and shares best practice to help raise standards in health and social care services. This website also provides a workbook and presentation for Standard 5 of the Care Certificate, at:

www.skillsforcare.org.uk/Documents/Learning-and-development/Care-Certificate/Standard-5.pdf

www.theadvocacypeople.org.uk/seap

SEAP (Support, Empower, Advocate, Promote)

www.mencap.org.uk/advice-and-support/services-you-can-count/advocacy

Mencap

www.mind.org.uk/information-support/guides-to-support-and-services/advocacy/what-is-advocacy/

Mind

www.gov.uk/government/organisations/disclosure-and-barring-service

Disclosure and Barring Service

www.safenetwork.org.uk

NSPCC safeguarding information and resources

www.ceop.police.uk/Safety-Centre/

Child Exploitation & Online Protection Centre (CEOP), for internet safety.

http://www.scie.org.uk

Social Care Institute for Excellence

www.hse.gov.uk/index.htm

Health and Safety Executive website – comprehensive information about health and safety in the workplace.

Unit R033
Supporting individuals through life events

About this unit
This unit examines the life stages from 5 to 65+ years, through childhood, adolescence, adulthood and older adulthood. Everyone's life is different and many different factors affect life stages in varying ways.

You are going to look at the changes associated with the development from childhood to older adulthood and the factors that can influence this development. You will examine expected and unexpected life events and the effect they can have on an individual's life. You will also research how individuals can be supported by service providers and practitioners.

Topic areas
In this chapter you will learn about:
1. Life stages
2. Impacts of life events
3. Sources of support.

OCR Cambridge National in Health and Social Care

How will I be assessed?

You will be assessed through a series of assignment tasks, which are set by OCR. The assignment will be marked by your tutor and then moderated by OCR.

For Topic area 1 you will need to:

- choose ONE life stage for your chosen individual, describing growth and development for that life stage
- explain how your individual's growth and development have been affected by two of each of the specified factors.

For Topic area 2 you will need to:

- describe two life events for your chosen individual
- explain the impact of ONE of the life events on your individual's physical, intellectual, emotional or social development
- explain how the impact of the life event affected the individual's needs.

For Topic area 3 you will need to:

- research the support available to your individual
- justify how the support will meet the individual's needs
- apply person-centred values of care.

Unit R033 covers three Performance Objectives (POs):

- PO2 Apply knowledge and understanding
- PO3 Analyse and evaluate knowledge, understanding and performance
- PO4 Demonstrate and apply skills and processes relevant to the subject area

Topic area 1 Life stages

Getting started

Think back to when you were five years old.

- How have you changed physically and intellectually?
- How have your language skills improved?
- What emotional and social changes have you gone through?

Remember PIES:

- **P**hysical – refers to the development of an individual's body
- **I**ntellectual – concerns an individual's thought processes such as thinking skills, understanding, learning, reasoning, comprehension and knowledge
- **E**motional – refers to an individual's feelings
- **S**ocial – concerns the individual's relationships with others

1.1 Life stages and development

Table 2.1 Key features of life stages

Life stage	Age
Childhood	4–10
Adolescence/young person	11–18
Young adulthood	19–45
Middle adulthood	46–65
Older adulthood	65+

Life stages and key milestones of growth and development for age groups: four to ten years (childhood)

During this life stage, children start to venture out of the home for whole days away from their carers/parents as they start school. Their physical appearance begins to change from their baby shape, and they begin to resemble a small adult.

PIES development across four to ten years (childhood)

Physical

- Between four and ten years of age, the body will grow taller and gain weight.
- As children take part in physical activities, muscles and bones become stronger.
- Strength and muscle co-ordination improve rapidly in these years.
- Facial features change and children lose baby teeth, to be replaced with permanent teeth.

Gross/fine motor skills

During this period of growth, both gross and fine motor skills develop rapidly. By the age of five, children can:

- hop, skip and jump
- stand on one foot for a few seconds
- throw and catch a ball, usually with two hands.

As they move towards ten years of age, children can:

- combine **gross motor skills** and **fine motor skills** more easily; for example, they can turn, spin and jump, such as in basketball/netball
- develop better hand–eye co-ordination; for example, they become more accurate when kicking a football into the goal, or throwing a ball at a target
- demonstrate improved agility, speed, co-ordination and balance.

> **Key terms**
> **Gross motor skills** The larger movements of arms, legs, feet or the entire body using the large muscles, for walking, running, skipping and jumping.
> **Fine motor skills** Smaller actions using the smaller muscles, such as grasping an object between the thumb and a finger when holding a paintbrush or pencil.

Figure 2.1 Children develop gross and fine motor skills

They continue to advance their fine motor skills, such as those needed for clearer handwriting and detailed artwork.

- By the age of ten, many will be able to draw and write with better control.
- Working on the computer or playing videogames will also be taken to a new level, as many children have the co-ordination and heightened reflexes to perform more difficult tasks.
- It is a good time for a child to be introduced to a musical instrument.

Intellectual

Although children can count by the age of seven, they do not understand how the logic of mass, volume and number work. Maths requires a wide range of skills and involves a broad vocabulary and variety of concepts.

Mathematical skills often build on one another – some children are strong in some types of maths but weak in others. By the time children are ten, they are usually skilled in addition and subtraction and are building skills in multiplication, division and fractions. They are at the stage where logical thinking is limited to what they can see.

Most children will have started to develop verbal reasoning skills from four to five years of age. A school teacher will help them to develop these skills. Verbal reasoning is important for learning concepts in physics or mathematics, as well as in literacy-based subjects.

From five to ten years, children develop a capacity to concentrate on one thing (directed thinking). At school they will carry out a variety of activities which will help them to learn and to understand the world

Unit R033 Supporting individuals through life events

around them. Adolescents will continue to learn and develop their skills, and this will continue into adulthood.

Between the ages of six and ten, most children should be able to write legibly and easily. At this age they are learning to read fluently.

Memory is the ability to acquire, store, and recall information or experiences across time. A person's memories:

- form the basis for their sense of self
- guide their thoughts and decisions
- influence their emotional reactions
- allow them to learn.

As such, memory is central to **cognitive development**. Memory performance generally improves with age. It is thought that memory continues to develop up until the age of 25–30 years.

Key term
Cognitive development
The construction of thought processes, including remembering, problem solving and decision making, from childhood through to adulthood.

Language

- By five or six years, children will often have good communication skills.
- By the age of five to seven years, most children can speak using correct grammar. They can use language in a range of social situations.
- By the age of ten, most children can talk easily to people of all different ages. They will keep a conversation flowing, by giving reasons and explaining choices. They will have speech patterns that are nearly at an adult level.

Communication skills develop throughout life as people learn to have a better command of language.

- Children at the age of five can use their language skills when learning to read, write and spell. They learn that the same word can mean two things, such as 'orange' the fruit and 'orange' the colour. Their vocabulary will be 2000–3000 words.
- By ten they enjoy reading. They may seek out magazines and books on subjects of special interest.

A person's vocabulary continues to grow throughout their life.

Emotional

Between four and ten years, children experience a growth of feelings. They must learn how to cope with these feelings just as if they were learning a new skill.

Playing with other children helps them with these feelings.

- By the age of five, children want to play with others and join in team games.
- By the age of ten, they have learned to cope with and control their feelings. They begin to develop their self-image and how they see themselves. They also become more independent as they realise that there is a life outside the home.

Activity
Memory task
Your teacher will place 10 to 20 objects on a tray.

- You have one minute to view the objects, then the teacher will cover up the tray.
- You then have one minute to write down all the items that you can remember.
- Count up how many items you have remembered, and report this to your teacher.
- Are there any items that were forgotten by the whole group?
- Discuss the implications for someone who could not remember any of the items.

OCR Cambridge National in Health and Social Care

Social

Children start to develop social skills from birth as they observe and bond with their parents, carers and siblings. Bonding is the intense attachment that develops between parents and their baby. Scientists are still learning a lot about bonding. They know the strong ties between parents and their child provide the baby's first model for close relationships and give them a sense of security and positive self-esteem. Once they start school, they meet lots of new people and make new friends. They might build a strong bond with their teacher at this age, who takes the place of a parent or carer in their eyes.

Children may start to form a special friendship as they reach the end of childhood, at the age of nine or ten.

Life stages and key milestones of growth and development for age groups: 11 to 18 years (adolescence)

This is a time of huge physical, emotional and social development, as young children grow into young adults. They leave the world of primary school and transition into a much larger senior school with many more pupils and teachers. Girls tend to mature earlier than boys.

PIES development across 11 to 18 years (adolescence)

Physical

Between the ages of 8 and 13 years, girls experience **puberty**. If there is not enough oestrogen in a young girl's body, she will not be able to menstruate properly. Menstruation continues throughout a woman's life, unless pregnant, until she reaches menopause. At this stage, the ovaries produce so little oestrogen that the lining of the womb fails to thicken up, and so periods stop.

> **Key term**
>
> **Puberty** The process of bodily changes that occur during adolescence, as a child grows into an adult capable of sexual reproduction.

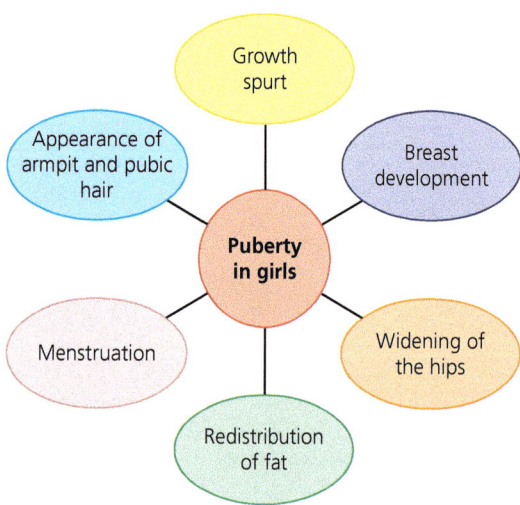

Figure 2.2 Puberty in girls

Unit R033 Supporting individuals through life events

Boys usually go through puberty between the ages of 9 and 14 years. Testosterone levels rise during puberty, peak during the late teen years, and then level off.

All adolescents might experience skin problems such as acne during puberty. This is caused by hormones secreted by the pituitary gland. The pituitary gland causes the production of oestrogen in girls and testosterone in boys.

Although they start puberty later than girls, boys often have a fast growing spurt and generally end up taller and heavier.

By the age of 11, most children will have developed their gross and fine motor skills, but they may develop them further by practice, for example, when playing sports.

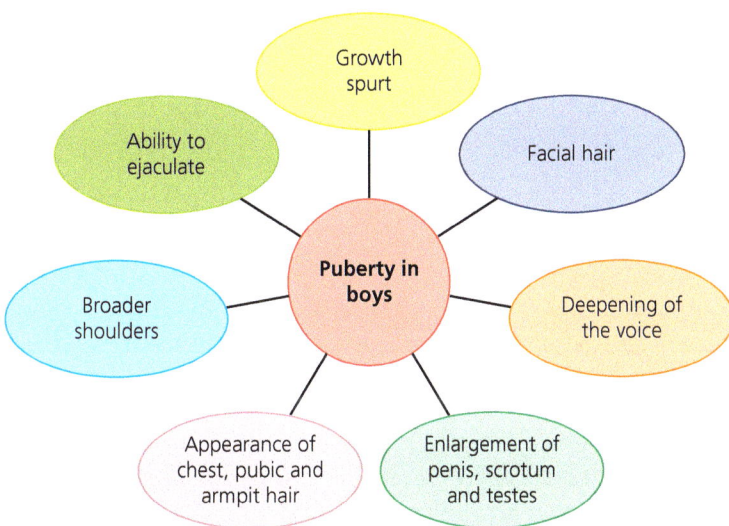

Figure 2.3 Puberty in boys

As shown in Figures 2.2 and 2.3, young people's appearance changes considerably during adolescence and they will begin to look like adults.

Case study

Chloe is 15 and is very small for her age. She is worried because her periods haven't started, and her body hasn't changed shape since she was a child. Her mother says she should not worry as she is a 'late developer'.

1 Discuss with a partner what advice you would give Chloe.
2 Feed back to the rest of the group. Were there any differences in opinion in your advice for Chloe?

Intellectual

At the age of 11, adolescents have started to use logic and **abstract thinking** to think through complicated ideas. This continues to develop throughout adolescence and into adulthood.

By 11, they become more fluent writers, increasing in speed; handwriting becomes more automatic as they develop their own style.

By 11–13 years, adolescents are reading to learn about their hobbies and other interests and to study for school.

- They comprehend more fully what they have read.
- They read fiction, including chapter books, and nonfiction, including magazines and newspapers.
- They learn to revise for examinations, and know what to do when they have to memorise facts and be able to use them.
- They may continue to use their examination techniques throughout their adult lives, particularly if they enter higher education after school.

> **Key term**
> **Abstract thinking** Being able to solve problems using the imagination.

Figure 2.4 Logic and abstract thinking develop throughout adolescence

Emotional

Adolescence is when hormones cause surges of positive and negative emotions, known as 'mood swings'. One minute a young person can be feeling incredibly positive, and the next moment they are feeling very down with negative emotions, such as feeling unpopular and that no one likes them. This is the time of life when a young person learns to regulate and control emotions, and to form secure relationships ready for adulthood.

Many adolescents have low levels of confidence and low self-esteem. They may not like what is happening to their bodies, and often they feel they have lost control of their emotions when they suffer from mood swings. They may feel depressed about their lives, especially if they do not fit in with their **peer group**.

Social

During adolescence, young people are more influenced by their peer group than by their family. They become increasingly independent as they rely more on their friends.

Adolescents want to fit in with the rest of their peer group, and often dress in similar clothes and behave in similar ways.

During adolescence, young people explore their sexuality and may have sexual relationships with other people. They may rebel against their parents or teachers, as they challenge acceptable ways of behaving.

> **Key term**
> **Peer group** A group of people, usually of the same age, who have similar interests, background and social status. A peer group can influence the behaviour of group members.

Life stages and key milestones of growth and development for age groups: 19 to 45 years (young adulthood)

During adulthood, people reach the peak of their physical performance, usually in their twenties and thirties. They are also at their most fertile. Physically, individuals are in the 'prime of their life' as they are at their best in ease of movement, lung capacity and strength.

PIES development across 19 to 45 years (young adulthood)

Physical

By the time people reach adulthood, they have reached their full height and have stopped growing. But habits and choice of lifestyle can affect an individual's physical development for the rest of their lives. Choosing a healthy diet and taking regular exercise will improve fitness and general good health. These habits will help to prevent diseases such as heart disease or cancer, and will last them into old age. Unhealthy choices, such as smoking, binge drinking, drug taking or eating a poor diet, can have a negative effect on health, and may cause avoidable disease or illness.

Intellectual

Intellectual skills such as logical thinking may continue to increase in early adulthood, if people use them. These skills are honed at work and used for decision making and problem solving. The young adult can build on their life experiences, allowing their thinking to become more flexible and enabling them to change and to adapt to different circumstances.

Emotional

During young adulthood, individuals start to build up their confidence and explore who they are. Becoming more confident is a result of leaving home, going to university/college or getting a job and becoming responsible for looking after themselves. The security of working and living in their own place adds to their confidence. People often get married or become partners with someone as they want love, security and companionship.

Social

In the early stages of young adulthood, individuals may spend a lot of their spare time socialising and trying to make new friends. The more that young adults socialise, the more comfortable they feel about social situations; they start to develop their social skills. They become more confident in large groups and as a result improve their communication skills. They may develop relationships of all types

Figure 2.5 In young adulthood, individuals may spend a lot of their spare time socialising

including close and intimate ones. This is an important stage for them where new bonds may be made. In turn, this can lead to an increase in sense of wellbeing and happiness.

Life stages and key milestones of growth and development for age groups: 46 to 65 years (middle adulthood)

Middle adulthood marks the end of the 'prime of your life' for most individuals. However, most middle-aged adults still have good health and not a notable change in their physical ability, although there are some minor changes, which may be hardly noticeable.

PIES development across 46 to 65 years (middle adulthood)

Physical

As individuals approach the age of about 60, they may experience early symptoms of ageing such as grey hair, wrinkles and long-sightedness, which means they need glasses for reading. They may also experience poor health such as cancer or heart disease. Women will go through the menopause usually between the age of 45 to 55. This means their periods stop so they will be unable to have children.

> **Research**
>
> Research information on the menopause. One place where you may find information is on the NHS website, for example:
>
> www.nhs.uk/Conditions/Menopause/Pages/Introduction.aspx
>
> 1 Explain what is meant by the menopause.
> 2 Explain the causes of the menopause.
> 3 Describe the symptoms of the menopause.
> 4 Why might women feel a sense of loss at the time of the menopause?

As people become older:

- muscle strength decreases, and muscles are not as firm as before
- reactions become slower
- skin elasticity is reduced, so that it wrinkles
- men and women can lose their hair
- posture can be affected as muscles become less flexible
- they may lose some flexibility.

Intellectual

In middle adulthood, individuals are often at the peak of their intellectual skills. They may gain promotion at work, reaching the highest position in their career. They may mentor younger individuals who are just starting their first job. Many people have now reached their career goals and may feel they can spend time developing hobbies and other interests outside of work which they may have put on hold to develop their career.

Although memory skills may start to decline in later middle adulthood, other intellectual skills such as abstract thinking and verbal skills may improve in middle age as individuals bring their life experiences and practical knowledge to situations.

Emotional

Middle-aged individuals may feel frustrated as they no longer feel as young and fit as they were. This can be in the form of a 'midlife crisis', when individuals reflect on their life so far. They may feel that life no longer offers them the opportunities it did when they were young.

Some individuals may feel content and happy with what they have achieved in their career. However, some people may feel dissatisfied and bored with their job and, because they are better off financially, they may want to retrain for a new career.

Social

Middle age is usually a time of greater financial security and many people feel they have more time and money to enjoy socialising. They may have made many friends throughout their working lives and have many social events to go to. Friendships are often well-established by this time in life. However, some people may have caring responsibilities such as looking after grandchildren or caring for aging parents, which can limit socialising.

Life stages and key milestones of growth and development for age groups: 65+ years (older adulthood)

Although older adulthood may seem a negative phase of life because of the ageing process, there are also positives:

- The older person can retire from work and spend their time as they wish, so they may take up new hobbies or go on out-of-season holidays.
- They may want to gain further academic qualifications, particularly if they were unable to do so during their younger years.
- Many older people remain independent for the rest of their lives.

PIES development across 65+ years (older adulthood)

Physical

Physical changes become more obvious in older adulthood.

Table 2.2 The effect of ageing on physical development

Body	Changes
Skin	• Wrinkles develop and skin loosens as it loses elasticity. • Skin becomes drier.
Hair	• Growth slows, and hair thins. • Men may go bald.
Hearing, smell and taste	• Senses deteriorate. • Appetite might be reduced.
Eyesight	• Long-sightedness may develop. • Cataracts and glaucoma may cause blindness if not treated.
Teeth	• Decay and gum disease can occur.
Lungs and respiratory system	• Lungs are less elastic, and respiratory muscles weaken. • Strenuous exercise is more difficult or impossible because of lack of lung capacity. • Respiratory disorders such as influenza or pneumonia have more serious effects.
Heart and blood vessels (cardiovascular system)	• Heart efficiency decreases, blood pressure may be raised, blood vessels are less elastic. • This can lead to cardiovascular disease such as stroke and heart attack.
Digestive system	• Indigestion or heartburn occurs, as saliva and digestive juices decrease with age. • Food takes longer to work through the digestive system as muscles are weaker and less efficient; this leads to constipation.
Urinary system	• Kidneys are less efficient at filtering waste products. • May need to pass urine more frequently; may be prone to urinary infections.
Reproductive system	• Menopause marks the end of reproduction for women.
Skeleton and muscles	• People shrink in height, as total bone mass is reduced. • In women, osteoporosis may result in fractured and broken bones. • Knee and/or hip problems can cause mobility problems. • Muscles become less flexible. • Balance can be affected. • Posture and mobility likely to alter.

Intellectual

Forgetfulness is a common complaint among older adults. As people age, they experience physiological changes that can cause slowness in brain function. It takes longer to learn and recall information. People often mistake this slowing of the mental processes for true memory loss. Many mental abilities are unaffected by normal ageing. People do not become less intelligent and can still learn new skills.

The causes of age-related memory are explained below:

- The hippocampus, a region of the brain involved in the formation and retrieval of memories, often deteriorates with age.
- Hormones and proteins that protect and repair brain cells and stimulate **neural growth** also decline with age.
- Older people often experience decreased blood flow to the brain, which can impair memory and lead to changes in cognitive skills.

Key term

Neural growth Any growth of the nervous system.

Unit R033 Supporting individuals through life events

It should be noted that not all older people will develop dementia.

Case study
Colin is 69. His partner has noticed that he has difficulty getting washed and dressed in the morning. He has started to repeat stories several times during the same conversation. Last week Colin set off to his daughter's house and got lost. He had a satnav device but couldn't follow the directions.

Archie is 72. Sometimes he has difficulty in finding the right word to use in conversation, but he can follow and hold a conversation. He recently forgot his wedding anniversary.

- Which person is likely to have dementia, and which one has memory loss?
- Give reasons for your answer.

Research
Research dementia and find out what the symptoms are. For example, you could look for information on the AgeUK website:

www.ageuk.org.uk/information-advice/health-wellbeing/conditions-illnesses/dementia/understanding-dementia

Emotional
When they reach retirement, the older person may feel less stressed and more relaxed.

- They may get a lot of pleasure and satisfaction in helping with their grandchildren.
- They may spend more quality time with their partner, family and friends.

However, sometimes older people feel lonely when they retire.

- This is especially true if their partner dies.
- They may start to lose their self-confidence if they have health problems.

Social
For many older people, this is the opening of a new chapter in their lives, where they choose what they are going to do.

- Older adults often have highly active social lives, as they have time to meet friends for coffee or lunch.
- Some people embrace new challenges, such as learning a new language, keeping fit or learning how to dance.
- They may join several different clubs, and enjoy the friendship and companionship as well as the activities.
- They may also enjoy travelling on organised trips for their age group.

Test your knowledge
1. What is meant by the term 'gross motor skills'? Give two examples.
2. What is meant by abstract thinking?
3. Name three changes that take place in girls' bodies during puberty.
4. Which is the longest development stage?
5. How does aging affect the urinary system?

Factors affecting growth and development across the life stages

There are many factors that affect growth and development across all the life stages. Some of these factors can be controlled by the individual (such as their diet) and some cannot (such as genetics).

OCR Cambridge National in Health and Social Care

Physical factors
Some physical factors can affect other physical factors; for example, lifestyle choices such as smoking can affect an individual's health.

Diet and nutrition
Food is essential for life and necessary for health and well-being. Having a well-balanced diet with a variety of nutrients helps people to stay healthy.

Nutrients are the component parts of the food we eat. They are chemicals that provide energy, support growth and repair, and support the normal functioning of the body. It is important to have the correct quantities of each nutrient so that people do not become undernourished and suffer deficiencies, or become over-nourished and obese. A balanced diet containing a variety of different foods will contain the correct nutritional quantities.

> **Key term**
>
> **Homeostasis** How the body adjusts to maintain a constant and steady state. For example, blood sugar levels are kept constant by the supply of insulin from the pancreas.

Table 2.3 The functions of nutrients

Function	Nutrient	What it does
Producing energy	Starchy carbohydrate	• provides energy for the body • provides vitamins, minerals and fibre
	Fat	• provides energy for the body
Growth and repair	Protein	• helps to build, maintain and repair body tissues • makes hormones, enzymes and antibodies • provides energy, if not enough is provided by carbohydrates
Prevention of disease	Calcium	• helps to maintain and build strong bones and teeth
	Vitamin C	• helps to heal wounds • helps to fight infection • helps to maintain healthy teeth, bones and blood vessels
	Vitamin D	• helps to form strong teeth and bones, together with calcium • supports the immune system
	Vitamin E	• prevents heart disease
	Vitamin K	• needed for blood clotting • helps wounds heal properly • prevents osteoporosis
Aid nerve function	Vitamin B12 Vitamin B6 Minerals	• help brain, nerves and muscles to function • help the body to use energy from food
Aid the excretion process	Fibre	• aids digestion • helps avoid constipation • contributes to maintaining bowel health
To act as a carrier for other nutrients	Fat	• carries fat-soluble vitamins A, D, E and K throughout the body in the bloodstream for use (absorption)
For cell formation	Vitamin E	• helps form red blood cells, muscles and other tissues
To protect and maintain cell **homeostasis**	Vitamins Minerals	• help regulate the many chemical processes in the body • iron helps to make haemoglobin in red blood cells and helps cells to use oxygen

Unit R033 Supporting individuals through life events

Activities

Physical activities are important across the life stages.

Regular daily exercise can help to:

- maintain the correct weight, as it uses up excess calories/kilojoules
- protect against heart disease.

Exercise has an effect on the body:

- There is increased blood flow to the major organs.
- Increased oxygen goes to the brain to help memory and learning.
- It improves large muscle strength and endurance.
- It increases flexibility.

For more information see Unit R035, Topic area 2.

Lifestyle choices

Lifestyle choices can have an immediate or a long-term effect. For example:

- If a person does not have enough sleep for one night, they will be tired the next day. However, if lack of sleep goes on for months, it will seriously affect many areas of their life.
- If a person smokes, it may seem to have little effect on them immediately. However, many years later, they may develop lung cancer.
- Drinking alcohol can cause liver damage, particularly if the individual binge drinks. It can also cause diseases such as bowel, stomach, mouth or throat cancers.

See Unit R035, Topic area 1, section 1.2 for further information on smoking and alcohol consumption.

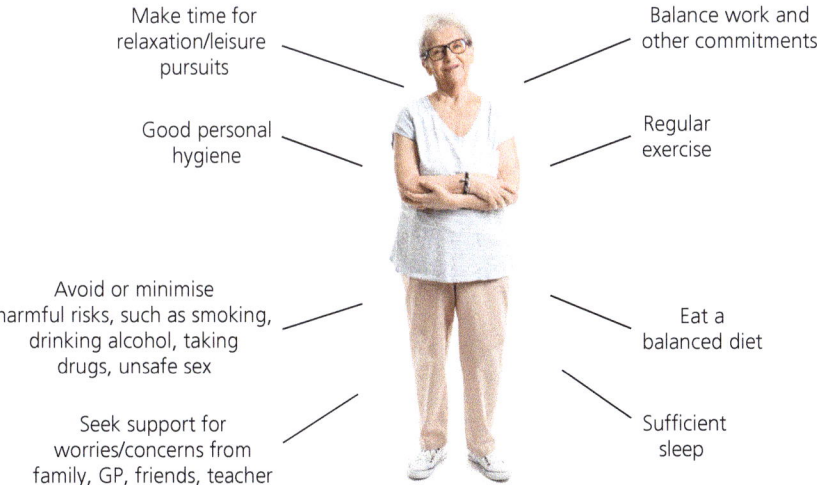

Figure 2.6 Positive lifestyle choices

Genetics

Genetics play a significant role in the development of certain birth defects.

- Every living being has cells containing chromosomes.
- When a human embryo is fertilised, it receives half of its chromosomes from the father and the other half from the mother.
- Birth defects may occur if more or fewer chromosomes are passed on to the child.
- Problems may also arise if any one of the chromosomes is faulty.
- Genetic birth defects in babies can occur even when both parents are healthy.

Examples of genetic disorders include spina bifida, some heart defects and Down's syndrome.

Physical and mental health

Obviously, physical and mental health play a large role in growth and development.

If someone has a long-term serious illness or feels unwell for long periods, then this will affect what they can achieve in their lifetime. This ill health could have a huge effect on their job prospects, their education and their financial prospects – it will be very difficult for them to reach their potential if they are unwell and in continuous physical pain.

Serious illness also has an impact on the rest of the family:

- One partner may need to have time away from work to look after their physically or mentally ill partner.
- Children sometimes become a carer for their parent. This could affect their education, as they miss school or don't have time for homework. They may also miss out on a social life as they cannot leave their parent.

Mental illness refers to a wide range of mental health conditions that affect mood, thinking and behaviour.

- Examples include depression, anxiety disorders, schizophrenia, eating disorders and addictive behaviours.
- Many people have mental health concerns from time to time.
- A mental health concern becomes a mental illness when ongoing signs and symptoms cause frequent stress and affect the person's ability to function in everyday life.

Unit R033 Supporting individuals through life events

Disability

Anyone can become disabled.

- Some individuals have **disabilities** from birth, such as spina bifida or cerebral palsy.
- Other individuals become disabled through accidents at other life stages, such as in a car accident or a serious injury at work.
- Others becomes disabled through illnesses such as cancer or diabetes.

Sensory impairment

Sensory birth defects affect the development and function of the sensory organs, including the eyes and ears, and can contribute to visual impairment and hearing loss.

- Many of these problems are caused by syndromes or inherited conditions, and often people with certain conditions experience problems with particular senses.
- Examples of sensory birth defects include cataracts, other visual conditions, blindness, hearing loss and deafness.

Social factors

Positive and negative relationships

Secure positive relationships, whether through marriage or civil partnership, are important to provide a safe social base for the family to grow and develop.

Positive relationships also help to prevent stress; for example, if an individual has had a bad day at school/work, they know they will feel better when they get home to people who care about them.

Relationships help individuals to maintain their self-esteem, which can prevent physical illness and help with mental and social well-being. Sometimes, however, separation or divorce is the only answer when a relationship breaks down and cannot be repaired.

Negative relationships can cause a lot of stress for the individual.

- There could be lots of arguments or lack of support.
- An individual may feel scared about upsetting the other partner. They may feel they would be abused or physically attacked if they do not do as their partner tells them to do.
- Their partner may not like them to meet friends or visit their family. At first, the individual may feel flattered by all the attention, until they realise they are being controlled.

> **Key term**
> **Disability** A physical impairment or weakness that affects an individual's ability to do daily activities.

OCR Cambridge National in Health and Social Care

Social inclusion/exclusion

Social inclusion is when an individual feels a valued member of their community.

- They feel they belong, as they share social relationships and interests, or are friends with others in the group.
- This social inclusion can help individuals to feel healthy. They are less likely to suffer from stress, as they can gain practical and emotional support from others in their group.

Individuals can be socially excluded from their community for many reasons, such as unemployment, disability or being on a low income.

- People who are disabled can be excluded if social facilities do not allow them the same access as other people; for example, lack of wheelchair access may exclude a wheelchair user from entering a building.
- Low incomes may exclude individuals from social groups, as they do not have spare income to spend outside their home.

Opportunities

An individual's life chances are the opportunities they have to reach their potential. However, not everyone has the same access to a wide variety of opportunities. For example:

- Some children are brought up in extremely poor circumstances and may return from school to look after other siblings. This means they cannot join any extra-curricular activities, or afford to go on school trips.
- Children may rush home from school to care for a parent who is disabled. This means that they may have adult responsibilities such as shopping, cooking and cleaning for the family.

Children in these circumstances may also have missed out on education, as they have to take time off school. This could affect their qualifications, and lead them to have a low-paid job.

Discrimination

Discrimination is the non-acceptance of other types of people. Discriminating against other people is illegal, and is usually the result of a lack of experience with other types of people.

Individuals are sometimes discriminated against because of their:

- social class
- education
- home and neighbourhood
- income
- race
- gender
- age, whether young or old
- disability
- sexuality and different sexual preferences.

> **Activity**
>
> Tara is 15 and had to change schools as her family moved to a different part of the country due to work. She has been at the school for 2 weeks and feels excluded as everyone has established friendship groups and nobody has made her feel welcome. She is too shy and quiet to approach a group on her own. Discuss how you and your friends could make Tara feel a part of her peer group.

Bullying

This can take many forms and can happen anywhere but can be a particular problem in schools, colleges and in workplaces. Bullies enjoy inflicting pain on other people as it makes them feel better about themselves. Bullying can take many forms:

- verbal abuse – e.g. calling people unpleasant names, or spreading untrue information about someone
- physical abuse – e.g. hitting, punching or tripping someone up
- threatening or intimidating behaviour – e.g. making the victim feel scared and powerless.

Emotional factors

Anxiety/fear

These emotions are closely linked but are not the same:

- Fear is the response to an immediate threat or dangerous situation – such as being physically attacked.
- Anxiety means worrying or having negative thoughts about a possible future event that may never happen – such as worrying about being physically attacked.

Most people feel fearful about a stressful situation, such as going for a job interview. But fear is not always a bad thing, as it helps an individual to be aware and alert to a situation.

However, anxiety can cause panic which can have a serious impact on an individual's quality of life.

- They may find it difficult to sleep.
- They might suffer from a panic attack – they start to hyperventilate (breathe rapidly), their heart rate increases and they may feel shaky and sweaty.

If anxiety becomes an ongoing and serious problem for the individual, they should visit their GP for help and advice.

Sadness/happiness

Feeling happy or sad can have an impact on an individual's health and well-being.

- Individuals who are happy are generally more likely to adopt a healthier lifestyle than those who are sad, as they feel positive about life.
- Happy people are more likely to have a stronger immune system and are less likely to suffer from minor ailments. They are also able to combat stress more easily because of their positive outlook.
- People who are sad are more likely to have negative thoughts about themselves and those around them.

Figure 2.7 Anxiety can lower an individual's quality of life

OCR Cambridge National in Health and Social Care

Grief

Grieving is an individual's response to loss. It may be the death of a loved one, such as a parent, partner or sibling, or indeed the family pet. Grieving may cause:

- anxiety
- sleeplessness
- depression
- panic
- tiredness
- loss of appetite
- withdrawal from friends
- stress
- increased risk of physical illness.

Attachment

Attachment in relationships is important throughout childhood and adolescence. It is essential for healthy growth and development.

Individuals who were securely attached to their parents/carers during childhood tend to be good at forming new relationships.

- They will feel secure because they have felt love and can begin to trust others.
- They are confident and will happily settle into school.
- They tend to go through adolescence easily.

Individuals who were insecurely attached can be dependent, clingy and jealous.

- Their moods might be unpredictable. They may be over-friendly one minute then angry and aggressive the next, so relationships may be strained.
- Relationships with parents may not be good, and there may be tensions at home.

Family security

For most people, whatever their age, the family is important for providing emotional stability, or an emotionally stable environment.

People should feel secure within the family home. It is a place where members can relax and be themselves. Young people should be able to test out relationships without fear of rejection.

Economic factors

Family income

Financial factors, especially income, play a big part in the quality of life for any person and their family. Whatever a person earns each week will be used to feed, buy clothes and house that family.

If the income is low, then the family may find it difficult to pay bills and buy food. There will be little disposable income, so the family will have few treats.

With such a low income, people will not have a lot of choice in what they buy to eat. They will want food to be filling so that their family does not go hungry, and this means they will tend to buy food rich in fat and carbohydrate as it is relatively cheap. This is not 'healthy' food, but it is what they can afford. Often a packet of biscuits is as cheap as one apple, and it will feed more of the family.

There has been a rise in food banks over the last few years which provide people on a low income with basic foodstuffs free of charge. The food is usually donated by members of the public and sometimes supermarkets contribute. Eating basic foods all the time will inevitably affect physical growth and development.

Figure 2.8 People on a low income can access basic foodstuffs through food banks

Employment

Some people have low wages, so although they work lots of hours, they might still find it difficult to buy food. They may be on a zero-hours contract, which means that their employer is not obliged to provide them with minimum working hours.

- This could mean that some weeks they have little work, so they receive little pay.
- They cannot plan for anything, as they do not know how much money they will receive from week to week.
- This can affect growth and development, as worrying about income can cause stress and anxiety. People may lose their self-esteem and confidence if they feel that their employment gives them low status in society.

Debts

Debt is when an individual owes money to someone.

- If an individual is struggling to manage on a low income, they may borrow a small amount each month on a credit card, but the money soon adds up to a large debt.
- They must then find money to pay something off the amount they owe on the card. This can cause stress and anxiety.
- They may miss payments, but the amount of the debt still goes up as they must pay interest on the money borrowed.

People sometimes borrow from illegal money lenders at a much higher rate of interest than that charged by the banks or credit card companies. They may find they are threatened with physical violence if they do not pay up on time.

Bills

Everyone has to pay household bills for items such as heating, rent or mortgage for housing, food bills, etc. When money is tight and people are struggling to pay their bills, this can sometimes lead to debt, as borrowing money seems to be the only option.

If household services are not paid for, they will be cut off – this means no gas or electricity for heating, hot water, light and cooking. This can have serious implications for growth and development: there may be no heating or cooking, so the family is cold and hungry, and likely to be underweight and more prone to infections.

Wealth

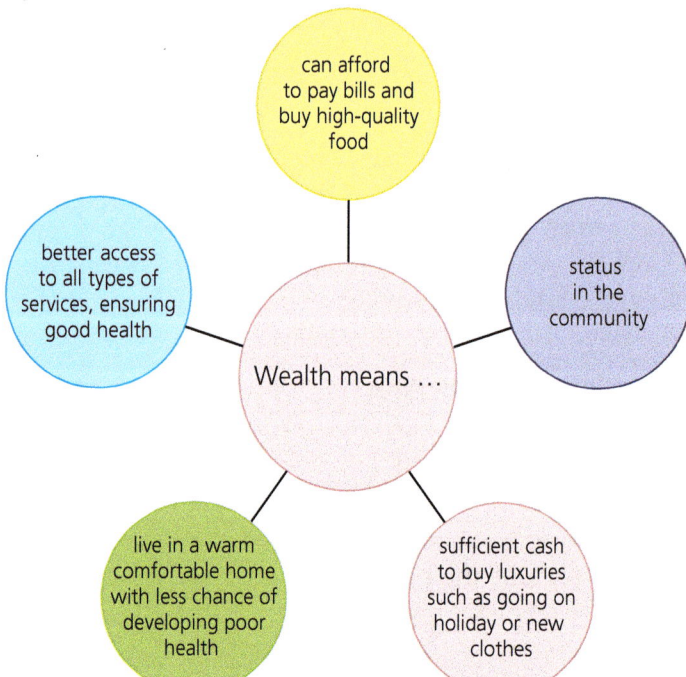

Figure 2.9 Wealth takes a lot of stress away from a family

Unit R033 Supporting individuals through life events

Education

A good education can open the door to a good, well-paid job, which means a decent income. People feel positive about themselves because of their job role.

Not everyone has the chance of a good education or of obtaining good examination results:

- Some children may miss school because they are a carer for a parent, or they are in poor health.
- There may also be a discouraging parental attitude towards school and education, which impacts on the child's chances.

However, people can gain qualifications at night classes or the Open University, which can add to employment chances.

Public/private health providers (services)

Access to health services can be unequal, as shown in Figure 2.10.

As well as free services provided by the NHS, individuals can also choose to pay for healthcare. Private healthcare is available in the form of private hospitals, dental services, podiatry, physiotherapy and many other health services.

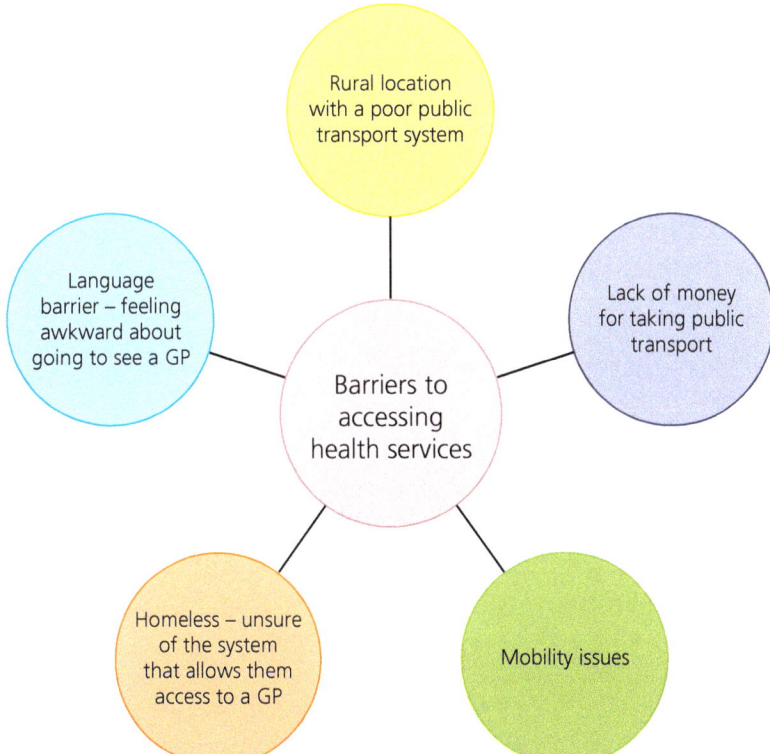

Figure 2.10 A well-educated person with a good income may not have these problems – they might feel more confident about asking for an appointment as they know their rights

Cultural factors

Culture refers to the ideas, customs, beliefs, values and ways of behaving shared by members of a community or a particular group or society. The culture/religion in which a person grows up can influence everything from developmental milestones and parenting styles to what kinds of hardship the person is more likely to face. Children learn the customs of their family's culture/religion during their childhood.

While biological milestones such as puberty tend to be the same across cultures, social milestones, such as the age at which children begin formal schooling or adolescents can go out without their parents, can differ greatly from one culture to the next. Some cultures believe in arranged marriages where girls are married early in their adolescence to a male of their parent's choice. Culture/religion affects individuals throughout their life span unless an individual decides to abandon them, but it is often difficult to do this.

Community

The community in which an individual lives can have a huge effect on growth and development. Much will depend on the location, cultural aspects and the social network within that community.

- It could be a tight-knit community, where neighbours look out for each other and offer help where needed.
- Alternatively, it could be the type of neighbourhood where people do not get involved with their neighbours.

Young people growing up in a wealthier community will have access to more facilities than an individual growing up in a poorer neighbourhood. Older residents also benefit from living in a wealthier community, as there might be more social facilities and easily accessible services.

Religion

Religious groups can affect how an individual behaves, as the religion has principles and rules for them to follow.

Religion emphasises:

- a moral code of behaviour – a set of rules to follow, and
- an ethical code of behaviour – understanding right from wrong.

These codes of behaviour encourage an individual to behave in a way that is controlled and acceptable in society. In this way, religion can help an individual to become a valuable and reliable member of their community.

Race

Black, Asian and minority ethnic groups (BAME) generally experience poorer health, more unemployment, lower incomes and poorer housing than the white population living in the UK.

Living in poor housing in a poorer neighbour can affect development and prospects, as there will be fewer facilities for individuals to access. They may have to travel out of their immediate area to access healthcare or a decent school.

These groups can be the subject of discrimination, as discussed above. This can negatively affect health and well-being, which can impact growth and development.

Gender identity

Gender refers to the expected norms, behaviours and roles associated with being a woman, man, girl or boy. Gender is a 'social construct', which means that expectations of gender differ between societies and can also change over time.

Some individuals do not feel that they belong to either gender, and do not accept that there are only two genders (binary – which means male and female). They might want to be known as non-binary, as they do not identify as male or female. They might not want to be called 'he' or 'she' but prefer to be called 'they'.

Gender influences someone's life opportunities; for example, men have tended to be promoted at work more often than women. This was because traditionally women stayed at home to look after children until they started school, and then tended to return to part-time work. Mothers also tended to take time away from work if their child was unwell. However, this has started to change, with many men sharing childcare or staying at home to look after their children while their partner goes out to work. However, women are still generally paid less than men, often for doing a similar job.

Sexual orientation

Sexual orientation is about who the individual is attracted to, both emotionally and sexually. This is not the same as gender identity – sexual orientation is about who the individual would like to have a relationship with.

Throughout their teenage years, adolescents are sometimes confused about their sexual orientation. They might be:

- emotionally attracted to their own gender but physically attracted to the opposite gender, or vice versa
- emotionally and physically attracted to their own gender and the opposite gender at the same time.

This leads to worry and confusion for them, as they might feel that they are different from everyone else in their peer group.

> **Activity**
> Carry out a quick poll in your class to find out the percentage of students who were looked after by their father while their mother went out to work. Does the percentage surprise you? Do you think if you asked children in Year 1 the percentage would be higher?

Environmental factors

Housing needs and conditions

- If children grow up in high-rise apartments without a garden to play in, they will be restricted in the games they can play.
- Cold, damp homes increase the likelihood of illnesses such as chest infections and pneumonia.
- Overcrowding can have a negative effect on health, as there is a greater chance of spreading infectious illness. It also affects other areas – there is no privacy for anyone to read, do homework, relax or watch television, which can cause stress and frustration.

Pollution (air, noise, light)

Air pollution can affect health.

- Exhaust fumes from vehicles such as cars and buses cause breathing problems, especially for people with respiratory difficulties or disorders such as asthma.
- Power stations, factories and waste products from gas central heating, cookers and fires also cause air pollution.

Noise pollution, land pollution and water pollution can also be dangerous to health.

- Landfill sites can cause water and land pollution, especially if toxic or clinical waste is buried.
- Opencast mining can cause noise and air pollution.

Light pollution can be a statutory nuisance, which means that it can be reported to the local council.

- Light pollution or excessive artificial lighting at night could disrupt an individual's natural sleep pattern.

Figure 2.11 Exhaust fumes contribute to air pollution and can cause breathing problems

Neighbourhood

Environmental factors can have a huge effect on development. Those living in poor and/or run-down areas may encounter:

- poor housing
- boarded-up shops covered in graffiti
- poor street lighting
- a fear of crime
- vandalism
- intimidating gangs on the streets.

All these factors can lead to stress, for both parents and children.

Unit R033 Supporting individuals through life events

Home environment (neglect and conflict)

Although the home should be a place of safety and security, this is not always the case. A child or young person could be neglected, meaning that their basic needs are not being met.

- They could be physically neglected – they do not have sufficient food so they are always hungry, or they cannot maintain their physical hygiene so they have body odour or dirty clothes.
- They could be emotionally or educationally neglected.
- There could be conflict, in the form of domestic violence, in their own home so the young person is always on edge. They may not be physically harmed but may have to witness violence between their parents/carers. This might lead to the young person having low self-esteem, feeling guilty or depressed.

Access to services

Sometimes access to services such as GPs, social services and benefit offices is difficult, and this can affect people's health and well-being. There are many reasons why people may not access services:

- They might have to rely on a bus service which only runs on certain days of the week, making it difficult to reach the services.
- They might work in low-paid jobs and cannot afford to take time off work.
- Women in different ethnic groups may feel uncomfortable with a male doctor, so may feel reluctant to seek help.
- Some people have poor literacy skills and have difficulty in reading, so filling in forms is impossible for them. They might feel embarrassed at their lack of education.

Test your knowledge

1. What is meant by homeostasis?
2. What is fibre used for in the body?
3. What does Vitamin E prevent?
4. What does Vitamin C help to heal, and what does it fight against?
5. Name three positive lifestyle choices.
6. What is the meaning of culture?

OCR Cambridge National in Health and Social Care

Topic area 2 Impacts of life events

Getting started

As a group, define expected and unexpected events. Now arrange the following life events into expected or unexpected events:

- starting school
- serious illness
- disability
- starting work
- menopause
- puberty
- changing jobs
- imprisonment
- accidents
- divorce
- marriage
- moving house
- bereavement
- having children
- redundancy
- retirement.

2.1 Life events and their impacts on individuals

Expected and unexpected life events

Life events can be expected or unexpected, and they can have a huge impact on an individual's development. Everyone has to cope with both types of events across the course of their lives.

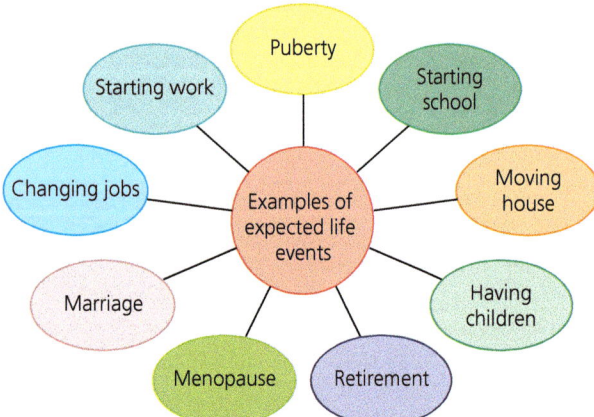

Figure 2.12 Expected life events

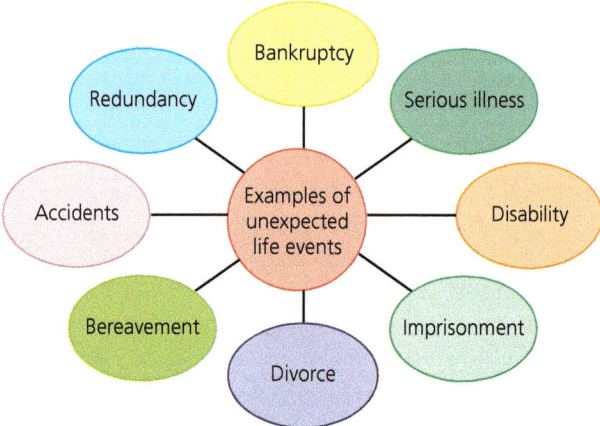

Figure 2.13 Unexpected life events

Physical events

Some physical events (such as puberty and the menopause) are an expected part of growing up, but others are unexpected (such as injury or an accident).

Accident/injury

Accidents can happen anywhere at any time, for example, at work, at home or when travelling. Some serious accidents can have a huge impact on an individual's life for many years or for the rest of their life. An accident or a serious injury could affect an individual physically, intellectually, emotionally and socially (PIES).

- Physically an individual may have problems walking, standing or carrying out tasks that need physical movement, such as dressing, carrying bags or picking up their child.
- Intellectually an accident could affect an individual by causing memory loss or loss of speech, impacting their ability to communicate.
- Emotionally the individual could suffer from stress and anxiety as well as depression as their life has totally changed. Their self-esteem could be affected, as they must adjust to their new situation of living with a disability.
- Socially they may feel embarrassed by their condition and not want to mix with friends. The individual may have to give up work and feel a failure for not being able to provide for their family.

Ill health

Long-term illness or physiological conditions can have a big impact on the physical, emotional, social and mental health of an individual. It could be a chronic illness where the individual will never be cured but will have to manage their symptoms.

Examples of chronic illnesses include asthma, motor neurone disease and cerebral palsy. People with these illnesses may need help and support to carry on with everyday life.

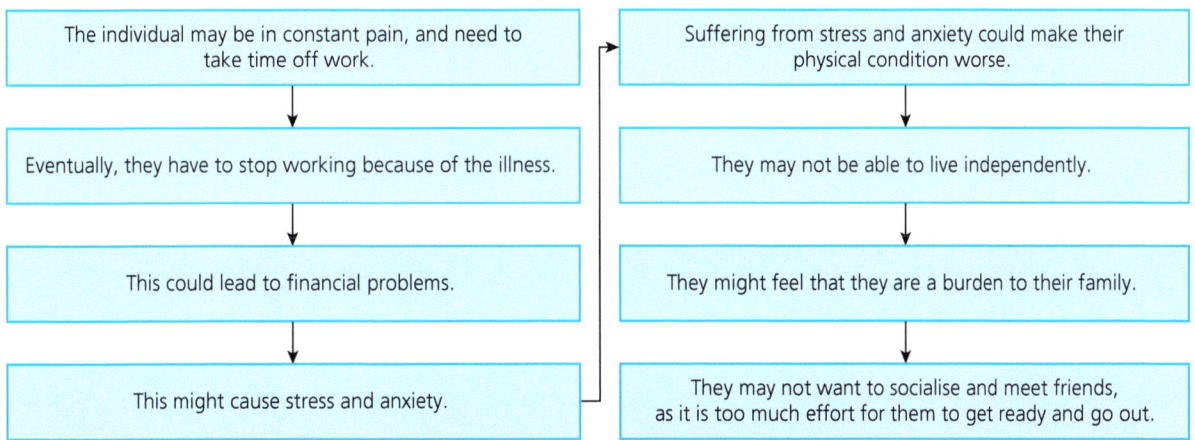

Figure 2.14 Constant pain/chronic illness can have a profound effect on an individual's life

Genetic disorders

Genetic disorders are caused by abnormalities in genes, and these disorders are present from before birth. Examples of genetic disorders include Fragile X, Down's syndrome and cystic fibrosis. Some of these disorders cause physical or learning disabilities, or both.

Individuals who have genetic disorders are sometimes slower at reaching physical development milestones, but with support such as physiotherapy they can start to catch up during adolescence.

They may be embarrassed or angry that they cannot do the same things as everyone else. They may find it difficult to socialise as they are less independent than others and because they feel different. Generally, individuals with genetic disorders need a lot of help and support in all aspects of day-to-day life.

Puberty

Although puberty is an expected life event, it can be a difficult time for both males and females as they may be embarrassed about the physical changes they are experiencing.

- Girls must learn to deal with menstruation, and they may feel worried that everyone knows that they have started their periods.
- Boys must deal with their voices breaking, causing others to make fun of them.
- There is also the worry for adolescents that everyone else has started to go through puberty, but they have not.
- Adolescents may start to question their sexuality, as their bodies change during puberty.
- Adolescents may also struggle to deal with their feelings, due to hormonal surges. They can be under pressure to start a relationship, to fit in with others in their peer group.

Menopause

This can be a difficult time for any woman.

- She may feel upset because she cannot have children, even if she did not intend to have any more.
- She may also notice the appearance of deep wrinkles and perhaps a weight gain.
- She may suffer symptoms such as hot sweats, mood swings and sleepless nights, which might be difficult to cope with. However, hormone replacement therapy (HRT) is available after consultation with a GP, which can help with these symptoms.

But there are positive aspects:

- She will no longer have to cope with periods and their symptoms every month.
- She may have a better sex life as she will not have to use contraceptives.

There may also be other changes in the woman's life that coincide with the menopause, as children may be leaving home to go to university, but ageing parents may need support.

Relationship changes

Everyone has relationship changes as they move through the different phases of their life. For example, an individual will make new friends as they move through school and into work or university.

Starting/ending relationships

Throughout their lifespan everyone has relationships – their first one with their primary carer. When they start school or nursery, children make friends with their classmates, and when older they may have a boyfriend/girlfriend and then a spouse or life partner. All these relationships are especially important as they make individuals feel good about themselves and develop their self-esteem.

Relationships meet social, emotional and sexual needs, and make individuals feel happy. They help to develop good health as relating to people can reduce stress and anxiety. Talking about problems with friends and family can help to solve issues as practical help and advice may be given.

However, ending a relationship, whether it is a friendship or a sexual relationship, can be difficult and hurtful for everyone concerned. Relationships could end because of an argument, because you have outgrown the friendship or because your interests have changed. Whatever the reason, it will be stressful and cause emotional pain.

Divorce/separation

According to the Office for National Statistics (ONS), 42 per cent of marriages end in divorce, and half of these divorces (21 per cent) occur in the first ten years. This can be a sad time, especially if one person did not want the marriage/partnership to end. But sometimes it is better than living in a tense atmosphere where one partner may feel a deep sense of unhappiness. Separation or divorce may be the only answer when a relationship breaks down and cannot be repaired.

Often people who have left a marriage/relationship feel very disappointed as they expected the marriage/relationship to last a lifetime. Divorce is an unexpected life event which can cause much upset and bitterness, and people may need some time to get over the emotional trauma. However, many divorced or separated individuals do remarry or find new partners.

Figure 2.15 Relationships help to develop self-esteem and reduce stress and anxiety

There is also the physical and emotional trauma of dividing up the home that both partners were involved in and finding new accommodation. The whole process can be very costly in financial and social terms.

People sometimes lose friends who take sides with one of the partners, excluding the other one.

Parenthood

When a pregnancy has been planned, parenthood is an expected event, but for others it can be unexpected. Parenthood is a huge change – life will never be the same again as the couple have gone from two to three, so their relationship has altered.

The birth of a baby is a joyful occasion for most parents, but it is hard work being a parent, as it carries a lot of responsibility.

- Parents are often tired as they lose sleep during the night when the baby needs to be fed or changed, or is teething or ill.
- The parents cannot just go out to meet friends as they must plan for a babysitter, and this could be costly.
- There may be a cut in income if one parent gives up their job to care for the baby. This cut comes when lots of equipment is needed, which can be expensive even if they buy second-hand.
- Babies need a lot of care and attention, and sometimes a partner may feel pushed out if they are not actively involved.

Bereavement

When a partner dies, there is upset and sorrow, and there can also be confusion about practical issues such as financial matters or how to run the home. The remaining partner could feel lonely and isolated, particularly if they had depended on their partner to take them shopping or out to other places. If the couple were together for many years, the remaining partner may become depressed and not want to leave the house.

The death of a parent will cause much upset for children too. They may need to look after the remaining parent, if they find it difficult to cope after their **bereavement**.

For an older person, losing a sibling or a good friend can be a life-changing event, as they feel that all their support has gone.

> **Stretch activity**
>
> Portia and Baz have been going out together for three years since they were in the sixth form at school. In her second year at university, Portia unexpectedly finds she's pregnant with Baz's child.
>
> Explain in detail the challenges that the couple face with this unexpected life event.

> **Key term**
>
> **Bereavement** Coping with change following the death of someone very close.

Unit R033 Supporting individuals through life events

Case study

Robbie is 17. Six months ago, his father was killed in a car crash when he was returning from work. Robbie seemed to cope well initially, and helped his mum to support his four younger siblings, who do not really understand what has happened. However, some days, he feels he cannot cope with all that is expected of him, and feels a sense of guilt about this.

Now his mother has suggested that he does not apply for university this year, as she feels he would be better off at home. He knows if he does not go this year, he will miss his opportunity to do what he wants to do with his life. Robbie really wants to go to a university away from home as he feels his mum is too dependent on him. He has tried to talk to his mum, but she just bursts into tears.

1. Robbie has asked you as a friend to speak to his mum about how he feels. Explain to his mum how Robbie's physical, intellectual, emotional and social health will be compromised if he does not go to university this year.
2. Explain any compromises that Robbie could make without affecting his own health and development. Give reasons for your answer.

Life circumstances

Changing life circumstances can occur at any time in our lives. Life is not always straightforward, and individuals learn that plans are sometimes interrupted by other events.

School starting/changing/exclusion

Starting school can be a traumatic experience for any child as they may fear leaving their parents/carers and their home to go into a new environment. It is a good idea for parents/carers to prepare the child by taking them to a playgroup before they are due to start school, so they become used to being away from home.

Teachers will need to reassure the child for at least their first week at school. If someone is unhappy at home or school or work, it can affect their emotional or social development or even physical development. For example:

- If a child is neglected at home, they could fail to thrive or gain weight.
- If a child or young person is bullied at school, then they may not want to go to school and may become physically ill from the anxiety of dealing with it.

Changing schools can have the same effect as starting school, because the child will be going into a new environment. Starting secondary school with a group of friends from primary school is much easier than changing schools because you have moved to a different area, which can be very difficult.

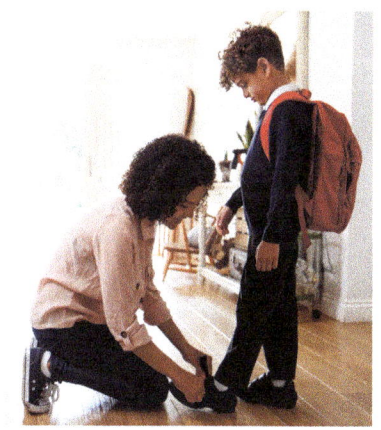

Figure 2.16 Children need to feel supported as they are starting school

OCR Cambridge National in Health and Social Care

If pupils behave badly and break school rules, they could be excluded from school. This can have a negative effect on the child, if they then start to mix with others who are taking part in criminal behaviour, such as shoplifting, stealing or vandalism.

Being excluded from school can cause mental health problems if the child has to look after themselves and isn't supported by their parents.

Redundancy

Apart from the financial implications, job loss or redundancy can mean a significant loss of identity and an individual's self-confidence may be eroded.

In addition, a person may feel excluded from society. Depending on the age, personality type, family and financial circumstances, individual reactions may range from mild, moderate to severe. The most common reaction to job loss is physical shock accompanied by some of the classic symptoms associated with grief – disbelief, denial, anger, feeling stunned, becoming withdrawn, loss of confidence and a feeling of low self-esteem. This is especially true if the individual is a younger adult who will then have to find another job to support themselves and their family.

With the retirement age rising, an older person who is made redundant may find it difficult to find alternative work. However, if the person was very near retirement age, they may not be as distressed.

Imprisonment

Obviously, this is an unpleasant unexpected life event.

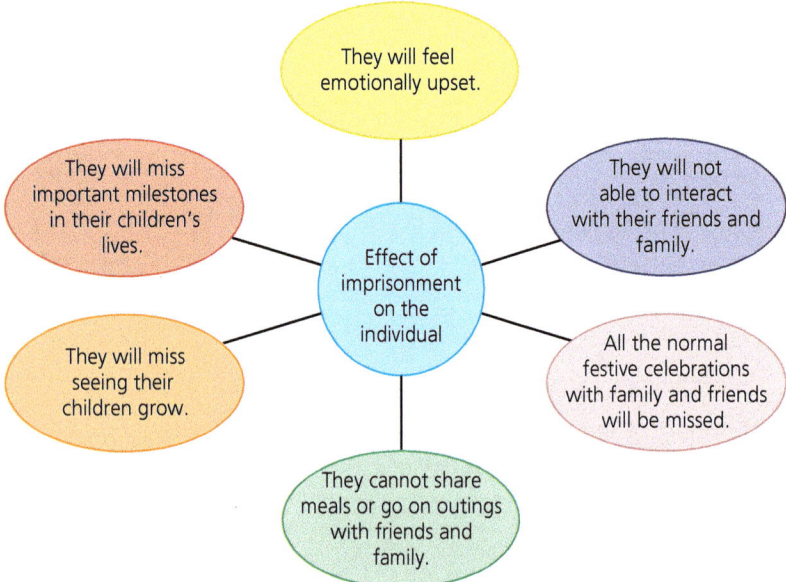

Figure 2.17 Imprisonment is an unexpected life event which can have major consequences for an individual

Unit R033 Supporting individuals through life events

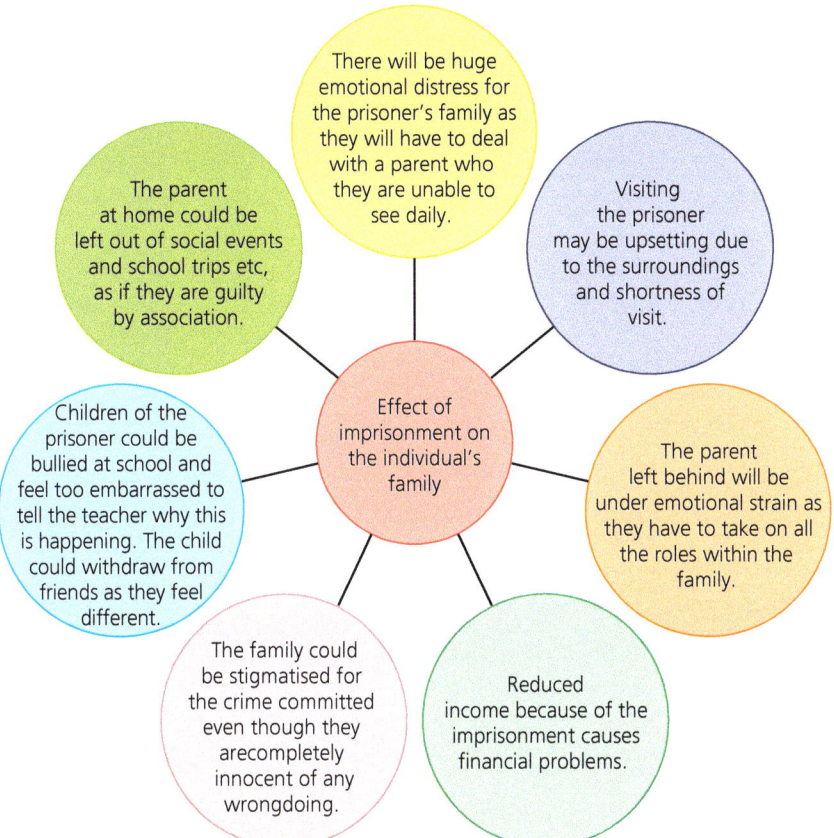

Figure 2.18 A prisoner's family has to deal with the consequences of their loved one being imprisoned

Retirement

Many older people are not retiring at 65 but are choosing to work for longer. Some of the downsides to retirement are explored below.

- Some people feel they lose their status and a sense of who they are when they retire. For example, a headteacher or a factory manager might feel that they have lost their place in society.
- People often feel a loss of purpose in their life, as well as a significant drop in their income. Most people's income will drop by half, or even more.
- Older adults may lose friends when retiring as they no longer see their work colleagues every day.
- Retirement can be a source of relationship stress. For example, a partner may be used to being by themselves during the day, and both parties could find it difficult to adjust to a new routine.

But the positive side of retirement is that the individual has more time to do what they enjoy. For example, they might meet friends for lunch, go for walks, start a new sport or take up voluntary work.

OCR Cambridge National in Health and Social Care

Bankruptcy

If someone has debts which they cannot afford to repay, they can apply for bankruptcy. However, bankruptcy will have lasting implications on the individual's life:

- Their credit rating will be affected so they will find it difficult to get any type of loan or credit.
- They are banned from certain jobs such as being an accountant, police officer, solicitor or Member of Parliament (MP).

The name of the bankrupt individual is recorded on a public register that anyone can access and search. Even utility services such as gas and electricity may be affected, as the individual will have to pay on a pre-payment plan or the service may insist on the installation of a meter.

Impacts that life events have on individuals

Individuals react differently to life events. The following tables give examples of the physical, intellectual, emotional, social and financial impact on individuals of:

- physical events
- relationship changes
- life circumstances.

Table 2.4 The impacts that physical events have on individuals

Physical events	Physical	Intellectual	Emotional	Social	Financial
Accident/ injury	There could be: • constant pain from injury • weight gain as they may not be as active • mobility problems if legs are injured • change in appearance if disfigured.	The individual may have to: • adapt to change if an accident causes a disability • learn new skills, such as walking with a stick or dressing using one arm • learn to live with impairment	The individual may feel: • grief that their previous life has ended, as they will never be the same as they were • anxiety as they wonder if they can cope with their impairment • stressed about going out of the house as they fear another accident • depressed as life has changed and there is no hope of improvement • low levels of self-esteem and self-image.	The individual may find that: • their lifestyle choices are limited as they cannot exercise the way they used to, e.g. running • personal relationships change as friends are embarrassed by the disability • family become tired and stressed trying to help with personal tasks.	The individual may find that: • their income changes – they may not be able to continue with their job so will have to rely on benefits • costs increase as they need help with certain tasks and may have to contribute towards care • there is a change in their wealth which will impact on family.

Unit R033 Supporting individuals through life events

Physical events	Physical	Intellectual	Emotional	Social	Financial
Ill health	There could be: • illness/tiredness, which means the individual needs to sleep during the day or go to bed early • weight loss as the individual feels too poorly to eat or has little appetite because of pain • changes to appearance as pain is reflected in the individual's face.	The individual may have to: • adapt to change as they become tired and cannot think clearly.	The individual may feel: • that their mental health is affected if they feel a burden to family and friends • depressed as they feel they are not the same as everyone else.	The individual may find that: • they have to cancel social outings as not feeling well • they lose touch with friends as they are too ill to socialise.	The individual may find that: • they cannot earn as much, therefore there is a change in wealth which will impact on family • their income changes if they can only work part time.
Genetic disorders	There could be: • illness/tiredness, which means the individual needs to sleep during the day or go to bed early • mobility problems.	The individual may have to: • cope with learning impairment from birth.	The individual may feel: • unaware of self-image depending on their condition, as this is how they have been since birth • angry that they are not the same as everyone else.	The individual may find that: • they have a limited number of friends, depending on their disorder.	The individual may find that: • they are unable to secure a job because of their learning disability, so may be dependent on benefits.
Puberty	There could be: • weight gain due to changing body shape.	The individual may: • start thinking like an adult, using logic and abstract thinking to solve problems.	The individual may feel: • stressed because of body changes • anxious because not as popular as others in their peer group • emotions are unpredictable.	The individual may find that: • they are making lifestyle choices to fit in with others in peer group, e.g. drinking alcohol, taking drugs • they feel angry at family.	The individual may find that: • they need more money to fund lifestyle choices • they have to buy sanitary products.
Menopause	There could be: • weight gain as hormones depleted • less elasticity in the skin which might cause wrinkles on their face • increased tiredness.	The individual may: • not be able to think as clearly as they used to.	The individual may feel: • depressed that child-bearing years are over • low self-esteem due to changing body and face • easily upset.	The individual may find that: • personal relationships are under stress due to feelings of anger.	The individual may: • reduce their working hours as they feel embarrassed by the symptoms they experience, or feel that they cannot do their job well enough because of the difficulty in thinking clearly.

Table 2.5 The impact of relationship changes on individuals

Relationship changes	Physical	Intellectual	Emotional	Social	Financial
Starting/ ending relationships	The individual may: • lose weight, if too excited to eat when starting relationship • put on weight as eating more through stress if ending relationship.	The individual may have to: • adapt to a new person in life.	The individual may feel: • their self-esteem is boosted if starting relationship • a blow to their self-esteem if ending relationship.	The individual may: • meet more people as they are going out with new partner • neglect family and friends.	The individual may: • spend more money buying clothes hoping to impress new partner • spend more money socialising.
Divorce/ separation	The individual may: • lose weight from stress.	The individual may have to: • change their job and learn new skills • get used to living on their own.	The individual may feel: • grief-stricken at loss of partner • anxious about living alone • depressed at end of relationship • low self-esteem as the partnership or marriage ends.	The individual may: • have to find new friends if current friends were originally friends of ex-partner • rely on family to help out with moving.	The individual may: • have a change in income • have to buy/rent accommodation on their own • have much less disposable income.
Parenthood	The individual may: • have sleepless nights with a new baby • find it difficult to lose pregnancy weight after birth.	The individual may have to: • adapt to a total change in lifestyle • learn new skills while caring for a baby.	The individual may feel: • stressed with new responsibility of caring for a baby • depressed, and suffer from postnatal depression • anxious about responsibility.	The individual may find: • their social life disappears as too busy caring for baby • they make a new group of friends from baby groups • family may help with occasional overnight stay so parents can get some sleep.	The individual may: • find it a very expensive time as lots of new equipment to buy • give up work to care for baby • need to pay childcare fees if parents go back to work.
Bereavement	The individual may: • have disturbed sleep because of their grief • lose weight as they are too upset to eat • loses interest in appearance.	The individual may have to: • adapt to person not being present • take on new tasks.	The individual may feel: • inconsolable with grief • stressed and depressed about what the future holds • low self-esteem if they feel alone and abandoned.	The individual may: • have no social life as they do not want to go out • depend on family for comfort.	The individual may: • have less income • have to pay for funeral • need advice on managing money.

Table 2.6 The impact of life circumstances on individuals

Life circumstances	Physical	Intellectual	Emotional	Social	Financial
School starting/ changing/ exclusion	The individual may: • feel tired because of stress • lose weight as too anxious to eat.	The individual may have to: • learn new routines • learn lots of new skills.	The individual may feel: • anxious until settled in • stressed about new environment and leaving parent • stressed at meeting so many new children.	The individual may feel: • excited at the opportunity to meet and make lots of new friends.	The individual may find: • the cost of uniform and school equipment is very expensive.

Redundancy	The individual may:
	• feel anxious about finding a new job, which causes them to:
	  • lose their appetite and lose weight
	  • be unable to sleep.
		The individual may have to:
		• reskill to get new job
		• adapt to new job environment.
			The individual may feel:
			• anxious about future
			• stressed about starting new job
			• depressed if new job is difficult to find
			• that they have lower self-esteem because of lost job.
				The individual may feel:
				• embarrassed to meet friends from their old workplace
				• not part of the team any more
				• they do not want to tell family in case they worry.
					The individual may find:
					• their income drops through losing job
					• a change in wealth if they use savings to pay bills
					• they need advice on managing money.

Imprisonment	The individual may: • lose weight due to total change of lifestyle • have a changed appearance because of weight loss and anxiety from being locked up • become unfit they can't exercise as much as they used to.	The individual will have to: • adapt to prison life • learn to follow prison routine.	The individual may feel: • that their mental health is affected by change in circumstances • depressed about putting family through this experience • anxious about mixing with other prisoners • frustrated as locked in cell for long periods.	The individual may feel: • deserted by friends • isolated if the family finds it difficult to visit • guilty for putting family through this experience • that they have very few lifestyle choices in prison.	The individual may find: • a drop in income as they cannot work • it is expensive for their family to visit them • any savings may be used up to meet bills.
Retirement	The individual may: • feel physically less tired.	The individual may: • find it difficult to adapt to new routine and plan their day.	The individual may: • have lower self-esteem if they valued their job role as an extension of themselves • feel depressed if they have few hobbies or interests to fill their time.	The individual may: • lose friends as they do not see them every day at work • find it difficult to adapt to being with their partner at home all day.	The individual may find: • money coming into household will drop as now on pension • they need advice on managing money.

OCR Cambridge National in Health and Social Care

Life circumstances	Physical	Intellectual	Emotional	Social	Financial
Bankruptcy	The individual may: • feel anxious about debt • be unable to sleep • lose appetite from anxiety and therefore lose weight • have a changed appearance because of weight loss and lack of sleep.	The individual may: • have to learn new skills if they start a new job.	The individual may feel: • that their mental health is affected by change in circumstances • anxious and depressed about putting family through bankruptcy.	The individual may find: • their lifestyle choices narrow as money is extremely limited • they lose friends who do not want to be associated with bankruptcy.	The individual may: • have little money due to circumstances of debt • need advice on managing money.

> ### Stretch activity
>
> Read through the section on the impacts of an accident on an individual.
>
> Without looking at the information, write a detailed account of how an active 24-year-old individual will cope with her injuries after breaking her back in a motorbike accident. She is unable to walk, so needs to use a wheelchair permanently. Every area of her life will be affected. Remember to include physical, intellectual, emotional, social and financial impacts in your answer.

Identifying individuals' needs based on the impacts of life events

Not everyone will need the same support when coping with life events. This explains why any organisation should tailor the help they can offer to an individual's specific needs.

Weight gain

Losing weight can be difficult at any time, but help can be accessed from the NHS. Going to the GP could be the first step on the weight-loss journey.

The GP or practice nurse will work out the individual's BMI (body mass index) to see how much weight they need to lose. Then the individual will be:

- set personal goals, such as how much weight they should lose each week or how much exercise they should have every day
- referred to a weight-loss programme with follow-ups every two to four weeks to discuss issues with the practice nurse
- directed to a local weight-loss group which might be run by the NHS, or they may have to pay to attend a commercial group such as WW (the new brand name for Weightwatchers).

Unit R033 Supporting individuals through life events

Losing weight with other people could be good, as other group members will be supportive. The NHS also has a weight-loss plan online, which can be accessed on:

www.nhs.uk/better-health/lose-weight/

Stress/anxiety

Stress and anxiety affect most people at some time in their lives.

- To deal with stress, an individual can book an appointment with their GP, who will talk through the issues and offer support and further suggestions of how to cope.
- If they feel they cannot wait for an appointment, they can phone 111 where someone will offer support.

There is online support which offers coping mechanisms for stress and anxiety. An example is:

www.nhs.uk/every-mind-matters/mental-wellbeing-tips/your-mind-plan-quiz

The individual must fill in a simple quiz which reflects their state of mind. The website then offers several suggestions to help, such as a 10-minute workout video to de-stress.

MIND, the mental health charity, also helps individuals with mental health issues such as anxiety and stress. Their website offers advice such as crisis-coping tools and there is a direct line an individual can ring:

www.mind.org.uk/need-urgent-help/

Loss of income

Citizens Advice (search online at: www.citizensadvice.org.uk) is a good place to start for anyone who has lost their income or is in danger of building up debt.

- They will help by offering advice on which benefits may be available to the individual and how to deal with debt.
- They will also help to work out a budget plan to help the individual deal with their loss of income and perhaps prevent them from getting into debt. The advantage of this service is that it is face-to-face contact.

The National Debt Line and the Stepchange Debt Charity also offer help and support.

MIND also has a money and mental health section on its website.

OCR Cambridge National in Health and Social Care

Learning impairment

Anyone who has a learning impairment due to the impact of a life event such as an accident can contact social services to ask for help and advice. They may be offered help at home, especially if they need help with their personal care, but they may have to pay for it, depending on their income.

If an individual prefers to continue to live independently, and does not want to go into residential care, they may have adaptations made to their home, such as a ramp, or a hoist to help them get out of bed.

Independent Living provides unbiased advice about a wide range of products and services to help with learning impairment, such as:

- mobility aids
- aids to help with cooking
- other aids designed for an individual to retain their independence.

> **Research**
> Search online for different companies offering aids to help people with dementia and cognitive impairment. The Independent Living website can be found at:
> **www.independentliving.co.uk**
> - Are you surprised by the number of different aids available?
> - Which aids do you think would be most useful to an individual with dementia or cognitive impairment?

> **Test your knowledge**
> 1. Give two examples of expected life events.
> 2. Give two examples of unexpected life events.
> 3. What is meant by bankruptcy?
> 4. Give two physical impacts that an accident/injury may have on an individual.
> 5. Give two emotional impacts of a divorce/separation on an individual.

Topic area 3 Sources of support

> **Getting started**
> Clive is 42 and broke his neck in a motorbike accident. He needs help to get up, shower and get dressed in the morning. He needs the same help to go to bed. However, during the day he can go out and meet friends.
>
> Clive plays wheelchair rugby. He often meets friends in the pub in the evening.
>
> Produce a support plan for Clive that would meet his PIES needs, including the following sources of support:
>
> - formal
> - informal
> - charities.

It is much easier for an individual to cope with life events if they have support and feel they can call on others to help them, even if it is just talking through their situation.

Unit R033 Supporting individuals through life events

3.1 Sources of support that meet individual needs

There are many different types and sources of support available for everyone. Some individuals prefer to rely on the help of their family and friends rather than organisations.

Sources of support

If a person doesn't have family or friends who can offer them support, they can access help and support from organisations.

Formal support

Formal care is care that is provided by paid health and social care staff, who are trained and are working in settings such as hospitals, residential care homes, nursing homes, children's services.

Hospitals

Individuals might be referred by their primary care provider (such as their GP) to a hospital. This is an example of secondary care, where individuals have planned operations or consultations with specialists (such as in **oncology** or **cardiology**).

However, if an individual is involved in an accident or has a sudden serious illness such as a stroke or heart attack, then an ambulance will bring that individual to hospital where their illness will be dealt with.

An individual might be referred to a specialist hospital for treatments such as organ transplants, paediatrics (children's specialists) or mental health services.

> **Key terms**
> **Oncology** A branch of medicine concerned with the diagnosis and treatment of cancer.
>
> **Cardiology** A branch of medicine that specialises in diseases of the heart.

Health centres

A health centre provides:

- medical services from GPs, practice nurses, health visitors, district nurses and possibly other staff such as a mental health nurse, depending on the area served by the health centre
- services such as minor surgery, weight-loss classes, antenatal classes or a baby clinic.

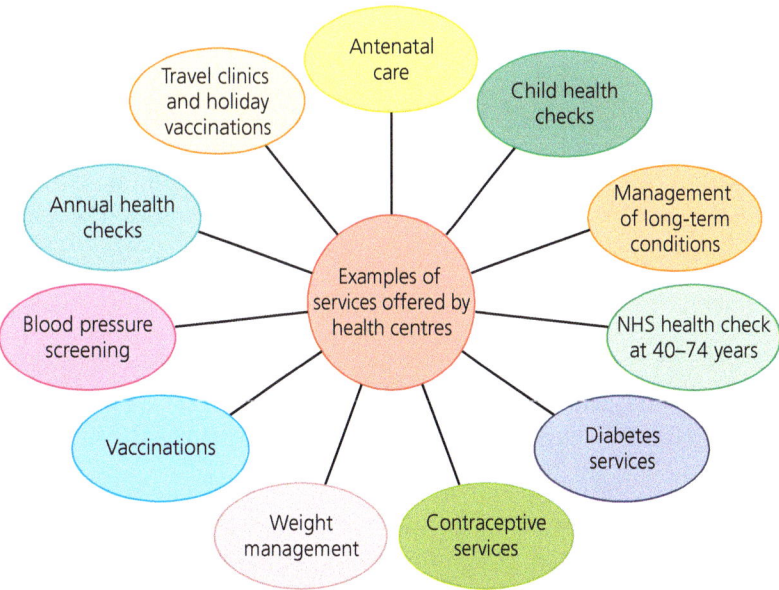

Figure 2.19 Health centres offer many services

Care homes

Care homes offer accommodation and personal care for individuals who require extra care and support, such as for individuals who cannot manage in their own homes perhaps because they are too frail to look after themselves. These types of homes are often called residential homes, and offer personal care such as help with dressing and going to the toilet.

Care homes aim to offer **holistic care**, and often have daily activities and outings for the residents. They offer security and companionship, and meet an individual's basic needs of food, shelter and warmth.

Day centres

Day centres offer a variety of services, usually for older people or people with disabilities:

- They provide a place where people can meet and socialise.
- Day centres also provide intellectual activities, such as group games such as bingo or individual games such as chess. For some individuals attending the day centre, these games will be too challenging, and they will need one-to-one intellectual stimulation such as looking at photographs to remember what happened in the past. This activity stimulates memories and may help them feel part of the group.
- There could be creative activities such as painting or knitting, which would also support physical skills and help with hand and finger mobility.
- Day centres can provide respite care for a few hours for carers. They can meet friends or go shopping, knowing that their loved one is safe.

Children's services

All children have access to a range of universal services depending on their age, needs and stage of development. Universal services are provided by several agencies such as education and health. Examples of practitioners involved in universal services include GPs, health visitors and school nurses.

A parent is likely to come into contact with children's services if:

- they have a child with additional needs (such as a disability)
- there are child protection issues, and children's services are worried that the child is likely to suffer harm.

If social workers are worried that the child may be harmed or is at risk of suffering harm, they must investigate. If it is found that the child has been harmed or is at risk of being harmed, family support may be offered to help the family.

> **Key term**
>
> **Holistic care** Looking after the whole person, i.e. physically, intellectually, emotionally, socially and spiritually.

Unit R033 Supporting individuals through life events

A needs assessment would be carried out by the children's services team at the local council. Depending on the outcome, the family may be offered:

- parenting classes
- a family support worker
- practical home help
- access to a Children's Centre.

The idea is that with extra support, the child will be safe from harm.

Hospices

Hospices aim to improve the quality of life and well-being of people who are at the end of their life. Anyone with a terminal condition can use a hospice. Staff look after the physical, intellectual, emotional, social and spiritual needs of their patients, helping them to live full lives until they die.

Each hospice offers different services related to the specific needs of their community, so each hospice is unique. They continue to adapt their services as needs change.

Hospices are usually funded by a mixture of state funding and funding from the public through fundraising and charitable events such as coffee mornings. They offer a range of services:

- Individuals can have hospice help at home, as staff go out into the community to offer help, support and advice for terminally ill people.
- They also offer respite care so that carers can have a break.

Figure 2.20 Sometimes people need formal support

Respite care

This is when an individual who cannot look after themselves, because of disability or illness, stays at an institution (such as a residential care home, hospice or nursing home) so that the main carer can have a rest. This is so that they do not become exhausted and unable to care for the person.

This break, usually for one or two weeks, allows the carer to have a break from caring for the individual. Day care can also offer respite care for one day a week.

Rehabilitation centres (addiction or injury)

Rehabilitation is a treatment that is designed to help the individual recover from an illness, injury, addiction or disease, so that they can return to health and go back to leading as normal a life as possible.

After an accident, a rehabilitation centre will help an individual to become as independent as possible in everyday life. Each individual will have an individualised programme to meet their specific needs, as people respond to treatments in a different way.

Informal support

Informal care is the care given by those who are not paid to do so.

Family/friends

In most cases, family and friends are unskilled care providers but will be available at times when practitioners are not. Informal care workers are likely to be:

- people the individual knows and trusts – they could be immediate family members such as husband, wife, partner, sons and daughters, who provide personal care to the individual such as washing, changing, cooking and serving meals
- extended family such as aunts, uncles, nieces and nephews, who might contribute by shopping or keeping the individual company
- neighbours who might help with chores such as gardening, shopping or fetching prescriptions
- close friends who may enjoy talking to the individual, or taking them out for coffee or for a walk if the individual is well enough.

Figure 2.21 Family might be the first place to turn for support

Religion/culture

Individuals who belong to a faith group are often well supported by that community. Other members of the group might visit the individual to keep them company, pray with them or help in any other way they can. They may keep them up to date with all the happenings in the faith group, and make them feel they are still part of the community. They may also help the individual's spiritual health.

Culture can affect the way in which individuals are supported at different stages of their lives, such as during pregnancy, birth, during childhood, adulthood, through illnesses and death. For example:

- In Arabic and Chinese cultures, it is common for female relatives instead of the father to be present at the birth of a child.
- In some cultures, family members may be deeply upset if a hospital consultant shares their concerns about a relative's ill health directly with the individual, instead of with their family.

Charity support

Charities fit into third-sector organisations that are not run for profit and are independent of the government. This third sector also includes community groups and self-help groups.

Table 2.7 Support offered by charities

Charity	Support offered
Relate www.relate.org.uk	• Provides information on every type of relationship, and on issues such as family problems, divorce, separation and money problems. • Provides sex therapy for couples. • Largest provider of relationship support across the UK. • Advice for new parents and step-parents. • Offers relationship counselling for couples and for all family members and situations. • Provides practical advice on divorce, such as living arrangements for children, helping children to live in two homes and introducing new partners to children. • Provides children and young people with help and advice about school, such as bullying, anxiety or other personal issues.
Gingerbread www.gingerbread.org.uk	• Provides advice and support for single parents. • Leading national charity, started in 1918. • Supports shared care between parents, as this is in best interest of the child. • Founding member of Kids in the Middle along with Relate, the Fatherhood Institute and Families Need Fathers, which aim to reduce conflict in families. • Campaigns on behalf of single parents across wide range of topics such as a fair welfare system, influencing government policy.
Cruse www.cruse.org.uk	• Provides support for people of any age suffering a bereavement. • Supports individuals through the grieving process.
Age UK www.ageuk.org.uk	• Provides services for older people. • The largest charity in the UK that specialises in support to older people. • Provides information and advice on a range of topics, e.g. health, finances, housing. • Raises awareness of issues faced by older people, e.g. accessing public services, living in safe communities. • Provides independent living aids such as personal alarms and stair lifts. • Provides training for those who support and provide services to older people. • Carries out research about adults in later life, e.g. the Disconnected Mind research project.
Mind www.mind.org.uk	• A national charity that has offered help and support to people with mental health problems for more than 60 years. • Lobbies government and local authorities to keep mental health at top of the agenda. • Raises public awareness and understanding of mental health issues through public campaigns. • Campaigns to improve services for people with mental health issues.
Specialist charities Examples: www.autism.org.uk www.diabetes.org.uk www.epilepsy.org.uk www.downs-syndrome.org.uk	• Specialist charities provide specialist information, training and advice to individuals, their families and professionals on a specific condition. • Examples of conditions supported by specialist charities are autism, diabetes, epilepsy, Down's syndrome.

The role of practitioners in providing support

Practitioners can be the only source of help for some individuals who do not have family and friends to offer advice and support. Even if they do have family and friends, they might not want to talk to them as it is too personal. Sometimes they need specialist support, and professional practitioners may be the best people to help as they have this expertise.

General practitioner (GP)

The GP (a doctor) is the first point of contact for individuals who live in the local community and require medical care or help. A GP will:

- diagnose the individual
- provide advice and information on illnesses and conditions
- prescribe medication needed for the condition
- recommend further treatment needed for the condition
- refer the individual to a specialist service and professionals, such as an oncology specialist if they suspect the individual might have cancer.

Nurse

A nurse is often based at a healthcare centre or a local surgery. Nurses will perform tasks such as:

- blood and urine tests
- carrying out health checks for people aged 40–74 years
- taking blood pressure
- giving injections
- follow up appointments after a hospital stay to check progress
- dressing patients' wounds
- offering family planning advice
- offering advice on a healthier lifestyle, such as giving up smoking and losing weight.

Midwife

Midwives work in hospitals or in healthcare centres, and are responsible for:

- supervising the antenatal care of pregnant women – monitoring the health of both the mother and her unborn baby, and offering advice on diet, exercise and other issues
- leading antenatal classes for expectant parents
- delivering babies
- postnatal care – they look after the mother and her baby until it is ten days old, then hand over care to the health visitor.

Health visitor

The role of a health visitor is to:

- look after the welfare of all children under five, checking their physical, intellectual, emotional and social well-being
- offer advice to parents on feeding, child development and other issues
- provide health education, and give advice on how to have a healthy lifestyle
- support people in their own homes, especially if they have a disability or are older.

Specialist doctor

Many doctors are trained in a specific area of medicine. There are specialist doctors across the whole range of medical conditions, such as:

- dermatologists, who specialise in conditions of the skin, nails and hair
- cardiologists, who focus on the cardiovascular system (heart and blood vessels).

Physiotherapist

Physiotherapists are usually based in hospitals or in the community, but also visit people in their own homes. They provide:

- exercises and other treatments to help individuals overcome issues caused by accidents or injuries or disease
- help with mobility, using manipulative and supportive exercises to build up muscle. For example, a person who has had a broken leg in a car accident may find it difficult to walk when they have the plaster removed, but the physiotherapist will help them to loosen up stiff joints.

Dietician

Dieticians usually work in community or hospital settings, but bigger healthcare centres might also employ one. They will:

- educate patients about eating a healthy diet in order to prevent ill health
- advise patients with specific diseases related to food intake, such as diabetes or heart disease, so that their condition improves or at least does not get worse.

Activity
Types of specialist doctor

As a group, think of all the types of specialist doctors and write them on the white board.

How many can you think of without researching them online?

Social worker

A social worker usually works for the local authority. They will:

- assess individuals' needs
- provide information and advice on the services that individuals require
- provide support to individuals with managing their lives
- arrange access to services that individuals require.

Counsellor

A counsellor can work for the NHS or privately. They will:

- allow individuals to explore the changes they would like to make in their lives
- enable individuals to improve their lives and access the support they need to do so
- refer individuals to other services and professionals.

Occupational therapist

Occupational therapists usually work in hospitals with individuals of all ages, but are also available in the community, rehabilitation centres and day care centres. They will:

- help individuals to relearn everyday living skills after they have had an accident or stroke
- suggest aids that may help the individual gain confidence, such as a walking frame
- suggest adaptations to the individual's home, such as a stair lift.

Healthcare worker

A healthcare worker works in a hospital, a healthcare centre or the local community, so their roles can vary depending on where they are based. In a hospital, they may:

- wash individuals, help them to dress and make them feel comfortable
- serve meals and help to feed individuals who cannot manage to eat by themselves
- help people to get out of bed and move around
- strip and make beds
- monitor individuals' conditions by taking their temperature, pulse, respiration rate and weight.

Figure 2.22 Helping to feed individuals is one of the healthcare worker's roles

If working in a healthcare centre, they may:

- sterilise equipment and restock consulting rooms
- receive training to do health checks
- process samples such as urine and blood ready to be sent off to the lab
- take blood samples
- do health promotion or health education work under the supervision of the nurse.

Charity workers

Although some people are in paid roles at charities, many of their workers are volunteers who may come from diverse backgrounds.

Charities can offer support and solutions for individuals' problems. While statutory or formal systems provide specialist and clinical care for health, charities think of all aspects of the individual, not just their physical and mental health. Some charity workers are at the heart of the community and support people on a daily basis.

The roles of informal care givers improving support

Family, friends and neighbours can offer a great deal of support when people are in need of help.

Physical needs

They can supply practical, hands-on help to meet physical needs; for example:

- If someone must go to hospital but has no means of getting there, a member of their family could take them.
- If an individual splits up with a partner, friends or family could help with moving all their belongings.

Intellectual needs

Sometimes when facing major life changes such as a divorce or a separation, people want advice to help them cope with the change of direction. Family members or friends could support them by:

- talking about their own experiences of divorce
- trying to help the individual to see a positive aspect of the situation
- helping them to budget for living in different accommodation.

Emotional needs

Individuals can rely on family and friends to want the best for them. They can trust them to provide an emotional haven where they can talk and discuss anything. This is a good emotional release for a person experiencing trauma, as they know they are being listened to and can share their problems.

Social needs

Mixing and talking with others is good for an individual's mental health and helps people to be able to cope with life changes. The family is the first group to meet the individual's social needs, and this continues for many people throughout their lives. Meeting a neighbour for a chat and a coffee can help someone's mental health by stopping them from feeling isolated.

How practitioners meet individual needs

Practitioners are trained to try and meet individuals' needs, which is shown in Table 2.8. They will also have further contacts with other organisations which may be able to help.

Table 2.8 The role of the practitioner in meeting individual needs

The role of the practitioner	Explanation
Enables/promotes independence	• One of the ways that practitioners can promote independence is to allow the individuals to have choice and encourage them to make decisions that affect them. • The practitioner should provide support if it is needed. • They can help the individual improve their mobility and their ability to carry out daily tasks such as dressing or making a meal. • This gives the individual confidence and raises their self-esteem.
Medical/mental health support	• Most medical practitioners will be able to provide the individual with medical support, such as referring them for further tests if necessary. • It is also important that medical staff have good interpersonal skills and listen to the individual, spending time to find out their worries and needs.
Care support	• If the individual is caring for someone else or just for themselves, the practitioners should ensure that they have all the help they are entitled to. • This can make a huge difference for the individual, to prevent them from becoming exhausted and unable to cope with all their responsibilities.
Respite care	• Respite care is a lifeline for individuals who may be caring for an individual every day. • This respite provides a break, for both the carers and for the individuals being cared for, from their usual routines to improve the quality of their lives and support their relationships. • These breaks can be organised by a social worker or a healthcare professional.
Financial support	• Practitioners working with individuals who require financial support must ensure that they are assessed for all the benefits and tax credits they are entitled to. • An individual may also be entitled to financial assistance with housing, housing adaptations or transport.
Advice and guidance	• It is important that practitioners give individuals advice and guidance that is accessible, as this allows for better choices. • Individuals feel more confident about making a choice if they have all the facts. • It is the duty of practitioners to make sure that individuals have all the information they need.

Unit R033 Supporting individuals through life events

Research and recommend personalised support based on individual needs

There are many different types of organisations which can offer support to individuals, some of which the individual may not even be aware of. For example, there may be voluntary and faith-based groups that may offer assistance.

Match support provision to specific individual needs

The practitioner should talk to the individual about the support they need in the different areas of their life.

Even though the local authority has a duty by law to provide **statutory care**, the individual may have to make a financial contribution towards their care needs if they have adequate financial resources. Alternatively, they may choose to pay for their care privately.

Individuals might find it more difficult to access services if they live in a remote location rather than close to a town. If they live in a rural location, it may be difficult to find a **domiciliary care agency** that has carers available to work in that area. So, availability in an area could affect the provision of services.

Costs could also be affected by the location of the individual who needs care:

- Even if carers are willing to travel long distances, the cost of this travel would need to be covered by the individual, and this might be too much for them.
- If the local authority is paying for the care, the amount of time taken for the carer to travel has to be taken into account: if the authority is paying for five hours of care and the travel takes two hours, the individual will only have three hours of care.

Co-ordinated care and treatment

Good care is based on an individual's needs. Most individuals receive care from more than one provider. Co-ordinated care is about the way services work together to make sure an individual's needs are met. For example:

- When a social care professional such as a social worker comes to assess the care the individual is receiving at home, they may notice that the individual is in more pain than usual.
- They might then contact the GP or district nurse to organise a home visit, so the individual can be reassessed for pain relief.

Justify choices made

Once the support needed by the individual has been agreed between the practitioner and the individual, there should be an explanation, with reasons, about why the choices made will be suitable to meet their needs.

> **Key terms**
>
> **Statutory care** Services that are provided and paid for by the government such as the NHS.
>
> **Domiciliary care agency** An organisation that provides care and support to individuals in their own home.

OCR Cambridge National in Health and Social Care

Apply person-centred values

A person-centred approach is to see the person as an individual, focusing on their personal needs, wants, goals and aspirations. The individual must be central to the whole process, with their support needs designed in partnership with the individual, their family and/or carers. The key principles of person-centred values are:

- knowing the person as an individual – listen to them, make them feel accepted and their opinions valued
- empowerment – allow individuals to make informed choices that are right for them
- respect the individual's values and preferences – appreciate a person's unique differences, needs, preferences, abilities, ethnicity, values and cultural background
- choice and autonomy – a holistic approach that supports the whole person across their physical, intellectual, emotional, social and spiritual needs
- respect and dignity – all caring relationships should be built on these
- empathy and compassion – the carer should try to understand how the individual is feeling and show concern.

Test your knowledge

1. What is meant by formal care?
2. What is meant by holistic care?
3. What is the purpose of respite care?
4. How can practitioners promote independence?
5. Give a definition of person-centred care.

Assignment practice

Aamir Chandra was born in Britain in 1953 after his parents arrived from India. He was a happy child who enjoyed playing with his two older brothers. He did well at the local primary school, passing the eleven-plus exam and going to the local grammar school.

He worked hard as his parents were keen for him to do well so he could get a good job when he left school. At the age of 18 he left school with good O level grades (equivalent to GCSEs) and A levels; he went on to university to become an engineer.

Aamir was 19 and had just started university when it was discovered that he had epilepsy which he knows about because his grandfather has it. Until this time he had not had any symptoms, and it came as a shock to the family as he was rushed into hospital when he had a seizure at university. When he came out of hospital, his parents supported him and the NHS gave him medication to help control his seizures.

When he was 22, he married a young woman chosen for him by his parents. Aamir and his wife were very happy in their arranged marriage, and had two sons and two daughters. Aamir earned a lot of money, so they were quite wealthy and lived in a quiet, rural neighbourhood. He was very keen to stay fit and active, so Aamir and his family ate a well-balanced diet and were enthusiastic tennis and cricket players. Sadly, Aamir had more episodes of epilepsy as he grew older, and it took time for the NHS to stabilise his seizures.

Aamir loved his job, but decided to retire at 62 as he had several grandchildren at this stage who he wanted to spend time with. He also wanted to spend time with his mother, who had lived with them since his father died.

Unit R033 Supporting individuals through life events

Task 1: Growth and development through the life stages

Topic area 1 is assessed in this task.

1 Describe the milestones of growth and development for one stage that Aamir has experienced, using PIES.
2 For the same life stage, explain how the growth and development of Aamir has been affected by:
   - two physical factors
   - two emotional/social factors
   - two economic factors.

Top tips

1 When you research and use information from books or websites, make sure it is referenced.
2 You must use the same life stage for both parts of Task 1.
3 You should use your own words in your description and explanation.

Task 2: Life events and sources of support for individuals

Topic areas 2 and 3 are assessed in this task.

Task 2a: Impact of life events on individuals

Topic area 2 is assessed in this task.

Ross is 49 years old and lives with his wife and two children. Ross married when he was 41, and his daughter was born two years later, followed by his son two years after that. His son Alfie has Down's syndrome. When Alfie was born, his wife gave up work to look after him. Ross worked offshore on an oil rig as an engineer.

Two years after Alfie was born, Ross was seriously injured when the car he was travelling in crashed on his way home from the oil rig. Ross is now quadriplegic (paralysed in his arms and legs) so he cannot move without assistance and needs lots of support to live his life. Ross has gained weight as he used to be highly active, but now he can barely move. He is stressed and anxious, as he feels his wife is carrying all the work of looking after Alfie.

1 Describe two life events that Ross experienced, including the life stage(s) when they happened.
2 Explain the impacts of one of these events on Ross at the time it occurred.
   You must consider the following impacts:
   - physical
   - intellectual
   - emotional
   - social
   - financial.
   If there is no impact for one of the above, you must explain why.
3 Explain the needs of Ross considering these impacts.

Top tips

1 The life events could be expected or unexpected, and be a result of a physical event, a relationship change or a change in life circumstances.
2 Use your own words in your description and explanation.
3 If you copy information from books, websites or course notes to support your own description or explanation, make sure it is referenced.
4 Remember that although you have to give two life events in the first section, you only have to explain the impact of one life event.

Task 2b: Research and recommend support to meet individual needs

Topic area 3 is assessed in this task.

In this task you will research and recommend personalised support to meet Ross's needs.

You must include the following in your report:

1 Information about the support that could meet Ross's needs, considering the following sources of support:
   - formal
   - informal
   - charities.

2 A recommendation of support to include:
- justification of your choices, to include how practitioners/care givers will support and meet Ross's needs
- how you have applied person-centred values of care.

Top tips
1 Your research could cover support available locally and/or nationally.
2 Include the three sources of support.
3 Use your own words in the report.
4 Record the sources of information you have used.

Synoptic links

Unit R033	Links with Unit R032: Principles of care in health and social care settings
Topic area 2: Impacts of life events	**Topic area 1:** The rights of service users in health and social care settings **Topic area 2:** Person-centred values **Topic area 3:** Effective communication in health and social care settings
Topic area 3: Sources of support	**Topic area 2:** Person-centred values

Read about it

Weblinks

www.ageuk.org.uk

For information on ageing, dementia and the menopause.

www.kidsdevelopment.co.uk/childrensintellectualdevelopment.html

Intellectual development in children aged 3–12 years.

www.stress.org.uk/what-is-stress

From distress to de-stress; all aspects of stress and how to manage it.

http://genetics.org.uk

Information on all aspects of genetics.

Reference books

Doherty, J. (2013) *Child Development: Theory and Practice 0–11*. Pearson.

Fisher A. et al. (2012) *Applied AS Health and Social Care*. Oxford University Press.

Gilmore K. et al. (2014) *The Little Book of Child and Adolescent Development*. Oxford University Press.

Sharma, A. and Cockerill, H. (2014) *Mary Sheridan's From Birth to Five Years: Children's Developmental Progress* (4th edition). Routledge.

Unit R034
Creative and therapeutic activities

About this unit

Creative activities and therapies with people and groups in health and social care settings can encourage physical and mental well-being, provide stimulation and enjoyment, and develop communication and social interaction skills. Therapies are carried out by trained professionals.

In this unit you will learn about the different types of creative and therapeutic activities that are available, and the different needs these activities address for children and young people, adults and older adults. You will also learn about the many benefits of participating in creative and therapeutic activities and how to encourage positive experiences for all those who take part in and support them.

Creative activities require careful planning and delivery if people and groups are to benefit from them. You will have an opportunity to plan and carry out a creative activity suitable for a person or group in a health or social care setting. You will also gain the knowledge and skills required to review a creative activity and make suggestions for improvements.

Topic areas

In this chapter you will learn about:
1 Therapies and their benefits
2 Creative activities and their benefits
3 How to plan a creative activity for individuals or groups in a health or social care setting
4 How to deliver a creative activity and evaluate your own performance.

OCR Cambridge National in Health and Social Care

How will I be assessed?

You will be assessed through a series of assignment tasks which are set by OCR. The assignment will be marked by your tutor and then moderated by OCR.

For Topic area 1, you need to:

- demonstrate an understanding of the different types of therapies used in health and social care settings
- describe different types of therapies, with examples
- explain the benefits of therapies to people in different settings.

For Topic area 2, you need to:

- demonstrate an understanding of the different types of creative activities used in health and social care settings
- describe different types of creative activities, with examples
- explain the benefits of participating in creative activities to people in different settings.

For Topic area 3, you need to:

- explain the factors that affect the selection of a creative activity
- demonstrate how to plan a creative activity to meet a person's or group's needs.

For Topic area 4, you need to:

- demonstrate an understanding of the skills/personal qualities required to encourage participation in a creative activity
- demonstrate how to deliver a creative activity with a group or individual
- evaluate how you planned and delivered a creative activity, with suggestions for improvement.

Unit R034 covers three Performance Objectives (POs):

- PO2 Apply knowledge and understanding
- PO3 Analyse and evaluate knowledge, understanding and performance
- PO4 Demonstrate and apply skills and processes relevant to the subject areas.

Unit R034 Creative and therapeutic activities

Topic area 1 Therapies and their benefits

Getting started
Creative and therapeutic activities in health and social care settings provide many benefits including enjoyment, stimulation, relaxation and a way of expressing thoughts and emotions.

- Make a list of three of your favourite interests or hobbies.
- Explain to a partner why you enjoy them and how they benefit you.
- Ask your partner what their three favourite interests or hobbies are, and listen to why they enjoy them and how they benefit them.
- Compare and discuss your answers.

1.1 Types of therapies used in health and social care

Types of therapy

Sensory
Sensory therapies are designed to stimulate the five senses of sight, sound, touch, taste and smell. They can be used for:

- relaxation
- managing stress and illness
- creating a pleasant experience for people.

Examples of sensory therapies can include aromatherapy, reflexology and massage.

Aromatherapy
Aromatherapy is a touch and smell therapy. It uses essential oils that are extracted from the roots, stalks, flowers, leaves or fruits of plants, for maintaining good physical and mental health and well-being. For example, lavender is one of the best-known essential oils that is used for promoting calmness and relieving tension.

Aromatherapy can be used in a variety of ways, such as:

- aromatherapy baths – essential oils added to water can help to relieve stress and tension (e.g. sandalwood oil), muscle aches and pains (e.g. sage oil)
- aromatherapy compresses – compresses soaked in water with essential oils added can be applied to different parts of the body to help to treat bruises and muscular aches and pains (e.g. hyssop oil)
- aromatherapy massages – essential oils applied to the body using massage techniques can promote relaxation and improve blood circulation throughout the whole body (e.g. juniper oil)

- aromatherapy steaming and inhalation treatments – essential oils can be added to a bowl of steaming water (e.g. eucalyptus oil for the relief of colds), or a pillow (e.g. camomile oil for encouraging relaxation and sleep)
- aromatherapy essential oil burners or vaporisers – water and essential oils are added to a bowl at the top of the burner and then a tea light underneath the bowl helps to evaporate the water and essential oils, and spread them around a room (e.g. orange essential oil can be uplifting, or peppermint and eucalyptus essential oils can improve focus and concentration).

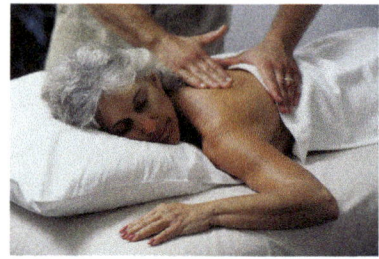

Figure 3.1 Sensory therapies can bring many benefits to health and well-being

Reflexology

Reflexology can promote physical and mental health and well-being. It encourages the body to relax and address any imbalances that may lead to stress and illness.

Reflexology is a touch therapy that involves using both thumb and finger techniques to apply pressure to specific areas or **reflexes** on the feet, lower leg, hands, face or ears that correspond with different organs and parts of the body when stimulated.

For example, in the reflexes in the feet:

- the toes are connected to the head and neck areas, including the sinuses, brain, eyes and ears
- the ball of the foot is connected to the thoracic area, including the lungs, heart and diaphragm
- the arch of the foot is connected to the abdominal area including the liver, stomach, small intestine
- the heel of the foot is connected to the pelvic area including the pelvis and **sciatic nerve**.

Reflexology can be used in the feet through a variety of techniques:

1. One hand supports the foot (this hand is referred to as the supporting hand). For example, if you are working on the left foot:
   - Use either your left or right hand to hold the top of the foot.
   - Place your four fingers across the top of the foot and your thumb on the sole.
2. One hand applies pressure to the foot (this hand is referred to as the working hand). For example, if you are working on the right foot, use your right or left hand to apply a variety of pressure techniques:
   - the rotating thumb technique
   - three different finger techniques that correspond with different reflexes you are working on
   - the pinch technique
   - the knead technique.

> **Key terms**
>
> **Reflex** An involuntary or unconscious response to a stimulus, such as the leg moving when the knee is tapped. In reflexology, the stimulus is provided when pressure is applied to the reflex area on the feet.
>
> **Sciatic nerve** A nerve that runs from your lower back through your hips, legs and down to your feet.

3   Use relaxation techniques that encourage the whole body to relax. For example:
    - the Achilles tendon stretch, to stretch the back of the leg and release tension
    - ankle rotation and loosening of the ankles to relax both ankles
    - the side-to-side technique to boost circulation and relieve tiredness
    - the spinal twist and wringing the foot techniques to reduce tension and relax the body from the neck down to the base of the spine
    - toe rotation to increase the flexibility of the toes and relieve tension in the neck and shoulders
    - the solar plexus technique, which is the main reflex area in the foot for stress and promotes relaxation of the whole body.

Research

1   Find out more about which parts of the body are connected to reflexology points in the feet. For example, you could look at the interactive foot map on the Association of Reflexologists' website:

    www.aor.org.uk/what-is-reflexology

2   Using this information, design a poster with an outline of either your left or right foot. Describe five feet reflexology points and their corresponding areas to the body.

Massage

Massage is a touch, sound and smell therapy. Different touches, pressures and speeds of different hand strokes are used to massage different areas of the body such as the face, hands and feet, as well as the whole body.

Massage encourages the relaxation of both the mind and body, and therefore works best in a quiet, warm, comfortable room with dim lighting.

Massage techniques can include:

1   A variety of hand massage strokes, such as:
    - stroking – with palms down and hands flat
    - circling – with palms down and hands flat like in stroking but moving in circles; one palm clockwise, the other anti-clockwise

- kneading – both hands flat, fingers together with thumbs stretched out wide; thumbs are used to push into, squeeze and pinch the skin towards the fingers; each hand follows the other over the same body area
- pummelling – make both hands into fists and keep your fingers relaxed; bounce them in a fast drumming movement, lightly up and down, one after the other
- knuckling – making your hands into loose fists, fingertips flat on the skin; roll them forward and turn them over so the knuckles push and slide into the skin.

2 Stimulating the sense of sound to relax the body and mind – the massage takes place in a peaceful and quiet area, or relaxing music or sounds are played, such as the sound of the waves in the sea.

3 Stimulating the sense of smell to relax the body and mind – oils are used to ensure hands slide in rhythmic movements and warm the skin during massage. Body massage oils can include sweet almond, sunflower or grapeseed, and facial massage oils can include avocado, evening primrose and jojoba.

Cognitive therapies

Cognitive therapies are designed to stimulate the mind and body. These therapies are based on the theory that our thoughts, feelings and behaviours are all connected and can influence each other. Examples of cognitive therapies include:

- hypnotherapy
- speech and language therapy
- mind-body healing
- reminiscence therapy.

Hypnotherapy

Hypnotherapy is a cognitive therapy that uses relaxation techniques so that:

- the **conscious** part of your mind is relaxed
- the **subconscious** part of your mind is open to suggestion, to encourage you to make positive changes to your life.

Hypnotherapy can be used to encourage people to give up habits such as smoking or to treat conditions such as **depression** or phobias, such as the fear of injections or needles.

Hypnotherapy techniques can include:

- relaxation techniques – such as lying down, counting down in your head from 100, focusing on your breathing by slowly breathing in through the nose and out through the mouth

> **Key terms**
> **Conscious** The part of your mind that is responsible for thinking, such as making decisions.
>
> **Subconscious** The part of your mind that works without your awareness or control, such as your breathing, your emotions and memories.
>
> **Depression** A medical condition causing low mood that affects your thoughts and feelings. It can range from mild to severe, but usually lasts for a long time and affects your day-to-day living.

- visualisation techniques to help associate memories with positive experiences instead of negative ones – such as remembering going on holiday as a child or remembering the details and smells of a favourite place
- positive thinking techniques – such as asking a person who has **body dysmorphic disorder** to repeat back under hypnosis 'I like my body, my body is beautiful'.

Speech and language

Speech and language therapy is used with children and adults who have difficulties with communication and/or with eating, drinking and swallowing. For example, speech and language therapy can be used to help:

- adults who have had a **stroke** to regain their ability to communicate with others
- children who have **cerebral palsy** and difficulties with swallowing when eating.

The **Royal College of Speech and Language Therapists (RCSLT)** has stated in their factsheet 'What is speech and language therapy?' that in the UK:

- nearly 20 per cent of the population experience communication difficulties at some point in their lives
- speech, language and communication needs are the most common type of special educational need in children aged 4 to 11
- around a third of people who have had a stroke will experience communication difficulties.

Speech and language techniques can include:

- articulation therapy – improves speech by correctly sounding out words such as through rhymes and/or songs
- oral motor therapy – strengthens the muscles needed for speaking, swallowing, eating and drinking by practising and observing the shape of the mouth and lips when saying the sounds 'a' or 'o', for example
- speech language intervention therapy – improves speech by encouraging putting words into sentences in the correct order through activities such as role play.

Mind-body healing

Mind-body healing uses the power of positive thinking. It is based on the theory that the mind and body are closely connected.

Mind-body healing can promote physical and emotional well-being by using the mind to influence the body through the thought process. For example, mind-body healing can be useful for managing stress and anxiety, and reducing pain such as backache and headaches.

Key terms

Body dysmorphic disorder A mental health condition related to a person's body image, where they are extremely anxious about their physical appearance and see themselves differently from how others see them. For example, they might see one or more parts of their body as too big or too small.

Stroke A life-threatening medical condition that occurs when the blood supply to part of the brain is cut off by a clot or bleed. Depending on the part of the brain it damages, it can affect how your body works, your communication and how you think and feel.

Cerebral palsy A lifelong neurological condition that is caused by damage to the brain before, during or soon after birth. This condition affects the body's movements and muscle co-ordination. Symptoms can include jerky uncontrolled movements, and stiff or floppy arms and legs.

Royal College of Speech and Language Therapists (RCSLT) The professional body for speech and language therapists in the UK.

OCR Cambridge National in Health and Social Care

Mind-body healing techniques can include:

1. Mindfulness meditation – focuses on controlled breathing and stillness. It also encourages making time to enjoy the present moment by focusing on the positive things happening in our lives now, rather than worrying about the things that have happened in the past or that may happen in the future.

2. Using the power of positive thinking – focuses on how you think to affect how you feel. For example, thinking positively and being optimistic about a situation will make you feel better and less anxious or stressed.

3. Using visualisation – focuses on your thoughts, words and actions, keeping them positive by visualising or creating positive pictures. For example, if you are going to a job interview, you can create a picture in your head of how you are going to present yourself successfully by:
   - thinking about the skills and qualities you have
   - visualising positive ways you could answer questions at the interview
   - visualising positive actions you can take at the interview to show your prospective employer that you will be a good asset to their company.

Reminiscence therapy

Reminiscence therapy is also known as life review therapy. It involves sharing memories, life experiences and stories from the past to promote well-being and mental stimulation. Reminiscence therapy can be useful to enable a person who has **dementia** to communicate with their family or friends.

> **Key term**
>
> **Dementia** A group of symptoms that affect how a person thinks, remembers, solves problems, uses language, communicates and carries out tasks and activities. They occur when brain cells stop working properly and the brain is damaged by injury, or by disease such as Alzheimer's.

Figure 3.2 What is reminiscence?

Reminiscence therapy techniques can include:

1. Discussions – introducing topics for discussion can stimulate conversations and encourage sharing of memories. Topics for discussion may include childhood holidays, pets, relationships with family and friends.
2. Photographs – introducing photographs from the past can evoke happy memories and may lead to a discussion of these. Photographs of favourite places, people such as family and friends, and events such as weddings and birthdays can be used.
3. **Life story work** – supporting the creation of life story work, that describes a person's life story through the use of photographs or other personal items such as a book or theatre tickets, can encourage the person to share positive memories, and provide useful and interesting insights into their life and interests.

Expressive therapies

Expressive therapies use the creative arts such as art, drama and music as a way of expressing thoughts and emotions. For example, some people who find talking therapies difficult may instead prefer to express their thoughts and emotions through the arts.

Art therapy

Art therapy can include drawing, painting, collage, colouring and sculpting. It involves self-expression and the examination of thoughts and emotions.

Art therapy techniques can include:

- spending time creating art – mixing colours for painting or using graphite or charcoal for drawing can be a leisurely experience, and can encourage people to discuss their feelings as they create
- sensory experiences – painting using hands and fingers or using clay when sculpting can be relaxing and calming for people
- discussion prompts – cutting out shapes, pictures and photographs to make collages can encourage discussions and the sharing of stories based on the images created.

Play therapy

Play therapy is used with children, young people and adults to help them express their emotions and help them with managing behavioural difficulties. For example, play therapy can be useful to help a child who is unwell in hospital to communicate how they are feeling and any anxieties they may have about their condition.

> **Key term**
>
> **Life story work** An activity that involves reviewing a person's past life events and developing a biography to understand more about the individual and their experiences.

Play therapy techniques can include:

- role play – role-playing events or situations that are traumatic or difficult such as bereavement can help with managing emotions, as the individual communicates how they feel at their own pace
- learning through play – play encourages children and young people to be creative and imaginative. It can also develop other skills such as sharing, turn taking and problem solving
- communication through play – encouraging communication through play can enable people to learn how to interact with others and form better relationships and friendships.

Figure 3.3 Learning through play

Express thoughts and emotions

As you have learned, art therapy can be a useful tool for encouraging people to express thoughts and emotions in a relaxed and enjoyable way without feeling pressurised. Expressing thoughts can help people to make sense of what is happening around them. For example, in art therapy:

- drama and role play can be a useful way to support a young person who is feeling overwhelmed about leaving home
- a young person can be supported to think through the steps they have to take, explore their emotions and improve their **self-esteem**.

Physical therapies

Physical therapies involve helping people to maintain, improve or recover their physical abilities that may have been affected through illness such as **arthritis** or due to injury such as a fall.

> **Key terms**
>
> **Self-esteem** How much a person values themselves and the life they live. High self-esteem is associated with people who are happy and confident. A service user with low self-esteem experiences feelings of unhappiness and worthlessness.
>
> **Arthritis** A medical condition that affects joints by causing pain, stiffness, swelling and reduced mobility of the joints.

Yoga

Yoga involves stretching exercises, controlled breathing and relaxation.

Yoga includes movements to promote physical strength and flexibility as well as relaxation of the body and mind. Yoga can:

- improve muscle tone and balance
- reduce symptoms of anxiety, depression and pain
- improve sleep and promote well-being.

Yoga movements, or poses, can help in specific ways:

1. The Sukhasana pose can help to relieve stress.
   - Sit cross-legged on a yoga mat with your hands on your knees and the palms facing up.
   - Then, keep the spine straight while you push the bones you're sitting on down into the floor.
   - Close your eyes, and inhale and exhale slowly.

2. The Cat-Cow pose can help to reduce back pain.
   - Get on all fours on a yoga mat with your hands directly below your shoulders and your knees directly below your hips.
   - Distribute your weight equally between your hands and spread your fingers wide.
   - When you inhale, arch your back and lower your chin to your chest, like a cat.
   - Then, exhale and lower your back down all the way to a scoop shape; lift your head, and tilt it back, like a cow.

3. The Vrksasana or Tree pose can help to improve your balance.
   - Stand straight, bringing your hands together in the prayer position and lifting them up over your head.
   - Then, while balancing on your right leg, bend the left knee out to the left side and press your left foot to the inner thigh of your right leg.
   - Hold for 30 seconds, then switch legs.

4. The Adho Mukha Svanasana or Downward-Facing Dog pose can help to improve flexibility of the spine, arms, shoulders and legs.
   - Place both your hands on the mat in front of you, palms down and placed slightly in front of your shoulders.
   - Place your knees on the ground directly under your hips.
   - Exhale slowly as you lift your knees off the ground and your hips up towards the ceiling.
   - Push the tops of your thighs back and stretch your heels down towards the floor.
   - Keep your head down between and in line with your arms.

5 The Balasana or Child's pose can help with relaxation and the reduction of tiredness.
   - Place both your hands on the mat in front of you, palms down and placed slightly in front of your shoulders.
   - Then, bend your knees and lower your hips to your heels as you bring your chest towards the floor and over your knees.
   - Lower your shoulders and head to the floor.
   - Place your arms along your sides, palms down, or you can support your head by folding your arms under your forehead.
   - Breathe and relax for as long as you need to.

Source: www.better.org.uk/yoga-poses

Tai Chi

Tai Chi was originally developed as a martial art in China and is also referred to as Tai Chi Chuan. It involves deep breathing and relaxation techniques with continuous, flowing movements.

There are many Tai Chi moves and styles:

1 Chen – this style combines fast moves with softer, gentle moves and is aimed at creating energy. The body maintains a low stance, while slow and fast moves are combined with circles and twists of the body and hands to build up energy. Fingers extend at a slight angle in this style.

2 Yang – this is the most common style and involves slow-paced moves that are gentle and circular. Fingers are spread lightly, and the rear foot is maintained at 45 degrees during the stances.

3 Wu – this style is controlled and involves a narrower stance. The rear foot faces forward, not at a 45 degrees angle, with the front knee bent and the back knee relaxed. Fingers are extended upwards and are loosely separated.

4 Sun – this style is an upright stance with compact movements and fast footwork. Hands are extended flat, with fingers slightly apart.

Reiki

Reiki is a Japanese technique commonly referred to as energy healing. It involves laying the palms of hands on a person to encourage physical and/or emotional healing.

In Japanese, the word 'Rei' means 'God's wisdom or the Higher Power' and 'Ki' means 'life force energy'. Reiki is a spiritual technique based on the belief that:

- Life force energy flows through every one of us.
- If it is low, it may lead to stress and ill health.
- If it is high, it can promote happiness and well-being.

Unit R034 Creative and therapeutic activities

There are many reiki techniques:

1 The hands-on technique – this can help to promote relaxation and relieve stress. Rub your palms together for a few seconds, and then, using the life force energy through your palms, place them on different parts of the body such as on the bones, joints, muscles or organs to promote healing.

2 The reiki meditation technique – this involves visualising the life force energy flowing through your body to the different parts that need healing. The mind is used for the healing process, instead of the palms of the hands. It is important that you're in a quiet place, free from distractions where you can relax and take slow, controlled deep breaths.

3 The live reiki technique – this involves feeling the life force energy flowing through the body from the moment you get up in the morning until you go to bed at night. It is something that is practised every day and is used to channel the life force energy to the specific parts of the body that need healing. This technique requires a high level of **self-awareness** and is usually practised after the hands-on and meditation techniques have been mastered.

> **Key term**
>
> **Self-awareness** The knowledge a person has of their own character and emotions.

Test your knowledge
1 What does 'sensory therapies' mean? Write down one example of a sensory therapy.
2 What does 'cognitive therapies' mean? Write down one example of a cognitive therapy.
3 What are four different types of therapies?
4 What type of therapy is art therapy?
5 What type of therapy is yoga?

Activity
Exploring therapies
1 Think about the range of therapies that you learned about and that are available in health and social care settings.
2 Choose two therapies that interest you.
3 Discuss why they interest you, what they involve, how they are used and why.

Benefits of therapies

Everyone of any age – older people, adults, teenagers and children – can experience positive benefits of different types of therapies used in health and social care settings. Positive benefits may include:

- physical effects on the body such as reducing pain
- intellectual effects on the mind such as improving concentration
- emotional effects such as improving self-esteem
- social effects such as improving interactions and relations with others.

Further examples of some of the benefits that different sensory, cognitive, expressive and physical therapies may bring to people are detailed in Tables 3.1, 3.2, 3.3 and 3.4.

Physical benefits

Table 3.1 Physical benefits of therapies

Type of therapy	Examples of physical benefits
Sensory	• Aromatherapy baths can help to relieve headaches, fatigue and muscular aches and pains by relaxing the muscles and stimulating the skin. • Reflexology can help to improve blood circulation by increasing the oxygenated blood reaching main organs and improving their functions. It can also help to improve sleep by calming the body and mind.
	• Massage can help to relieve pain by stimulating the release of the body's **hormones** called **endorphins**. Massage can also help to improve movement by increasing flexibility in the joints.
Cognitive	• Mind-body healing encourages deep relaxation that in turn can help to lower blood pressure and reduce the effects of pain. • Speech and language therapy can improve the co-ordination and functioning of the muscles responsible for speech and swallowing.
Expressive	• Art therapy can help to improve manual dexterity by using controlled hand movements and hand–eye co-ordination when painting or drawing or sculpting. • Play therapy encourages physical movement because it can encourage the body to move and position in different ways such as through crawling, stretching, walking, running, sitting up/down, standing up, lying down.
Physical	• Yoga poses that encourage the body to move in different ways can help to increase muscle strength and improve flexibility and mobility. • Yoga poses can also encourage increased blood flow to the heart thus improving blood circulation, lowering blood pressure and improving heart function. • Tai Chi can help to improve posture and balance because it involves continuous movements. The stances involved can also increase strength in the body's leg muscles. • Reiki improves the body's physical systems and its functions such as breathing, digesting and sleeping. • Reiki can provide pain relief from migraines and **sciatica**.

Key terms

Hormones Chemical substances produced in the body by the endocrine glands and transported in the blood to other organs in the body. Examples are adrenaline, oestrogen, testosterone.

Endorphins Chemical substances produced by the brain to reduce pain.

Sciatica A condition where the sciatic nerve, which runs from the lower back to the feet, is irritated or compressed, causing inflammation, numbness and pain.

Unit R034 Creative and therapeutic activities

Intellectual benefits

Table 3.2 Intellectual benefits of therapies

Type of therapy	Examples of intellectual benefits
Sensory	• Aromatherapy, reflexology and massage can improve focus and concentration because these therapies make the person feel relaxed and calm. • Being in a relaxed and calm state also benefits the mind by enabling it to be more creative.
Cognitive	• Speech and language therapy can improve communication skills by helping people regain their language skills and develop new ways of communicating, such as by using gestures and signing. • Reminiscence therapy can improve communication skills by encouraging conversation. It can also improve long-term memory by recalling events from the past.
Expressive	• Art therapy can help to improve imagination, creativity and concentration by focusing on self-expression of thoughts and emotions.
	• Play therapy improves communication skills because it encourages the use of **verbal** and **non-verbal communication** and increases awareness and understanding of what others are communicating.
Physical	• Tai Chi can improve cognition, including memory and concentration, because its techniques focus on carrying out complex flowing movements and breathing techniques. • The reiki meditation technique can help with improving concentration by encouraging focus on the breathing so that the body and mind become relaxed.

Key terms

Verbal communication Using words to speak or talk with others.

Non-verbal communication Messages that are conveyed without words, such as body language and facial expressions including eye contact, body movements and hand gestures.

Figure 3.4 What are the benefits of speech and language therapy?

Emotional benefits

Table 3.3 Emotional benefits of therapies

Type of therapy	Examples of emotional benefits
Sensory	• Reflexology can help with maintaining a sense of well-being because it treats the individual's whole person, both their body and mind. • Massage can help to reduce stress and anxiety by soothing and calming the mind. In addition, the hormone **cortisol** is released during massage, and its purpose is to lower stress levels in the body.
Cognitive	• Hypnotherapy increases self-awareness by encouraging the individual to examine themselves, their habits and any changes they wish to make to their lifestyle, such as to lose weight, stop smoking or stop drinking alcohol. • Reminiscence therapy can enhance a person's sense of well-being, because when the individual shares something positive and worthwhile about themselves, this can make them feel listened to and valued.
Expressive	• Art therapy can help to reduce depression and grief by encouraging the expression of thoughts and emotions that are difficult to acknowledge or talk about. • Play therapy can increase self-awareness and improve self-esteem and confidence – it encourages friendships, and increases people's understanding of how others perceive them and how their actions can impact on others.
Physical	• Yoga involves controlled breathing and relaxation which can help to reduce stress by reducing the amount of the hormone cortisol that the body produces. • Yoga can also reduce anxiety and panic attacks because it encourages a sense of peace and calmness. • Tai Chi can also help to reduce stress and anxiety because its techniques focus on deep breathing and relaxation. Slow breathing and movements can also have a positive effect on the nervous system and the hormones that regulate moods. • Reiki promotes a sense of deep relaxation which can lead to lower stress levels, reduced anxiety and alleviate depression and grief.

> **Key term**
>
> **Cortisol** The body's main stress hormone secreted by the adrenal glands found at the top of the kidneys.

Social benefits

Table 3.4 Social benefits of therapies

Type of therapy	Examples of social benefits
Sensory	• Aromatherapy, reflexology and massage promote a sense of well-being. This can lead to increased confidence when meeting, interacting and connecting with others.
Cognitive	• Mind-body healing promotes the use of positive thinking that will lead to effective co-operation when socialising and working together with others. • Reminiscence therapy can help with forming relations and connecting to others, because it can produce useful insights into a person, including their interests, likes and dislikes.
Expressive	• Sharing opinions and views on art during art therapy can improve social connections with others who share a similar interest. • Play therapy can improve understanding of rules and moral behaviours by encouraging patience, respect for others and empathy. • Play therapy helps to develop skills such as listening, turn taking, taking responsibility, working together and co-operation with others who may have different thoughts and opinions.
Physical	• Tai Chi improves physical and emotional well-being. It can therefore encourage positive interactions with others, through improved mood and motivation. • Reiki helps with improving co-operation and interactions with others by encouraging focus on the present, becoming more grounded and therefore responding to others in a supportive and positive manner.

Case study: Therapies at Highview

Highview is an adult day care centre providing care and support for older people and people with dementia. The centre helps people to meet new friends and do activities they enjoy. There are many activities available, based on people's needs, preferences, hobbies and interests. The staff team would like to introduce something different and are considering different types of therapies.

Imagine you have been asked to carry out some research on the different types of therapies used in health and social care settings.

1 Describe two types of therapies you think could be used at Highview and your reasons why.
2 For each therapy, explain their benefits to people.

Key term

Empathy The ability to identify with another person's situation and understand how they may be feeling or thinking.

Test your knowledge

1 What is one physical benefit for service users of participating in a therapeutic activity?
2 What is one emotional benefit for service users of participating in a therapeutic activity?

OCR Cambridge National in Health and Social Care

Topic area 2 Creative activities and their benefits

> **Getting started**
>
> Creativity is the ability to challenge, question and explore. It involves taking risks, playing with ideas, keeping an open mind and making connections where none are obvious.
>
> Source: Victoria and Albert Museum of Childhood
>
> Think about an occasion when you were creative. Perhaps you wrote a poem or designed a piece of clothing or took part in a craft activity.
>
> - How did you feel when you were doing the creative activity?
> - What did you learn?

2.1 Types of creative activities and their benefits

Creativity involves:

- expressing yourself
- reflecting your individuality and your uniqueness
- being imaginative
- trying and exploring new activities
- enjoying and learning.

Types of creative activities

Creative activities can be:

- physical
- intellectual/cognitive
- emotional
- social
- sensory
- imaginative.

We'll explore each of these here.

Physical

Physical activities involve people moving around and using their bodies and muscles to express themselves, remain healthy and pain-free.

- Sports, physical education, exercise, armchair exercise, gardening and dance can promote **gross motor skills**, such as balance and co-ordination.

> **Key term**
>
> **Gross motor skills** The larger movements of arms, legs, feet or the entire body using the large muscles, for walking, running, skipping and jumping.

Unit R034 Creative and therapeutic activities

- Jigsaw puzzles, woodwork, painting, drawing, sewing, knitting, embroidery, crochet, bead and jewellery making are good ways to exercise the brain, increase cognitive function and develop **fine motor skills**.

Recreational activities are another type of physical activity that can take place both indoors and outdoors, with children, young people and adults. Examples are music and movement, parachute games, ball games, trampolining, swimming, walking, climbing and cycling.

Intellectual/cognitive

Intellectual activities can help to promote **language and cognitive development** in children and adults. Examples of intellectual/cognitive activities include:

- a group of children reading stories
- group discussions
- doing crossword puzzles
- taking part in quizzes
- poetry
- storytelling
- writing stories and plays
- reminiscence
- listening to the radio and music
- playing board games such as Pictionary
- doing jigsaw puzzles
- ICT.

Key terms

Fine motor skills Smaller actions using the smaller muscles, such as grasping an object between the thumb and a finger when holding a paintbrush or pencil.

Language and cognitive development Learning language and cognitive skills, such as understanding and using words, communicating, thinking, remembering and problem solving.

Figure 3.5 Reading and writing can help to promote language and cognitive development in children and adults

Emotional

Emotional creative activities can help people to understand and express their emotions or feelings. Examples include storytelling, group discussions, painting, craft work, photography and mime. Taking part in these activities can be a safe way for people to:

- talk about their feelings of frustration or anger
- explore topics or areas that they find difficult or too upsetting to talk about.

Social

Social creative activities encourage positive relationships, and enable people to communicate, interact and meet with others, and exercise their bodies and minds. Examples are singing, dancing, drama, role play, mime, quizzes, bingo, card games and board games.

Group experiences such as painting, cooking and discussions can help with promoting social and mental well-being by encouraging people to interact with others and make new friendships.

Sensory

Sensory creative activities stimulate the five senses of sight, sound, touch, taste and smell. They enable people to experiment with different textures, smells and sounds, and provide opportunities to communicate and interact with others. Examples are gardening, painting, clay, cookery, and exploring sand and water.

Sensory creative activities can help people who have a visual or hearing impairment, or both, and/or have difficulties with moving around in their environments. They may find it more difficult to explore and take an interest in activities that are not known to them, but that does not mean that they cannot explore, be creative or use their imagination.

Imaginative

> *Imagination is more important than knowledge.*

Source: Albert Einstein

This type of creative activity encourages people to use their imaginations to act out, role play and/or create different scenarios. This can improve people's mental health and mood, and can enhance positive interactions with others. Imaginative creative activities can also help with developing children's and adults' language and communication skills.

Examples of this type of activity include:

- reading
- junk modelling
- young people dressing up and taking part in a role play
- making a scrapbook or collage making

Unit R034 Creative and therapeutic activities

- dance and drama workshops
- older adults creating a display about their local area using photographs, paintings they have done and craft models they have made.

Benefits of creative activities

Participating in creative activities can benefit children, young people, adults and older people in a variety of ways and at different times in their lives. The benefits of creative activities can vary from one person to another, depending on their experience of the activity and the extent to which the activity addresses their specific needs; you will learn more about this in Topic area 3 of this unit.

Figure 3.6 What are the benefits of participating in a creative activity?

Key terms

Dexterity The ability to perform an action with the hands skilfully.

Agility The ability to move the body quickly and easily.

Table 3.5 shows the range of potential benefits that creative activities can bring.

Table 3.5 The benefits of participating in different types of creative activities

Type of creative activity	Skills and areas developed	Examples of benefits
Physical	Fine motor skills – small skilled actions that require the use of muscles, such as an individual cutting and sticking to create a collage. Gross motor skills – large skilled actions that require the use of muscles, such as an individual jumping up and down. Circulation – activities that increase the heart rate and improve the circulation of the blood around the body, such as walking, swimming and chair-based exercises.	• improved dexterity • increased strength in muscles, i.e. in fingers, hands, wrists, toes • improved hand–eye co-ordination • improved agility • improved mobility • improved strength in muscles in the body • improved balance • increase in fitness • exercises the heart, lungs and muscles of the body • improved breathing • reduction of pain and discomfort, i.e. swollen feet and legs • improved pain management • reduction of tension, stress and anxiety • improved relaxation • improved sleep and appetite

OCR Cambridge National in Health and Social Care

Type of creative activity	Skills and areas developed	Examples of benefits
Intellectual (cognitive)	Mental stimulation – activities that exercise and stimulate the brain, such as doing crossword puzzles, taking part in a quiz or learning a new language. Work independently – activities that promote independent learning, such as role play, making posters, creating 3D models. Creative skills – activities that encourage people to explore, experiment and promote self-expression, such as mixing paints, storytelling and dance.	• prevent and/or slow down memory loss • maintain and improve memory • maintain and improve concentration • relieve boredom • learn new skills • ability to plan daily activities • ability to make your own choices • improved communication • problem solving • improved imagination • development of life skills
	Communication skills – activities that enable people to engage and interact with others, such as visiting places, drama activities, painting and drawing. Language skills – activities that provide people with opportunities to develop their speech and language skills, such as reading, singing and storytelling.	• increased self-awareness • improved verbal communication • improved written communication • ability to express how a person thinks and feels • learning • improved speech • improved listening skills
Emotional	Self-esteem – activities that enhance people's well-being and promote positive mental health such as walking, listening to music, dance. Express emotions – activities that provide opportunities for people to express and/or talk about their feelings, such as creative writing, poetry, drama and painting.	• feeling valued • feeling empowered • improved confidence and **self-worth** • improved self-esteem and self-concept • improved motivation • having a sense of achievement • develop new interests • improved emotional stability • being able to express emotions • reduction in anxiety and low mood • relieves tension and stress
Social/moral benefits	Social interaction – activities that provide opportunities for people to be actively involved in the lives of others, such as visiting family and friends, joining a group, going to the park. Developing friendships – activities that provide opportunities to interact and develop relationships with others, such as playing games, group storytelling and art projects.	• being able to work in groups/teams • improved relationships • staying connected and sharing experiences with family and friends • being able to make friends and maintain friendships more easily • developing new relationships • engagement • interaction with others (which reduces boredom) • improved social network • experiencing how to receive and provide support can promote a sense of belonging • reduction in boredom • learning new rules • following and learning rules • learning right and wrong • modelling appropriate behaviour • preparing children for starting school

Key term

Self-worth Confidence and value in your own abilities and qualities.

Unit R034 Creative and therapeutic activities

Test your knowledge

1. What are two types of creative activities?
2. Write down one example of a social creative activity.
3. What type of creative activity is painting?
4. What is one physical benefit of participating in a creative activity?
5. Write down one example of how participating in an intellectual activity can improve a person's problem-solving skills.
6. What are two communication skills that could be improved by participating in a creative activity?
7. Write down two examples of creative activities that can enable people to express their emotions.
8. What are the social/moral benefits of participating in creative activities?

Activity

The benefits of participation

As a whole group, discuss the benefits and skills developed by participating in the following creative activities:

- dance (physical activity)
- storytelling (intellectual/cognitive activity)
- painting (emotional activity)
- singing (social activity)
- sand and water play (sensory activity)
- junk modelling (imaginative activity).

Topic area 3 Plan a creative activity for individuals or groups in a health or social care setting

Getting started

People's experiences of creative activities will vary, depending on how the activities are delivered and whether they had positive or negative impacts.

Think about a creative activity you or someone else you know participated in.

- Write down positive and negative points about how this activity was carried out, and the reasons why.
- Share your findings with a partner.
- Compare and discuss answers.

3.1 Factors that affect the selection of a creative activity

Having learned about the different types of creative activities there are for people in health and social care settings, you will now find out more about the needs of people that these activities address.

All people are unique and therefore have diverse needs. This is why it is important to offer a range of creative activities that can be adapted to meet people's abilities, religious/cultural beliefs and gender.

OCR Cambridge National in Health and Social Care

Individual abilities

Creative activities in health and social care settings such as in hospitals, nursing homes, day centres and support groups are also important to benefit people's **p**hysical, **i**ntellectual, **e**motional and **s**ocial development, commonly referred to as **PIES**.

It's important to understand that these areas of development do not occur in isolation, they are interrelated and affect one another. Some more information about PIES development areas is shown in Figure 3.7.

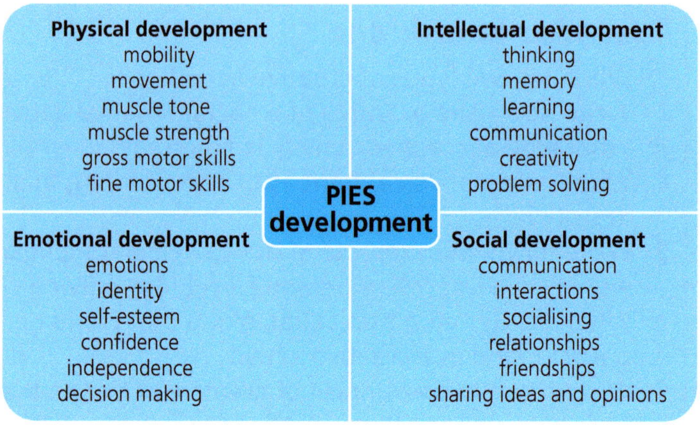

Physical development
mobility
movement
muscle tone
muscle strength
gross motor skills
fine motor skills

Intellectual development
thinking
memory
learning
communication
creativity
problem solving

PIES development

Emotional development
emotions
identity
self-esteem
confidence
independence
decision making

Social development
communication
interactions
socialising
relationships
friendships
sharing ideas and opinions

Figure 3.7 PIES development

Physical

Table 3.6 Creative activities to support physical abilities

Challenges related to physical ability	How creative activities could support these challenges
A child or young person who has cerebral palsy may have difficulty moving their body in a co-ordinated way when walking or running, and may have to use a wheelchair.	• Creative activities that encourage movement and co-ordination, such as dance and exercise, can help the child or young person to develop stronger muscles and improve their balance.
Children and young people with **attention deficit hyperactivity disorder (ADHD)** often have high energy levels.	• Physical activities that encourage high levels of activity, such as running, cycling and hiking, or team sports like football and basketball, will ensure the child moves around and is focused. • Michael Phelps, the Olympic swimming gold medallist, was diagnosed with ADHD when he was a child. Taking part in swimming provided him with the focus and goals he needed to achieve.
Adults who have physical disabilities may want to maintain their physical health by keeping the muscles and joints in their body strong. Maintaining mental well-being is also important, and closely linked to good physical health and well-being.	• Creative activities such as aerobic exercise, gym sessions, swimming and trampolining will support physical and mental health.
Adults may have a range of different medical conditions such as **diabetes**, obesity, high blood pressure, mobility difficulties, depression or anxiety. They might benefit from creative activities designed to improve and maintain good mental and physical well-being.	• Activities could include nature walks, specially designed gym sessions, relaxation and yoga classes.
Older adults who experience a lack of mobility, or limited mobility, find that physical creative activities are important to their overall physical and mental well-being, because they improve their self-esteem.	• Aerobic exercises in water can support people's bodies while reducing additional pressure on muscles and joints. • Chair exercises, where the individual carries out exercises while sitting down, can strengthen bones and muscles, and can improve a person's balance. • Relaxation exercises, including yoga, can provide an overall sense of well-being.

Intellectual

Table 3.7 Creative activities to support intellectual abilities

Challenges related to intellectual ability	How creative activities could support these challenges
Creative activities can help children and young people with **learning difficulties** to become more independent and confident in their own abilities.	• Drama and role play can help a child or young person who has learning difficulties to interact with others and develop their communication and social skills. • Trying new activities can also help children and young people to learn and develop new skills.
Children or young people who have special needs may need additional help because of an illness or medical condition, or an emotional or learning difficulty or disability that prevents them from learning and developing in the same way as other children or young people of the same age who do not have special needs.	• Art activities that enable children to use their creativity and explore their senses, such as clay and dough modelling, water and sand play, can provide a good focus for children who have difficulty concentrating and participating in activities.
Adults who have special needs can also experience difficulties with communication, which can be related to speech and language, social skills and/or behaviour.	• Creative activities such as cooking, gardening, exercise and visiting cafés with friends can help to develop people's confidence, social skills and self-esteem.
Creative activities can support older adults who have dementia or who experience memory loss.	• Completing life story work, using photographs of the people and places that are important in their lives, can exercise the memory. • Gardening activities, including indoor planting and window boxes, are also good for exercising the senses. • Meeting others to reminisce and creating memory boxes can be creative and enjoyable.

Key terms

Attention deficit hyperactivity disorder (ADHD) Symptoms include a short attention span, constant fidgeting and impulsive behaviour.

Diabetes A condition where the amount of glucose in the blood is too high because the body cannot use it properly.

Learning difficulties A type of difficulty in processing some types of information, such as dyslexia. A person's general intelligence is not affected.

OCR Cambridge National in Health and Social Care

Emotional

Table 3.8 Creative activities to support emotional abilities

Challenges related to emotional ability	How creative activities could support these challenges
Children and young people who have a visual or hearing impairment, or both, may have difficulties with (or lack confidence when) moving around in their environments. They may find it more difficult to explore and take interest in activities that are not known to them, but that does not mean that they cannot explore, be creative or use their imagination.	Creative activities that have been designed to meet the visual, hearing and tactile (related to sense of touch) needs of children and young people who have sensory impairments can provide: • a sense of achievement • opportunities to learn a new activity • opportunities to experiment with different textures and sounds • opportunities to be with other children. For example: • Painting a large-scale mural encourages children to use their hands, feet and whole bodies as the painting tools, rather than brushes. • Woodwork can encourage young people with visual and hearing impairments to work together to create objects that can be used by them and others. This fosters feelings of self-worth and purpose.
Children and young people who have behavioural conditions such as **obsessive compulsive disorder (OCD)** or ADHD can at times be difficult to engage due to their repetitive and disruptive behaviours.	• Creative activities such as painting and needlework can help children and young people who have OCD to relax and remain calm, reducing their anxiety levels and changing their focus onto more positive behaviours.
Adults who have hearing and/or visual impairments may benefit from spending time in a sensory garden where they can experience an outside space using their senses.	Some sensory gardens include: • scented plants • fruit that can be eaten • water features that can be listened to • sculptures that can be touched.

Figure 3.8 How can outdoor experiences benefit the senses?

> **Key term**
>
> **Obsessive compulsive disorder (OCD)** An anxiety disorder characterised by obsessive thoughts and compulsive activities.

Unit R034 Creative and therapeutic activities

Social

Table 3.9 Creative activities to support social abilities

Challenges related to social ability	Examples of creative activities that could support these challenges
Creative activities can provide opportunities for children and young people to meet others of their age who have similar interests, and to relax and learn new skills.	• cinema groups • drama workshops • music activities that involve playing different instruments and creating a range of different rhythms and sounds are sociable activities
Adults with mental health needs and who may experience anxiety or depression can find that participating in creative activities can help with building their confidence, interacting with others, making friendships and learning new skills.	• photography • painting, drawing and ceramics • creative writing and poetry
Adults who have sensory impairments may benefit from a range of creative activities to provide mental and physical stimulation, enjoy hobbies and meet other people.	• music workshops where they can learn how to play an instrument • drama and dance • pottery and crafts
Adults who have hearing impairments may enjoy opportunities for creative expression.	• art activities such as pottery and ceramics • acting and miming activities.
Older adults who experience dementia or memory loss can benefit from creative activities that encourage them to stay active and meet other people.	• visiting favourite places

Case study: Meeting people's needs through creative activities

Sarah has cerebral palsy and is married to Geoff, who has learning difficulties. They have a daughter, Siobhan, who is four years old and has special needs relating to her speech and communication.

Sarah and Geoff attend a social group that meets once a week in their local area. The social group offers opportunities for making new friends, meeting lots of different people and trying out a range of activities. This evening, Sarah will be attending the dance workshop and Geoff will take part in the poetry group.

Sarah and Geoff have made arrangements for Siobhan's childminder, who also has a child of her own, to look after Siobhan for one evening a week. Bowling, parachute games and musical chairs are some of the group activities they have suggested Siobhan enjoys taking part in.

1. How many different types of creative activities are available to Sarah, Geoff and Siobhan?
2. What needs do you think the dance workshop may address for Sarah? Why?
3. How can the poetry group address Geoff's learning difficulties?
4. What other types of creative activities may address Siobhan's speech and communication needs? Why?

Figure 3.9 How can group activities encourage positive interactions?

OCR Cambridge National in Health and Social Care

Individual's religious/cultural beliefs

All people are unique and have their own specific religious and cultural **beliefs**. These might be different from your own. Selecting a creative activity that not only meets a person's abilities but also recognises and values their religious/cultural beliefs is essential for:

- showing good practice
- providing high-quality, safe and effective support
- respecting a person's rights
- supporting a person's rights
- empowering a person and raising their self-esteem.

Religious beliefs refer to beliefs and rituals associated with a religion, and cultural beliefs refer to beliefs about particular traditions, customs or **values**. For example:

- In some religions and **cultures**, a young person may only be able to participate in a swimming activity if they cover their head or body fully.
- Some people may pray at specific times every day, so it is important that the times when activities are held take people's customs into account.

People's religious/cultural beliefs may also relate to the food they eat, the art they like and the music they listen to. For example:

- When planning a cooking activity, it is important to respect a person's beliefs about handling and/or eating meat, **kosher**, **halal**, vegetarian and vegan foods.
- Make sure that people's beliefs and backgrounds are reflected in paintings, drawings, songs and music. In some religions and cultures, pictures of plants and trees are seen as important; in others, sculptures are considered important.
- The lyrics of songs and musical instruments can also reflect different beliefs and will vary between different cultures.

Gender

Creative activities should also provide opportunities for people to express their **gender identity** and be free from **gender stereotypes**. Selecting a creative activity that recognises and takes into account a person's gender is essential for:

- showing good practice
- treating a person with dignity
- treating a person with respect
- supporting the promotion of **equality** and **diversity**
- supporting **anti-discriminatory practices**.

Key terms

Beliefs Ideas that are accepted as true and real by the person that holds them. They could be religious or cultural.

Values Those things in our lives that we value as very important. They can include, for example, our family, our friends, our health, our freedom and our rights.

Culture Refers to particular ideas, traditions and customs practiced and shared by a group of people, usually from a particular country, community or society.

Kosher Foods that are permitted to be eaten under Jewish dietary laws, and that can be used as ingredients when preparing food.

Halal Foods that are permitted to be eaten under Islamic dietary laws. An animal can only be eaten if it has been slaughtered in a particular way.

Gender The socially constructed characteristics of men and women such as roles, expressions and behaviour.

Gender identity A person's sense of their gender and how they feel; this may not be the same as the sex that they were assigned at birth i.e. male, female or **non-binary**.

Unit R034 Creative and therapeutic activities

When a person shows a particular interest or ability in a creative activity, this should be encouraged, without thinking about their gender. If they are not encouraged, this can limit their opportunities to learn and develop, and make them feel they cannot be themselves.

- If you are planning a book club, ensure that the characters in the books or stories challenge gender stereotypes – such as female drivers, male nurses, women playing football, men sewing.
- Plan for indoor and outdoor creative activities to appeal to all children. You can do this by not colour coding any of the equipment used, i.e. with pinks, reds, blues.
- Divide individuals into groups/teams alphabetically rather than by their gender, so that they feel free to do any activity they want to.
- Make sure that creative activities are inclusive of gender, so that you respect people's rights and support their gender identities. For example, when you plan a creative activity, think about how you communicate and the language you use. Some people may prefer gender-neutral pronouns such as 'they', 'them' and 'their' instead of 'she', 'he', 'hers' and 'his'.
- You can offer different types of physical, intellectual, emotional, social, sensory and imaginative creative activities to a person of any gender. Activities should be selected for the individual's abilities, interests, beliefs and benefits that it will bring to them, rather than their gender.

Figure 3.10 How do you support individuals' interests?

Key terms

Non-binary A person who does not identify as only male or only female; they may identify as both male and female or as neither. The + in the acronym **LGBTQ+** is used to emphasise the diversity of sexualities and gender identities.

LGBTQ+ This stands for Lesbian, Gay, Bisexual, Transgender, Queer, Questioning, Intersex, Allies, Asexual and Pansexual.

Gender stereotypes An oversimplified idea of how people are expected to behave, based on their gender. An example is expecting all boys to only enjoy playing with toy cars, while all girls will only enjoy playing with dolls.

Equality This means treating people fairly and valuing them for who they are. Everyone should be provided with the same rights and opportunities, and this should not be affected by their age, ability, gender, culture or religion.

Diversity The differences individuals and groups have from each other such as appearance, gender, disabilities, cultural or religious background.

OCR Cambridge National in Health and Social Care

Figure 3.11 How do you express yourself?

> **Key term**
>
> **Anti-discriminatory practices** Practices that prevent discrimination from occurring, by treating people equally, fairly and lawfully, and are not affected by their age, gender or culture.

Benefit of the activity to the individual

It is important to understand the factors that affect the selection of a creative activity. You need to consider how it benefits the individual, as well as how it meets the individual's abilities, beliefs and gender.

As you have learned in Topic area 2, section 2.1 in this unit, the benefits of creative activities may include:

- physical benefits – improved strength and fitness
- intellectual benefits – mental stimulation and learning new skills
- emotional benefits – improved self-esteem and confidence
- social/moral benefits – developing new relationships and modelling appropriate behaviour.

You may find it useful to review your learning of the benefits of different types of creative activities. The case study that follows will help you to explore the benefits of creative activities to the individual.

Unit R034 Creative and therapeutic activities

Case study: The benefits of Right Now

Stefan is part of a youth production company called Right Now – a theatre-based project aimed at 16–25 year olds who have, or are experiencing, mental health issues. The project encourages young people to be involved in all aspects of the development and performance of drama productions and plays, as a way of enabling them to express how they feel about the aspects of their lives that are affected by their mental health needs.

Stefan decided to join Right Now because his mental health had made him feel isolated from other young people of his age. Participating in the group has enabled Stefan to:

- feel more confident in his own abilities
- make new friends who he feels relaxed and comfortable with
- learn new skills
- reduce his boredom
- develop his imagination and creativity.

Stefan has also noted that his periods of mental illness have reduced significantly.

1. How has participating in Right Now impacted positively on Stefan?
2. How may participating in creative activities improve young people's mental health needs?
3. Are there any other potential benefits to young people with mental health needs of participating in projects such as Right Now?
4. Participating in Right Now has enabled Stefan to learn new skills. What skills do you think he may have learned? Why?

Activity

Selecting a creative activity

1. Think about someone you know well, such as a relative or a friend.
   - Select a creative activity you think they would like to try.
   - Explain how it meets their individual abilities, including their religious/cultural beliefs and gender.
   - How could their individual abilities and gender affect the creative activity they try?
2. Reflect on your own abilities and gender. Do these affect the creative activities you participate in?

3.2 How to plan a creative activity to meet individual abilities

In order for creative activities to be of maximum benefit, it is very important to:

- plan and deliver them in a structured way
- review them for their effectiveness on a regular basis
- remember that people's experiences of creative activities will vary, depending on how the activities are delivered and whether they had positive or negative impacts.

Aims of the creative activity

Good planning for a creative activity begins with deciding on the aim, or purpose, of the activity, in terms of what you hope to achieve. For example:

- Would you like the activity to improve a child's fine motor skills?
- Do you want to provide developmental opportunities for adults with a learning disability to be able to read more confidently and independently?

Test your knowledge

1. Write down two examples of how individual abilities may affect the selection of a creative activity.
2. Write down two examples of opportunities for people to express their gender identity during a creative activity.
3. Why is it important when selecting a creative activity to consider how it benefits a person?

OCR Cambridge National in Health and Social Care

The purpose specific to an individual or group

Once you have set out the overall aim of the activity, you can then begin to think about how to achieve the aim by breaking it down into a series of objectives or targets that are realistic and achievable. For example:

- showing a child how to hold a crayon correctly
- being able to support a young person with a learning disability to put on a sock correctly
- supporting a group of older adults to learn and perform a song.

You may have heard of the acronym SMART (Specific, Measurable, Achievable, Relevant and Time bound). This is often used as a way of ensuring that all objectives can be achieved and measured:

- **S**pecific – clear details about what you plan to do
- **M**easurable – clear outcomes that can be measured
- **A**chievable – realistic in terms of what can be achieved and agreed
- **R**elevant – relevant to the individual's needs and overall aim
- **T**ime bound – achievable within the agreed timeframe.

Not having SMART objectives may mean that the activity is not achieved and people's needs remain unmet. This could lead to a negative experience.

Timescales

It is useful to agree on an overall timescale for the activity to be delivered and a target timescale to achieve each objective. A target timescale could include:

- the preparation time required to set up the activity
- the time it will take to clear away
- the completion time for the activity
- the time of day, i.e. morning or afternoon.

Doing this will mean you can monitor closely whether each objective is going to be achieved. If it is not, then you can take early action to make necessary changes. For example, each objective could be broken down into individual timescales of 10 to 15 minutes, with an agreed timescale for the whole activity of 45 minutes.

Remember the following points:

1. Allow sufficient preparation time for the activity – if you don't do so, you might start the activity late. This looks unprofessional and could also result in people feeling bored or getting distracted from the purpose of the activity.
2. Allow enough time – if you don't do so, the activity might be rushed, and people might feel that they have not had sufficient time to participate in a meaningful way.

3 Have enough time to clear away after the activity – if you don't do so, it may lead to resources such as scissors, knives and paints being left out and causing a potential danger to others who find them.
4 Take into account the time of day when the activity takes place – if you don't do so, some people might be unable to attend and/or the required staff to support the activity might not be available.

Resources needed

You must think about the materials and equipment you will need for the activity. This will depend on the chosen activity and also the needs of the people involved.

Figure 3.12 What resources would you need for a baking activity?

For example, if you are supporting a group of four children to bake a cake:

1 You will require a copy of the recipe for each of the children.
2 The recipe might need to be made available as a specialist resource, such as in large print, a talking recipe, a coloured overlay for a child who has a visual impairment, or include photographs for a child who has learning difficulties.
3 Utensils may have to be adapted, such as with large handle grips, and be made available for both left/right handed use.

4 You will also need:
- ingredients for the cake
- equipment for making the cake, including non-slip mats
- protective equipment such as aprons
- access to tables and chairs
- access to a kitchen and an oven
- washing-up facilities
- a cloth to wipe the tables clean
- a broom to sweep the floor afterwards
- plates to put the cake on.

5 The materials need to be ready to use, and there should be enough of each one. Not having the correct materials, or not having enough materials, can prevent the activity from taking place or mean it takes too long to achieve within the agreed timescales. It may also reduce the time available to deliver the activity.

Costs

You also need to be aware of the costs for running an activity. Not doing this may mean that you do not have the materials or people you need for the activity to be effective and run smoothly. For example:

- How much do the materials cost?
- How many people will you need to run the activity?
- Will you need to pay for a venue? If so, how much?

You will also need to know what the total budget available for the activity is, and ensure that you remain within this. You might be able to use some materials (such as paper, crayons, printing, ink, cooking ingredients) for more than one activity. If so, you will need to share out the cost.

Table 3.10 shows a costing that has been done by a domiciliary agency worker. She is planning an activity with an older man who has mobility difficulties. They are going out for lunch to build his confidence while walking supported.

Table 3.10 Costing for an activity with an older man who has mobility difficulties

Type of cost	Actual cost
Carer (2 hours)	£19.80 × 2 = £39.60
Car travel (mileage)	0.45p/mile × 5 miles = £2.25
Lunch	£10.80 **Total cost: £52.65**

Unit R034 Creative and therapeutic activities

Space and accessibility

Having sufficient space to deliver the activity and a setting that can be easily accessed by the individual or group will further ensure that it is suitable for their needs. For example, a person who uses a wheelchair will need space to be able to move around the setting freely.

Having sufficient staff and helpers is essential to:

- provide people with the support they require to participate in the activity
- ensure the activity takes place in a safe environment.

Safety

It is important to follow safe working practices in accordance with legal requirements, in order to safeguard your own and other people's safety and well-being.

Following safe and legal working practices

The Health and Safety at Work Act 1974 (HASAWA) is the main piece of health and safety legislation that applies and forms the basis of all health and safety legislation.

The aims of the Act are to protect:

- the health and safety of employees
- others who may be affected by work activities.

Being aware of the legal requirements is very important so that you can:

- protect people, yourself and others' well-being
- provide a safe environment free from harm, danger and abuse.

Research
Health and safety legal requirements for creative activities

Research the health and safety legal requirements for protecting people from danger, harm and abuse when carrying out creative activities. You will find the **Health and Safety Executive (HSE)**'s website a useful source of information:

www.hse.gov.uk

You could also find out more information from staff who work in health and social care settings.

Key term

Health and Safety Executive (HSE) The official supervisory body for the health, safety and welfare of people in work settings in the UK.

OCR Cambridge National in Health and Social Care

Minimising risks

Although it is very important for activities to be enjoyable and successful, they must also be safe and protect people, groups and others involved in the activity from actual and potential harm, danger or abuse.

It is good planning to consider what might go wrong during the activity, or what may cause a potential danger or harm. Taking this into account before the activity minimises the risks of any danger, harm or abuse occurring.

It is important that all people participating in the activity:

- have access to clear information about what dangers, harm and/or abuse may exist
- know how to recognise the signs of these
- know what organisational procedures must be followed if and when these do arise, including who to approach for help and advice.

A risk assessment is a method used to minimise risks and protect people from harm. It should help you to think about:

- what could go wrong with an activity
- how to identify suitable ways of controlling risks by eliminating, reducing or minimising the risks of harm occurring to people and others present when the activity is taking place.

The HSE recommends an approach where you carry out the risk assessment process in five steps, as follows.

1. Identify the hazards associated with work activities.
2. Identify who could be harmed by the hazards.
3. Identify the control measures, how you manage the risks and whether the risks can be further reduced.
4. Record the findings of your risk assessment and inform those at risk about the controls that you have put in place.
5. Review the risk assessment on a regular basis.

It is important that you carry out a risk assessment every time you carry out an activity, even if it is the same activity. Figure 3.13 shows a risk assessment for an arts and crafts activity carried out in a care setting with young people.

Protective equipment

When planning a creative activity, you might need protective equipment. This refers to the equipment that is worn by the individual, volunteer or staff member to protect against the spread of infections, such as disposable gloves in case of allergies and plastic aprons when handling food. These can provide a barrier for infections that could be spread through your hands and clothing.

Unit R034 Creative and therapeutic activities

Activity	Hazards identified	Controls to eliminate or reduce the risk	Likelihood of an accident happening	Risk rating
Painting	Spillage of paint on floor	• Young people work in small groups, with one volunteer and one support worker per group. • All spillages are cleared immediately.	Likely	Medium
Sticking – using glue	Contact with skin, mouth and eyes	• One glue stick to be made available per group. • Glue stick use to be supervised for every young person. • Precautions to be explained to young people.	Not likely	Low
Cutting – using scissor	Cuts	• Approved craft scissors to be made available per young person. • Scissor use to be supervised for every young person. • Precautions to be explained to young people.	Not likely	Low
Risk assessment signed by:	M Hayes (Support Worker)			
Risk assessment agreed with:	D Mills (Manager)			
Date of risk assessment:	17/01/22			
Review date of risk assessment:	17/04/22			

Figure 3.13 Example risk assessment for an arts and crafts activity

Protective equipment can also be used to protect from harm, such as:

- oven gloves if cooking hot food
- appropriate clothing such as enclosed shoes and a waterproof jacket if completing an outdoor walking activity.

Safety of equipment

It is very important that any equipment you use for the activity is:

- maintained correctly, so it is safe for you and others to use
- used safely by trained people and in line with the manufacturer's instructions
- appropriate for the job.

Not doing so may result in accidents and/or injuries.

OCR Cambridge National in Health and Social Care

Contingency plans for emergencies

Making plans for what to do in the event of an emergency during an activity is very important, so that you can respond effectively. **Contingency planning** for emergencies involves asking yourself the following three questions:

1 What might happen? (e.g. a fire, an accident)
2 What do I need to do if it happens? (e.g. follow the fire/accident procedure)
3 What can I do to prepare for the emergency? (e.g. attend training, read through policies and procedures, simulate a fire emergency or accident scenario, inform people and others at the beginning of the activity)

> **Key term**
> **Contingency planning** A process that takes account of possible future events, i.e. emergencies.

Communication

Communication is very important and underpins the success of all activities: without good communication, even the best of activities will not be a success.

Good communication will inspire others to achieve and do their very best. You must take into account verbal and non-verbal communication methods, as well as written and electronic communication.

Appropriateness to individuals

Ask yourself the following questions when planning a creative activity.

1 How appropriate is it for the individual/group?
   - Will the individual/group be able to understand it?
   - Does it meet everyone's needs?
   - Will the individual/group receive the message you are communicating in the way it is intended?
2 How clear is the information provided?
   - Will the individual/group understand the purpose of the activity?
   - Will the individual/group understand what they are required to do?
3 Is communication encouraging and motivational? This includes what is spoken, what is conveyed without words, what is expressed, how questions are answered. You can make sure your communication is encouraging and motivational by:
   - communicating about what is important to others
   - communicating positively by using words, expressions and non-verbal communications that are positive and empowering.

Methodology to be used

You can organise creative activities in a variety of ways.

Demonstration

Leading by example in a demonstration can:

- be motivating – you can demonstrate how to do the different aspects of the activity. Is the activity going to involve people working on their own, in pairs or in small groups? (If in pairs or groups, how long for and why?)
- help with learning – people can visualise what's required. This can be a particularly useful method to use if it's a new activity that they haven't tried before such as dancing, craft work or cookery.

Group work

Group work lends itself well to role-playing. It provides opportunities for people to:

- work together with others as a team
- interact and appreciate one another's points of view
- practise skills.

For example, group work might be a good option when carrying out creative activities such as drama, mime, sewing, reminiscence and walking.

Individual contribution

During a painting activity, asking people to work on their own and then to share this with the person sitting next to them can encourage them to be creative and original. It might also help them to take into account another individual's perspective.

Independent working can be useful when planning creative activities such as poetry, writing and photography.

Feedback methods

Obtaining feedback about a creative activity can help you to:

- measure whether and how its aims have been met
- increase your awareness and learning of the positive and negative aspects that have been experienced
- develop even better and more enjoyable activities in the future.

Methods for obtaining feedback must be planned and may include asking questions, using questionnaires and gathering witness testimonies.

Asking questions

Questions can be asked during and at the end of the creative activity. You can ask questions specific to the activity and the individual/group you are working with, and at different stages of the activity – at the beginning, in the middle and at the end.

For example, during a creative activity such as gardening:

- You may ask a person whether they are enjoying the activity, to give you an indication of how well the activity is working.
- If it isn't working, then this gives you an opportunity to ask the individual further questions such as: Why aren't you enjoying it? What changes could be made?
- The individual may tell you that they don't enjoy or find it difficult to bend down to re-pot plants.
- You could suggest they place the plants on a table instead, to avoid bending, or move to one of the raised bed areas where minimum bending is required.

By using the individual's feedback to make these changes, you are providing a positive experience for the individual, who will be able to fully participate.

Feedback can also be obtained from the individual/group at the end of the creative activity, either on a one-to-one basis or in small groups. You can find out about their overall experience, such as:

- how the activity benefited them
- what difficulties they encountered
- what aspects of the activity they liked or didn't like
- what learning and/or knowledge they gained
- whether they'd like to participate in the activity again.

Remember also while asking questions to observe what the individual/group's body language is telling you – do they look happy, and like they've enjoyed themselves?

Figure 3.14 What feedback methods do you prefer, and why?

Unit R034 Creative and therapeutic activities

Questionnaires

A questionnaire is another method of obtaining feedback from the individual/group and can inform your planning of creative activities. Questionnaires are prepared in advance and can be given out to complete anonymously.

Questionnaires can be developed to capture feedback about specific areas, such as:

- preparation of the activity – were the aims of the activity set out at the beginning met? Did the activity start on time?
- delivery of the activity – were the resources you needed for the activity made available to you? Did you have enough support to participate in the activity?
- closure of the activity – did the activity finish on time? Were you asked at the end of the activity your ideas for how the activity could be improved?

Witness testimony

Witness testimonies can be another useful method of obtaining feedback. This involves being observed carrying out a creative activity by someone who understands your work role, such as a supervisor or manager.

The person observing, or witness, can be a useful source of information for capturing feedback that perhaps cannot be obtained from others, such as your skills in:

- preparing and clearing the activity away
- communicating with participants and colleagues
- supporting participants during the activity
- dealing with any difficulties that may have arisen during the activity
- encouraging participants' feedback during and at the end.

Witness testimony can be a useful, subjective first-hand account of your skills, knowledge and qualities.

> **Test your knowledge**
> 1. Why is it important to plan the aim(s) for a creative activity?
> 2. What are the benefits of using group work and individual contribution when planning a creative activity?
> 3. What are two health and safety issues that may arise during the delivery of a cookery activity?

Synoptic link

Unit R034	Link with Unit R032: Principles of care in health and social care settings
Topic area 3: Plan a creative activity for people or groups in a healthcare or social care setting	**Topic area 3:** Effective communication in health and social care settings

Topic area 4 Deliver a creative activity and evaluate your own performance

Getting started

Think about a creative activity you have participated in and enjoyed.

- Who was delivering the creative activity?
- What did you like about the person delivering the activity? For example, did they have good communication skills? Were they interesting, kind, cheerful or funny?
- How did the person delivering the activity encourage you and/or others to participate?

4.1 Skills/personal qualities required to encourage participation

Skills

You need a range of skills and personal qualities to deliver a creative activity effectively. Table 3.11 provides you with more information and examples of some of the skills required to encourage participation when delivering creative activities.

Table 3.11 Examples of skills required to encourage participation

Skills required to deliver a creative activity	Examples of how the skill encourages participation
Effective communication requires four different types of skills that practitioners must be able to understand and use when delivering a creative activity: • verbal • non-verbal • written • specialist. You will find it useful to refer to Unit R032 Principles of care in health and social care settings, for more information about the meaning of effective communication. Not communicating effectively can: • lead to misunderstandings • make people less likely to want to participate in creative activities.	• Using a high and enthusiastic tone when you introduce a music and movement activity to a group of people can make them feel excited and keen to try it. • Using non-verbal communication, such as a smile and a nod of the head when supporting a person to participate in collage making can make them feel supported and want to interact with you. • Using clear language and an easy-to-read layout when you write a cookery recipe for a group of people can lead them to take an interest in the activity and participate. • Using specialist communication such as Makaton when explaining how to participate in a game of Pictionary to a person with a learning disability will help the individual to understand and therefore participate in the activity.

Unit R034 Creative and therapeutic activities

Skills required to deliver a creative activity	Examples of how the skill encourages participation
Supporting inclusion when delivering a creative activity requires practitioners to provide opportunities for people to participate and be involved regardless of any differences they may have. The skills required for supporting inclusion include: • treating everyone fairly • respecting their differences. Not supporting inclusion can lead to: • people's rights not being supported or respected • people being excluded from participating in creative activities.	• Delivering a sand and water activity that takes into account people's preferences such as where to deliver the activity (i.e. inside, outside, in a quiet area) can make them feel valued, respected and included. • Empowering a person by valuing their contributions to a poetry or song writing activity can encourage them to feel comfortable and confident to participate. • Making specialist resources available when delivering creative activities – such as easy grip tools, picture cards and software applications – can enable people with a range of needs to communicate more effectively and participate.
Being responsive when delivering a creative activity requires practitioners to respond clearly and directly to: • different people and groups • changes and difficulties that may arise. The skills required for being responsive include being positive and constructive. Not being responsive can lead to people and groups not enjoying activities and not wanting to participate.	• Responding positively and calmly to a person who is not enjoying playing a board game can mean they feel they can approach you and tell you how they are feeling and what they don't like about it. In this way, you can make the necessary changes for them to participate in this activity or a different one. • Responding immediately and clearly to a person who is using offensive language when participating in a sports activity will mean that they will understand that their language is unacceptable and will not be tolerated. In addition, the group will see that you are working in a positive way and reinforcing good practices. • Responding to an unexpected emergency when delivering a creative activity by staying calm and getting help, while ensuring other practitioners provide reassurance, can mean that the rest of the group will continue to participate and have a positive experience. An unexpected emergency might be someone becoming unwell.
Being empathetic when delivering a creative activity is a skill that requires practitioners to understand how someone else may be feeling or thinking. Not being empathetic can lead to people and groups not feeling supported and understood, and less likely to participate.	• Being empathetic, by using kind and reassuring words, towards someone who is finding it difficult to feel confident when participating in role play will mean that you will encourage them to participate, as they will feel supported by you. • Being empathetic, by showing respect and sensitivity towards someone who has dementia, and who finds it difficult to remember how to knit, will make the individual feel that you have shown a genuine interest in them, and they will be more likely to continue with the activity. • Being empathetic towards a group of people who have different needs and preferences by ensuring the creative activity takes these into account, might mean that people will be less likely to get distracted or lose interest in the activity.
Being organised when delivering a creative activity is a skill that requires practitioners to manage their time effectively and prepare in advance of the activity being delivered. Not being organised can lead to: • people feeling devalued and not respected • a situation where practitioners look inexperienced and unprofessional, which can create distrust and lead to a lack of participation.	• Being organised when delivering a junk modelling activity by preparing all the resources needed in advance will mean that you can engage with people at the start of the activity and focus on supporting them to participate. • Being organised when delivering a painting activity by ensuring that you have sufficient paints, pots and brushes, which are set out before the activity begins, will mean that the group can participate in the activity and choose the materials they will need. • Being organised when delivering a creative activity by leaving sufficient time at the end to ask the group for their feedback will mean that the group will feel involved and that their views and ideas are important. They will therefore be more likely to participate again in another activity.

> **Key terms**
>
> **Tone** The way something is said, such as cheerfully, empathetically, angrily or sarcastically.
>
> **Written communication skills** Aspects of written communication, which can include the typeface and font size used for the text, use of grammar, punctuation and spelling, formal or informal styles of writing, and the language used.
>
> **Specialist communication skills** Communications with people who have a wide range of needs, i.e. Braille (used by people who are blind or visually impaired and are unable to access materials in print), BSL (used by people who are deaf or hearing impaired), voice-activated software (used by people who have difficulties with their mobility (their ability to move) or in using a keyboard to type due to a **physical disability** or a learning disability).
>
> **Physical disability** A condition that affects and limits the way a person moves and their ability to perform physical activities.
>
> **Makaton** A form of communication that uses signs and symbols to help adults and children who have difficulties with speech to communicate.
>
> **Learning disability** A reduced ability to think and make decisions, as well as difficulties with everyday activities.

Personal qualities

You have learned about the different skills that are required for delivering creative activities. Now you are going to explore in more detail the different personal qualities that are needed for participation and that are essential for practitioners to have.

Cheerfulness

A cheerful and friendly manner will mean that you will seem approachable, and can show the individual or group that you have a genuine interest in them and in the activity you are delivering.

For example:

- A practitioner who has a cheerful manner when storytelling or delivering a reminiscence group will enable the people in the group to feel comfortable and want to participate.

Being friendly is also more likely to reassure and encourage people to participate in new activities that they haven't tried before.

Having a sense of humour can also be a good way of creating a happy and relaxed environment where activities can be enjoyed.

Patience

Being patient when delivering creative activities to people and groups is essential for ensuring that they can participate at their own pace. For example:

- A practitioner who is patient when supporting a person with a physical disability to take part in armchair exercise will enable them to participate at their own pace, as independently as possible and without feeling rushed.

> **Activity**
>
> **Skills for delivery**
>
> The skills required for delivering a creative activity are learned, practised and developed.
>
> - How many of the skills in Table 3.11 do you think you have?
> - Can you think of other skills which might be also be important?

Unit R034 Creative and therapeutic activities

Being patient will also mean that people will learn to trust you and work with you. They are more likely to feel more confident to further develop their existing skills and interests, and to learn and explore new ones.

Being patient involves taking the time to actively listen to what the individual is expressing so that you can get to know them. For example:

- A practitioner delivering a social activity such as singing or dancing can get to know and understand a person by observing their body language and facial expressions while they participate in the activity and during feedback.

Caring

A caring approach when delivering creative activities will have a positive impact because it will provide comfort and support to the individual or group. For example:

- A practitioner with a caring approach towards a person who may be feeling anxious or not very confident in participating in an activity they haven't tried before can reassure them, and encourage them to continue with the activity.

Being caring also involves being able to show empathy, i.e. genuine compassion and understanding. For example:

- A practitioner who is committed to ensuring that a group activity such as bingo or a quiz meets people's different and unique abilities, including their religious/cultural beliefs and gender, will be more likely to encourage people's participation because they will feel included and involved.

Respect

Showing respect when delivering creative activities involves communicating respectfully. A practitioner delivering an imaginative activity such as drama can do this by:

- introducing themselves to the group
- knowing each individual's preferred name in the group
- getting to know each individual and their likes and dislikes
- treating everyone fairly and equally.

A respectful approach will mean that people will feel that you are treating them like a unique person.

Respect can also be shown by asking the people and/or group for their feedback, their views, ideas and any concerns they may have about a creative activity they've participated in. In this way they will feel listened to, valued and, more importantly, respected as people. They will therefore be more likely to continue to participate in activities.

OCR Cambridge National in Health and Social Care

Willingness

A genuine desire and commitment to care for and support people to participate in creative activities is another important personal quality that involves putting the wishes and preferences of people at the centre. For example:

- A practitioner can support a person with a physical disability to mobilise in the garden so that they can take part in all aspects of a group gardening activity. They do this by asking, listening and respecting the support the individual would like. This empowers the individual to be in control of how they participate, and will encourage their participation.

Being willing also involves practitioners responding to changes in people's likes, dislikes and preferences so that people's needs are met. For example:

- A practitioner who takes into account changes to a person's fitness levels or cognitive abilities will be more likely to encourage active participation.

Without all these essential skills and personal qualities, it would not be possible for practitioners to encourage participation in creative activities or provide support to people and groups with diverse needs.

Figure 3.15 Which personal qualities do you have?

Unit R034 Creative and therapeutic activities

Research

Identify a healthcare or social care setting job role that interests you.

- Research the skills and personal qualities that are required for this job role.
- Reflect on how these compare to the skills and personal qualities that are required to encourage participation with a group or individual when delivering a creative activity.

You will find it useful to refer to the following websites:

www.healthcareers.nhs.uk

the NHS's website for job roles in healthcare

www.skillsforcare.org.uk

the Skills for Care's website for job roles in social care

4.2 Deliver a creative activity with a group or individual

Delivering a creative activity requires a good knowledge of who the activity is aimed at. You will also need a range of skills and personal qualities to make it effective, safe and enjoyable for everyone. For a creative activity to be successful, you must know how to:

- introduce the activity
- supervise the activity
- collect feedback from participants.

Introduce the activity

A good introduction to an activity will help to 'set the scene' for the group.

Aim(s)

- Your introduction should provide an overview of the activity and what you hope to achieve. This needs to include the purpose of the activity – i.e. its aim(s) and an overview of the tasks so that it is clear what the activity is about and who it is for.
- An introduction to the activity should also include an introduction of who you are, including your name and why you have chosen the creative activity you will be delivering. This will help to encourage the group or individual to engage with you. It is also a good idea to spend some time asking the group or individual to introduce themselves.
- For example, if you are delivering a group activity, you could ask the group or individual to say/express their name and share an interesting fact about themselves. This will not only help to make everyone feel more comfortable with each other but also provide a good basis for working with the group or individual.

OCR Cambridge National in Health and Social Care

Content
- Your introduction should include details of the main content of the creative activity. This could include a demonstration of how to carry out the activity and how to use any equipment that will be needed. This gives the group or individual further information about what the activity will involve.
- Introducing the content of the activity must also include details of how any support needed will be provided and made available, so that the group or individual can understand how their needs will be met.
- Finally, when introducing the activity it is important that all health and safety requirements are explained to the group or individual and are met. This could involve explaining what to do in the event of the fire alarm sounding, and the precautions to take when using electrical equipment and items such as scissors and knives.

Settle the individuals so that they are prepared to carry out the activities
- Your introduction should settle everyone so that they are prepared to carry out the activities. This could include ensuring that they are comfortable, i.e. in terms of where they are sitting, and whether they've used the toilet facilities, so that they are ready to carry out the activity.
- Settling people must also include checking that they have understood what the activity will involve and that they agree to participate in it. This is also an opportunity for you to clarify anything that hasn't been understood and answer any other questions people may have.
- Finally, when introducing the activity, it is important that people have the support and equipment they require. Not doing so may mean that they decide not to participate. This could involve checking with people whether they require any additional support or any other items or equipment.

Supervise the activity

After introducing a creative activity to a group or individual, it is essential that the activity is supervised so that it is safe and benefits everyone. To supervise the activity effectively, it is important to carry out the steps outlined here.

Encourage participation
You can encourage participation, for example, by:
- providing one-to-one support for a person who is finding it difficult to crochet by showing them how to do it
- using encouraging words with a group that is feeling tired during a long walk

Unit R034 Creative and therapeutic activities

- being patient with a person who is finding it difficult to read
- using encouraging body language with a group of people participating in a reminiscence group
- actively listening to a group of people in a storytelling activity
- demonstrating how to use mime to a person who has never done it before
- participating yourself in a dancing activity and encouraging other people to do the same
- encouraging people to take part in a quiz by acknowledging their contributions
- using hand-over-hand techniques for encouraging people to participate in sand and water play
- providing examples of different painting techniques to encourage a group of people to paint for the first time
- sharing fun modelling ideas to encourage people to participate in junk modelling.

You will also find it useful to review your learning from Topic area 4, section 4.1 in relation to the skills and personal qualities required to encourage participation in creative activities.

Intervene when necessary

You can intervene during a creative activity, for example, by:

- offering to support a person when they are unsure about how to carry out a task by themselves
- suggesting the individual has some time away from the activity when they are getting frustrated
- being assertive and not tolerating any physical or verbal harm directed towards you or anyone else
- acting immediately when an activity may result in a person placing themselves, you or others in danger.

Provide support

You can provide support during a creative activity, for example, by:

- providing emotional support and reassurance to a person who is anxious about trying a new social activity
- physically helping a person who is finding it difficult to use a piece of equipment such as a chisel during a woodcraft activity
- responding to a person's questions about what task to complete next
- encouraging the group or individual to continue with the activity by providing them with positive feedback about their progress so they are motivated to continue.

OCR Cambridge National in Health and Social Care

Maintain safety

You can maintain safety during a creative activity, for example, by:

- minimising any risks that could have the potential to cause harm, such as ensuring the cooker's safety lid is put down after use during a cookery activity to prevent any injuries being caused, or clearing away all equipment at the end of an activity
- wearing gloves when using glue during a craft activity to prevent any allergies or injuries
- checking all equipment before use, to ensure it is safe to use and therefore unlikely to pose a danger
- ensuring there is sufficient space when delivering an activity to avoid people injuring themselves by being close to each other or to furniture and fixtures
- acting immediately if there is a spillage on the floor, to avoid anyone slipping over and injuring themselves
- seeking additional support if you are unable to deal with an unexpected incident on your own.

You will also find it useful to review your learning from Topic area 3, section 3.2 in relation to the safety aspects to consider when planning a creative activity.

Keep to timescales

You can keep to timescales during a creative activity, for example, by:

- allocating a specific time to each of the tasks the activity involves, including preparation time and clearing away time
- reviewing and, if necessary, adapting the allocated times for each task so that the whole activity remains within the agreed timescale
- adapting the activity as you deliver it so that you can ensure you keep to the required timescales.

You will also find it useful to review your learning from Topic area 3, section 3.2 in relation to managing timescales when planning a creative activity.

Replenish resources/materials

You can replenish resources/materials during a creative activity, for example, by:

- carrying out visual checks during the activity to check if any resources/materials are running low
- ensuring you can easily access additional resources and materials during the activity if you need to – perhaps these could be stored in a lockable drawer or cupboard
- planning in advance for any resources/materials that you may need to order, so that they arrive in sufficient time.

Unit R034 Creative and therapeutic activities

You will also find it useful to review your learning from Topic area 3, section 3.2 in relation to the resources needed when planning a creative activity.

Collect feedback from participants

The closing stages of a creative activity involve allowing for time either during or at the end of the activity to collect feedback from participants.

Table 3.12 gives examples of how to collect feedback.

Table 3.12 Methods of collecting feedback

Method of collecting feedback	How to do this
Asking questions	Ask the participants questions during the activity when completing a task or at the end, such as: • What did you like, and why? • What didn't you like, and why? • What could have been done differently? • Is there any other support you require? Think about how to record their responses so that you can collate them and assess: • how the activity was received by participants • areas that require improvement.
Questionnaire	Ask the participants to complete questionnaires at the end of the activity. You will need to decide whether you want participants to put their names on their questionnaires or complete them anonymously. When the participants have completed the questionnaires, you will need to: • collect them together • review participants' responses to assess what worked well and what needs to be improved.
Witness testimony	Collect witness testimony from observations that others have made during the creative activity. These observations may be: • written down for you to read through • shared with you verbally, or • recorded for you to listen to. You will need to think about what information is important and relevant in terms of feedback for the creative activity.

You will also find it useful to review your learning from Topic area 3, section 3.2 in relation to feedback methods when planning a creative activity.

OCR Cambridge National in Health and Social Care

Case study: Dee's best practice guide

Dee is an activities co-ordinator in a residential home and has many years of experience in carrying out creative activities with older people. She has provided a document with the best practice principles of how to carry out creative activities to help guide her team. Read through the best practice guide below and consider how you can use it to guide you with your practice when carrying out a creative activity.

1 Summarise the best practice principles to follow when introducing a creative activity.
2 Give two examples of how you can settle people so that they are prepared to carry out the creative activity.
3 What are the potential consequences of not following health and safety requirements during a creative activity?
4 Give two examples of how you can encourage participation and provide support to participants during a creative activity.
5 Give two reasons why it is important to obtain feedback from participants.

Practice guide for creative activities

Introduce the activity

To try to grab participants' attention straight away, have an introduction activity that shows the group the equipment they are going to use.

- Ask them to guess what activity they think it might be, and why.
- Then encourage them to look at the equipment and pick it up.
- For example, place pens, paper, scissors and glue on each table and then ask each group to guess what they are going to do.

Then give an outline of the creative activity, its aim(s) and what it will involve.

- Check that individuals understand what you're telling them.
- Show them what the end product may look like – for example, a collage.

Next, explain that you are going to demonstrate each of the tasks first so they can model your actions.

- Use pictures, photographs and diagrams to convey your message about what each task involves and/or the equipment to use, such as craft or cookery utensils.

It is important that individuals feel settled and comfortable so that they are prepared to carry out the activities.

- You could sort individuals into smaller groups and check with each of them that they have everything they need.
- Checklists are a useful tool to make sure that participants are clear about what they are doing.

In order to help individuals focus on the activity, make sure the environment is suitable.

- There should be sufficient space and lighting.
- The room should not be too hot or too cold.
- The environment should not be too noisy.

Start the activity by showing the group a picture or singing a song.

Supervise the activity

Close supervision of the activity is important to ensure that it is going to plan, and health and safety requirements are being met.

- Always make sure that health and safety requirements are being met – keep all areas hazard-free, and avoid the risks of danger, harm and abuse.

It is important to observe participants' behaviour and amend activities if required.

- If a participant is not enjoying an activity, support them to choose another activity while the remaining participants in the group continue with their activity.
- If participants wish to extend the creative activity, encourage them by suggesting ideas, demonstrating appropriately and communicating effectively.

Be aware of the amount of resources or materials you are using.

- Allow sufficient time to replenish materials during the activity.
- Aim to replenish resources before they run out so that participants can continue with the activity.

The end of the activity is just as important as the beginning. You want each participant to complete the activity having enjoyed it and achieved what they set out to do. Not doing so can be frustrating for participants, so it is vital to keep to timescales.

- Leave enough time to clear away.
- You can incorporate clearing away into the end of the activity.
- Encourage participants to have an active role in this.

Collect feedback from participants

At the end of the activity it is important to discuss with the participants how they found the session.

- Ask them what worked and what did not.
- Observe what their body language is telling you – do they look happy, and have they had fun?

Think about how you are going to collect the feedback.

- You need to use the feedback to assess your performance and how well the activity worked.

4.3 Evaluation

The quality and value of a creative activity will depend on your planning, delivery and evaluation of it. Evaluating a creative activity can help you to measure:

- whether and how its aim(s) have been met
- what aspects have worked well, and why
- what aspects have not worked well, and why
- what improvements could be made, and why.

How to evaluate your own performance

Evaluating your own performance when delivering a creative activity will increase your awareness and learning of the positive and negative aspects that have been experienced. It will also help you to develop even better and more enjoyable activities in the future.

Use feedback

You can evaluate your performance when delivering a creative activity by exploring the feedback and ideas shared by the individual/group and others such as support staff, witnesses, your supervisor or manager.

Feedback from individuals/groups

This kind of feedback may be in the form of comments when you're delivering the activity, such as:

- thanking you for the support provided
- giving ideas for other types of support they require.

This can be very useful feedback because it will show you how the activity you've delivered has directly impacted on them – for example, has it made them feel more confident, or helped them to make new friends?

The individual/group can also provide you with their views about the support they received to participate in the activity; for example:

- having a large print handout enabled a person to become more independent when following a recipe during a cookery session
- having large grip handles on gardening tools enabled the group to carry out more planting outdoors.

Feedback from support staff, witnesses and your supervisor

This kind of feedback can provide you with a good insight into your strengths and weaknesses. For example, they may comment on:

- how you interact with participants
- the effectiveness of the methods you use to explain different aspects of the creative activity
- the range of your skills and personal qualities.

Their ideas and suggestions can be used to improve your work practices. They can also encourage you, and advise you how to develop your delivery of creative activities.

How to use feedback

It is important to use the feedback you've obtained, both good and bad, constructively so that you can evaluate your performance and improve your practice.

For example, you can use the feedback received by identifying whether there were any common themes or comments shared.

Some of the feedback you receive may highlight weaknesses in your performance. This might make you feel uncomfortable, but it is important not to feel upset and instead think about it, be open to it and learn from it. If you disagree with feedback, ask for more detail so that you can fully understand it.

To use feedback effectively, you need to be:

- positive and showing respect for the opinions of others
- willing to learn from it
- prepared to act on it and make improvements.

Self-reflect

Being able to self-reflect is important because it involves you thinking honestly about your practice, and not being afraid to question your practice so that you can continue to improve it. It also involves being aware of how your work practice impacts on participants.

You can self-reflect on a creative activity either:

- while you are delivering it – this is known as 'reflection *in* action', or
- after you have delivered it – this is known as 'reflection *on* action'.

Reflecting on a creative activity *while* you are delivering it requires you to be able to think on your feet and improve the activity while you are delivering it. Reflecting on a creative activity *after* you have delivered it requires you to be committed to learning from the experience and then making improvements.

You can evaluate your performance at work through self-reflection by:

- spending time thinking back over a creative activity and evaluating it – for example, whether its aim(s) were met, to what extent and how
- examining in detail how you carried out the creative activity and the reasons why – for example, in terms of the preparations you made or the support you provided to participants
- assessing the impact the creative activity had on you and the participants – for example, what you learned about yourself and the skills/knowledge areas developed by the participants

OCR Cambridge National in Health and Social Care

- examining any difficulties that were experienced during the activity as well as any positive developments that happened that you were not expecting – for example, not having sufficient resources, or participants engaging, not only with you but with each other during the creative activity
- identifying your strengths – for example, communicating effectively with participants when introducing a creative activity, or managing your time effectively when delivering a creative activity
- identifying your weaknesses – for example, setting clearer aims for a creative activity so they are understood, or being more organised when collating feedback from participants
- developing new areas of learning – for example, learning more about different types of creative activities, or new approaches to supporting participants who may experience anxiety during creative activities.

Figure 3.16 Do you make time to self-reflect?

Review strengths and weaknesses

As part of your evaluation, you need to review the strengths and weaknesses of your planning, your communication skills and how you encouraged the participation of the individual or group.

Your planning

You can evaluate your performance by reviewing your strengths and weaknesses in terms of your planning of the creative activity. You can consider the following:

- The aspects of your planning that were effective and the reasons why these aspects of your planning worked well. For example, you could self-reflect on the process you followed for planning the activity or the skills you used.
- The aspects of your planning that need improving and the reasons why these aspects of your planning were weak. For example, you could consider the feedback you received or the effect that these aspects of your planning had on the delivery of the activity.

Your communication skills

You can evaluate your performance by reviewing your strengths and weaknesses in terms of your communication skills. You can consider the following:

- The communication skills you have. For example, you could self-reflect on the different communication skills you used during the creative activity and the impact they had on communicating effectively.
- The communication skills you don't have or that need improving. For example, you could consider whether you experienced any difficulties communicating during the activity, including the reasons why.

Unit R034 Creative and therapeutic activities

Encouraging participation of the individual/group

You can evaluate your performance by reviewing your strengths and weaknesses in relation to how effective you were in encouraging participation of the individual/group. You can consider the following:

- The methods that were effective in encouraging participation. For example, you could consider what methods and skills you used and the reasons why these encouraged participation.
- The other approaches you could have taken for encouraging participation. For example, you could self-reflect on at what points during your delivery of the activity encouraging participation was difficult and the reasons why, or other methods that could have been more effective.

Suggest improvements

You can evaluate your performance by suggesting improvements for what you could have done differently and/or better, not only to benefit the overall delivery of the activity but also the participants' experience of it.

Suggesting improvements can also improve your performance, because it:

- makes you more aware of your own abilities and limitations
- helps you continue to improve your work practice.

What you would do differently and why

You may decide that when you deliver the creative activity again you want to make some changes. For example, you might decide to:

- use more pictures when introducing the content of the activity – so that it is better understood
- provide more practical support to participants – so that you can increase their participation
- collect feedback from participants at the end of the activity only – so that you have more time to spend with participants during the activity.

Once you've decided what you would do differently, and why, ensure you put these improvements into practice. Then, start the review cycle again by comparing the second time you deliver the activity with the first time, and think about what improved as a result.

You will need to identify your evidence that the activity improved and think about how you are going to capture the evidence (i.e. comments, photographs of people, products displayed).

> **Test your knowledge**
>
> 1 What are two important aspects to consider when introducing a creative activity?
> 2 What are two important aspects to consider when supervising a creative activity?
> 3 Write down two examples of how to maintain safety when delivering a creative activity to a group or individual.
> 4 Write down two examples of how to use feedback to evaluate your performance.
> 5 Write down two ways to self-reflect when evaluating your performance.
> 6 What are two benefits of reviewing your strengths and weaknesses when delivering a creative activity?

OCR Cambridge National in Health and Social Care

You will also need to consider what benefits resulted from the improvements, and whether you need to make further improvements to the activity if you deliver it again.

Synoptic links

Unit R034	Links with Unit R032: Principles of care in health and social care settings
Topic area 4: Deliver a creative activity and evaluate your own performance	**Topic area 1:** The rights of service users in health and social care settings **Topic area 2:** Person-centred values **Topic area 3:** Effective communication in health and social care settings

Assignment practice

Ivy Day Centre offers up to 45 places per day, Monday to Friday, to older people who want to meet other people and participate in a range of activities. Activities offered are set out in a weekly programme and are based on people's interests, needs and preferences. Activities include bowls, darts, gardening, puzzles, quizzes, music and singing.

The team at the day centre consists of 1 day-services manager, 3 senior care officers and 18 care officers. The team also provide support to people who wish to access local services in the community, such as the hairdresser, shops, chiropodist, dentist and doctors' surgery.

Task 1: Produce a plan for a creative activity

This task covers:

- Topic area 3.2 How to plan a creative activity to meet individual abilities.

You are a care officer at Ivy Day Centre, and your manager has asked you to produce a plan for a creative activity of your choice for the people who attend the day centre. It is hoped that your plan can be used as an example of good practice for other staff who will also be planning creative activities.

Top tips

1. Note the social care setting on which the model assignment is based and ensure your response is relevant, i.e. a day centre for older people.
2. Your plan must include understanding and evidence of:
   - the aims of the creative activity
   - timescales
   - resources needed
   - safety considerations
   - how you plan to communicate with the participants
   - methodology you plan to use
   - feedback methods you plan to use.

Unit R034 Creative and therapeutic activities

Task 2: Carry out a simulation/deliver a creative activity

This task covers

- Topic area 4, section 4.1 Skills/personal qualities required to encourage participation
- Topic area 4, section 4.2 Deliver a creative activity with a group or individual.

Your manager at Ivy Day Centre has asked you to deliver the reminiscence group activity that you planned.

Top tips

1. Note the social care setting on which this model assignment is based, and ensure your response is relevant, i.e. a day centre for older people.
2. Delivery of a creative activity would ideally take place with people or a small group within an actual health or social care setting.
3. If the creative activity is to be delivered in a simulated environment, participants in the role play must be able to demonstrate realistic characteristics of the intended group.
4. The creative activity should take between 15 and 30 minutes, and include evidence of:
   - an introduction to the activity
   - supervision in the following areas: encouraging participation, intervening when necessary, providing support, maintaining safety, keeping to timescales, replenishing resources/materials
   - your communication skills
5. All evidence gathered must observe confidentiality.
6. A witness testimony from your employer can be included.
7. A teacher observation record will also need to be completed by the teacher.

Task 3: Evaluate your performance carrying out a simulation/delivering a creative activity

This task covers:

- Topic area 4, section 4.3 Evaluation.

Your manager at Ivy Day Centre has asked you to evaluate the reminiscence group activity that you simulated/delivered.

Top tips

1. Note the social care setting on which this model assignment is based and ensure your response is relevant, i.e. a day centre for older people.
2. The evaluation of your performance must be based on feedback and self-reflection received.
3. The evaluation must include evidence of:
   - your strengths and weaknesses in the following areas – planning, communication skills, encouraging participation
   - suggestions for improvement
   - use of feedback.

Task 4: The benefits of therapies and creative activities to the needs of the individual/group

This task covers:

- Topic area 1, section 1.1 Types of therapies used in health and social care
- Topic area 2, section 2.1 Types of creative activities and their benefits
- Topic area 3, section 3.1 Factors that affect the selection of a creative activity.

Your manager at Ivy Day Centre has asked you to consider the needs of the group you chose in Task 1 and consider which therapeutic interventions might be of benefit to them. Your manager has asked you to give a presentation to the rest of the team with your findings.

OCR Cambridge National in Health and Social Care

> *Top tips*
> 1. Note the social care setting on which the model assignment is based and ensure your response is relevant, i.e. a day centre for older people.
> 2. You could use Microsoft PowerPoint to help you develop your presentation. If you do, remember to make the text on your slides clear and large enough so that it can be read by all.
> 3. Your presentation must include evidence of:
>   - a description of different types of therapies and an explanation of their benefits in relation to PIES for people/the group you chose in Task 1
>   - a description of different types of creative activities, an explanation of the factors that affect the choice of activity and an explanation of their benefits in relation to PIES for people/the group you chose in Task 1.
> 4. A witness testimony from your tutor who has observed you deliver your presentation must also be included.

Read about it

Weblinks

www.ageuk.org.uk

Age UK – information about activities for older adults.

www.alzheimers.org.uk

Alzheimer's Society – information about activities for people who have dementia.

www.aor.org.uk

The Association of Reflexologists for information about reflexology including what the therapy involves.

www.a-t-c.org.uk

The Aromatherapy Trade Council for information about using aromatherapy essential oils.

www.bapt.info

The British Association of Play Therapists for information about what play therapy is, what's involved and the benefits.

www.britreflex.co.uk

The British Reflexologist Association for resources on reflexology including books, hand and feet reflexology charts, DVDs and online courses.

www.gcmt.org.uk

The General Council for Soft Tissue Therapies (GCMT) is the governing body in the UK for soft tissue therapies including massage.

www.hse.gov.uk

Health and Safety Executive – information about risk assessment.

www.hypnotherapists.org.uk

The National Council for Hypnotherapy (NCH) is the UK's leading professional association for hypnotherapists and provides information about the practice of hypnotherapy in the UK.

www.mind.org.uk

Mind is the UK's leading mental health charity, providing services for better mental health including information about mental health disorders including body dysmorphic disorder.

www.nammt.co.uk

The National Association of Massage and Manipulative Therapy (NAMMT) for information and guidance on massage techniques.

www.reikifed.co.uk

The UK Reiki Federation for information and resources on what reiki is.

www.rcslt.org

The Royal College of Speech and Language Therapists for information, guidance and resources on speech and language therapy and techniques.

www.sense.org.uk

Sense – information about activities for children and adults who have sight and hearing loss.

www.thesma.org

The Association of Soft Tissue Therapists for resources and information on soft tissues therapies including massage.

Online information guides

www.alzheimers.org.uk/site/scripts/documents_info.php?documentID=115

Staying Involved and Active – information guide about staying involved and active for people who have dementia (Alzheimer's Society, 2016)

OCR Cambridge National in Health and Social Care

www.alzheimers.org.uk/get-support/staying-independent/activity-ideas-dementia

Taking Part: Activities for People with Dementia – information booklet about activities for people who have dementia (Alzheimer's Society, 2016)

www.bhf.org.uk/informationsupport/support/healthy-living/staying-active

Staying Active – information about why it is important to be active (British Heart Foundation, 2018)

Reference books

Agar, K. (2008) *How to Make Your Care Home Fun: Simple Activities for People of All Abilities*. Jessica Kingsley Publications.

Bowden, A. and Lewthwaite, N. (2009) *The Activity Year Book: A Week by Week Guide for Use in Elderly Day and Residential Care*. Jessica Kingsley Publications.

Hall, N. (2016) *Hand Reflexology for Practitioners*. Singing Dragon.

Hall, N. (2013) *Principles of Reflexology*. Singing Dragon.

Unit R035
Health promotion campaigns

About this unit

Although health education plans can be costly, they can help save billions of pounds for the NHS in the long term. Health campaigns empower service users by giving them information that helps them make life-changing choices which could improve their health and well-being.

In this unit you will learn about the public health challenges faced by the UK, the approaches used to encourage health and well-being, and their importance to society. You will study the factors that affect a healthy lifestyle and the way that campaigns can be designed to target different groups of people.

You will also learn how to plan and deliver your own small-scale health promotion campaign and how to evaluate your planning and delivery.

Topic areas

In this chapter you will learn about:

1. Current public health issues and the impact on society
2. Factors influencing health
3. Planning and creating a health promotion campaign
4. Delivering and evaluating a health promotion campaign.

OCR Cambridge National in Health and Social Care

How will I be assessed?

You will be assessed through a series of assignment tasks, which are set by OCR. The assignment will be marked by your tutor and then moderated by OCR.

For Topic area 1, you need to:

- explain why you have chosen your public health challenge
- understand why it is important to address public health challenges.

For Topic area 2, you need to explain:

- the factors that could influence the health and well-being of the target audience
- the barriers to leading a healthy lifestyle
- the benefits of following the health promotion campaign.

For Topic area 3, you need to:

- produce a plan for a health promotion campaign
- demonstrate your understanding of its aims and various aspects such as timescales, resources and safety.

For Topic area 4, you need to:

- introduce and deliver the campaign while demonstrating your communication skills
- evaluate your strengths and weaknesses
- use feedback to suggest improvements.

Unit R035 covers three Performance Objectives (POs):

- PO2 Apply knowledge and understanding
- PO3 Analyse and evaluate knowledge, understanding and performance
- PO4 Demonstrate and apply skills and processes relevant to the subject areas.

Unit R035 Health promotion campaigns

Topic area 1 Current public health issues and the impact on society

Getting started

Think about when you started nursery or junior school. If you cannot remember, do you have a younger brother or sister who has recently started nursery?

- What type of infections did you catch?
- Can you remember being absent from school with an upset stomach after others in school had had the same complaint?
- Why do you think you got these childhood illnesses?
- Did you 'grow out' of these regular infections? Why do you think that was?

Share your thoughts with a partner, then discuss with the rest of the group.

1.1 The importance of a healthy society

Health is important to everyone at every life stage – infancy, adolescence or later adulthood. Money cannot buy health, but lifestyle choices can affect it.

Local health promotion teams (from the clinical commissioning groups (CCGs)) base their campaigns around nationally set health events. For example, the 2022 NHS calendar of national health and well-being campaigns included events for:

- No Smoking Day in March
- National Walking Month in May
- Organ Donation Week in September
- Anti-Bullying Week in November.

There are downloadable resources on the NHS website for all these campaigns (such as posters and leaflets), which can be used by local health promotion teams.

Reasons why a healthy society is important

Some of the reasons why it is important for society to remain as healthy as possible are explored in this section.

Control of communicable diseases

Communicable diseases are infectious diseases which are caused by **pathogens** such as **bacteria**, **viruses** and **fungi**. These communicable diseases are spread from one person to another.

Key terms

Pathogen A bacterium, virus, fungus or parasite that can cause disease. Often more simply known as germs.

Bacteria Microscopic single-celled organisms which exist everywhere. Many are harmless and some are good for our bodies, but some cause bacterial infection such as salmonella which causes food poisoning. Cholera and tuberculosis (TB) are also caused by bacteria.

Virus Tiny pathogens that need to enter the cells of a living being to be able to multiply. An example is rhinovirus, which causes the common cold. Other examples of viruses include influenza and COVID-19.

Fungi Organisms that include yeast, moulds and mushrooms. Fungal infections usually affect the skin; examples are athlete's foot, ringworm or candida (thrush).

Issues around controlling communicable diseases range from patients picking up infections such as **MRSA** in hospital to controlling outbreaks of infectious diseases such as measles, smallpox, influenza and COVID-19.

A communicable disease can develop after the person becomes infected by a pathogen through:

- inhaling droplets from another person's cough or sneeze
- direct contact with the person carrying the pathogen
- contact with contaminated fluids such as blood, mucus, saliva
- consuming contaminated water or food
- receiving a bite from an insect or animal carrying the pathogen.

Throughout history, more deaths have been caused by infectious/communicable diseases than any other cause. Examples are:

- the Black Death in the fourteenth century
- the 1918 'Spanish' influenza pandemic (where the numbers who died were more than those killed in the First World War)
- COVID-19, which began in 2020.

There have been many outbreaks of other communicable diseases, although not causing as many deaths – such as diphtheria, polio, scarlet fever, smallpox, tuberculosis and typhoid.

The following measures helped to eradicate some diseases:

- The development of sanitation and clean water helped to eradicate diseases such as cholera.
- Antibiotics and vaccines were developed after the Second World War.
- The establishment of the NHS in 1948 enabled people to get free healthcare treatment.

The rapid spread of COVID-19 throughout the world in 2020 demonstrated the importance of keeping communicable diseases under control.

- It stretched the UK's NHS hospitals to the limit, as they struggled to cope with the number of patients needing treatment.
- This meant that many treatments (such as knee or hip replacements) had to be cancelled as wards were turned into COVID-19 wards.
- Some people who had symptoms of serious conditions such as cancers were afraid to go into hospital because they were worried they might catch COVID-19.

People with healthy immune systems are generally less likely to catch some communicable diseases, as their bodies will be able to fight it off.

Key term

MRSA This is often called a superbug as it is highly resistant to treatment. It usually affects people who are weakened by surgery or illness.

Research

Communicable diseases that have been eradicated in the UK

In small groups, choose one of the infectious diseases from:

- diphtheria
- polio
- scarlet fever
- smallpox
- tuberculosis
- typhoid.

Research the disease, and produce a short handout/PowerPoint presentation containing the following information:

- whether it is caused by bacteria or a virus
- how the disease is transmitted
- symptoms of the disease
- how vaccines have reduced the deaths from the disease.

Unit R035 Health promotion campaigns

Decrease the cost of care

In 2019/2020, the overall budget for the NHS in England was £134 billion. Most of this money was spent on the day-to-day running of NHS services (approximately £120 billion), with the rest (approximately £14 billion) spent on health initiatives, education, training and building new hospitals.

The NHS could save money if people improved the ways they looked after themselves. This is because the NHS provides many treatments for preventable illnesses, such as:

- illnesses caused by obesity (e.g. diabetes)
- cancers caused by smoking (e.g. lung cancer).

The NHS wants people to be better educated about their lifestyle choices, so that they can remain in good health.

Decrease sickness and dependency

The Department of Health and Social Care published a report, *Prevention is better than cure*, in 2018. It states that if the choices an individual makes reflect current health advice (see Figure 4.1), then many illnesses and diseases are preventable. If the person's illnesses/sickness are reduced, they are more likely to be independent and able to look after themselves.

One of the aims of this report is to provide community support for older people to be independent and live in their own homes for as long as possible.

By following the advice in Figure 4.1, people will maximise their health and prevent illness for as long as possible.

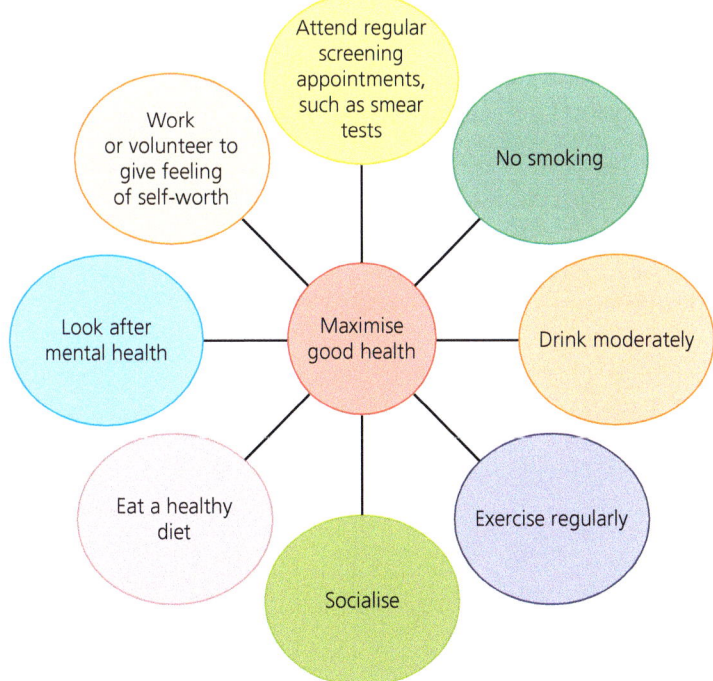

Figure 4.1 Ways an individual can maximise good health

Activity

Five steps to good mental health

Search the UK Government website for this guidance document: *Five Ways to Mental Well-being*. You can find it at this webpage:

www.gov.uk/government/publications/five-ways-to-mental-wellbeing

In pairs:

- Read through each one of the five ways.
- Exchange ideas with your partner on what you did most recently to connect, be active, take notice, keep learning and give.
- Were there any of the five that you failed to meet?
- Has it made you more aware of what you should be doing to help you achieve good mental health?
- Did you find this useful?

OCR Cambridge National in Health and Social Care

Increased life expectancy

According to the Office for National Statistics (ONS), between 1960 and 2010 the average lifespan increased by ten years for males and eight years for females. This was due to the reduction in infant and childhood **mortality** rates in the first half of the 20th century.

- In 1950, the life expectancy was 68.69 years for males.
- In 2019, life expectancy at birth was 79.4 years for males and 83.1 years for females.

However, life expectancy rates have slowed down with relatively low increases compared to the previous decade. *Prevention is better than cure* has the aim that life expectancy increases by at least five years by 2035. But to meet this increase of life expectancy, there are several public health challenges that must be met.

1.2 Public health challenges for society

Current challenges to public health

Obesity

Public Health England (PHE) considers obesity to be one of the biggest challenges. In the UK:

- 63 per cent of adults are above a healthy weight
- 32 per cent of these adults are obese
- 1 out of 3 children leaving primary school is overweight
- 1 out of 5 of those children is obese.

Obesity is a term that is used to describe a person who is very overweight with a lot of body fat. Obesity is generally caused by consuming more calories – particularly in fatty and sugary foods – than the individual burns off through physical activity. The excess energy is then stored by the body as fat.

Obesity is an increasingly common problem, because many modern lifestyles often promote eating excessive amounts of cheap, high-calorie food and spending a lot of time sitting at desks, on sofas or in cars. It is often easier to order a high-fat takeaway than cook from scratch.

Key term

Mortality Death.

Test your knowledge

1. What is a communicable disease?
2. List three ways a person can become infected with a communicable disease.
3. Name two of the Government's five ways to good mental health.

Unit R035 Health promotion campaigns

In March 2017, PHE worked with the food industry to reduce the amount of sugar in foods that children love (see Figure 4.2).

Figure 4.2 Food categories that contribute most to children's sugar intake

The Government is taking the obesity challenge seriously. In November 2020, the Department for Health and Social Care launched a public consultation on a proposal to ban online adverts for foods high in fat, sugar and salt. This consultation has now been extended to apply to television, magazine and newspapers adverts. The aim is to tackle the obesity crisis and get the nation fit and healthy.

If individuals follow a healthy eating plan such as the Eatwell Plate on page 194, then they are less likely to become obese because they will be filling up with fruits and vegetables rather than high-fat, high-sugar foods.

OCR Cambridge National in Health and Social Care

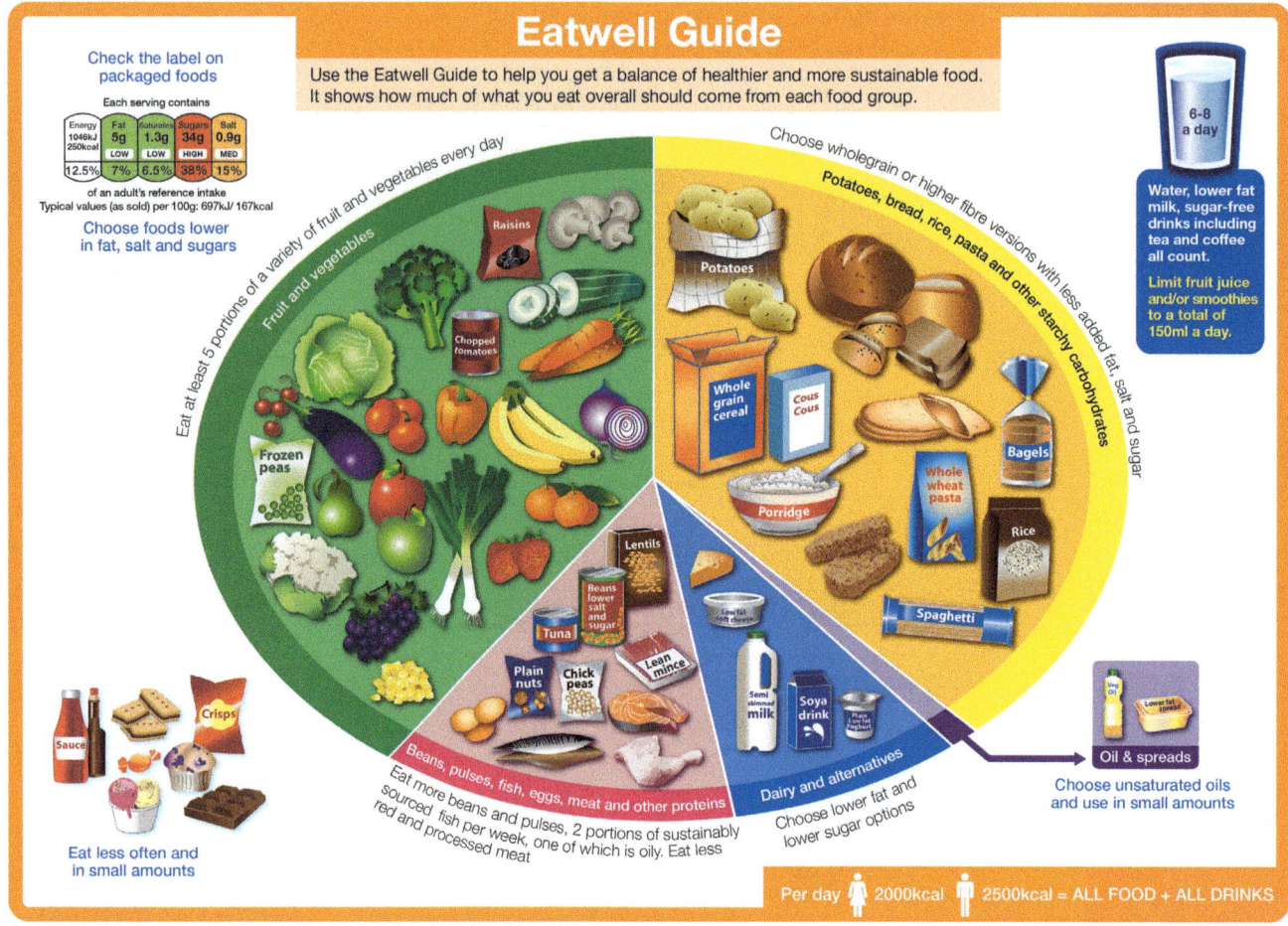

Figure 4.3 The Eatwell Plate

Table 4.1 A summary of the challenges of obesity

Challenge	Who is impacted	Impact on individual and society
• To encourage people to eat healthily without too many high-fat, high-calorie, ready-prepared meals so they lose weight.	• everyone at all life stages	• money spent in NHS for obesity-related sickness and ailments • poor quality of life • reduced life expectancy • days lost from work • early death

Body mass index (BMI) is used to indicate if an individual is under or overweight. BMI can be calculated by dividing a person's weight by the square of their height.

Unit R035 Health promotion campaigns

To calculate someone's BMI, use the following formula:

BMI = weight (kg) divided by height (m)²

Here is an example:

- Height is 1.752 m, squared (1.75 × 1.75) = 3.06 m²
- Weight is 80 kg
- BMI calculation: 80 divided by 3.06 = 26.14
- So the BMI result is: 26.14.

Using Table 4.2, you can see that the person with a BMI of 26.14 is overweight.

Table 4.2 BMI measures: what they mean

BMI	Significance
Less than 18.5	Underweight
18.5–24.9	Healthy
25–29.9	Overweight
30–39.9	Obese
40+	Morbidly obese

Stretch activity

BMI results: what do they mean?

1 Calculate the BMI of the people listed in this table. They are all adults.

Name	Weight (kg)	Height (m)	BMI	Ideal weight to achieve BMI of 18.5–24.9
Bern	48	1.56		
Baz	73	1.61		
Kourosh	99	1.93		
Samadara	45	1.47		

2 Comment on each BMI result. Is each individual underweight, overweight or an ideal healthy weight?
3 Complete the final column of the table by calculating the weight that each individual should be to achieve a healthy BMI.
4 Work out approximately how much weight each person should gain or lose to achieve a healthy BMI.

Flu and viruses

People tend to think that flu or influenza is not a serious illness, but many people die from flu every year. According to PHE, over 27,000 people died from flu in 2017/18, but the figure for 2018/19 reduced to over 24,000. This was partly due to the flu vaccination programme. However, every flu season is different due to the different strains of flu and some years are worse than others, resulting in more deaths.

Flu is easily transmitted from person to person. It is usually spread by coughs and sneezes, so it is important that people eligible for the flu vaccine take it.

OCR Cambridge National in Health and Social Care

The following groups of people are vulnerable to severe symptoms if they catch the flu, and so are offered the flu vaccination every year:

- aged 50 or over
- have certain health conditions
- pregnant
- in long-stay residential care
- the main carer for an older or disabled person who may be at risk
- live with someone who is at high risk from COVID-19 (on the NHS shielded patient list)
- frontline health or social service providers.

Delivering the flu vaccine to these people should prevent them from becoming seriously ill and being admitted to hospital for treatment. Flu epidemics have a major impact on hospitals, especially during the winter months, as many people are admitted and health services sometimes struggle to cope.

Table 4.3 A summary of the challenges presented by flu and viruses

Challenge	Who is impacted	Impact on individual and society
• To encourage uptake of flu vaccine.	• those with health conditions • frontline health and social care service providers • anyone aged over 50	• money spent by the NHS on hospital admissions • NHS struggles to accommodate flu patients • unnecessary early deaths • days lost from work

Alcohol consumption

When someone drinks beer, wine, or another alcoholic drink, the alcohol quickly enters the bloodstream. The alcohol then breaks down and is distributed throughout the body, affecting the brain and other tissues.

Alcohol can have an adverse effect on all the body systems. Consuming too much alcohol brings higher risks of the following physical conditions:

- various cancers such as mouth, throat, oesophagus, larynx, breast and liver
- a stroke
- heart disease
- liver disease
- pancreatitis
- reduced fertility
- diabetes
- depression and anxiety.

Unit R035 Health promotion campaigns

If an individual regularly drinks more than the recommended weekly amount of alcohol (14 units over the week for adults) over a long period, they risk damaging their health. There is no guaranteed safe level of drinking. If consumed occasionally and in moderation, alcohol may not be a problem – but the more the individual drinks, the greater the health risks.

As shown by the list of conditions above, the cost of alcohol consumption to the NHS is huge. But it is not just the NHS who pays the price for this; many workdays can be lost if people take time off work because of alcohol-related illness or ill health.

Table 4.4 A summary of the challenges of alcohol consumption

Challenge	Who is impacted	Impact on individual and society
• To encourage people to drink responsibly and keep within recommended guidelines.	• young people • adults • older adults	• NHS cost of alcohol-related diseases/accidents • early deaths • abuse of family when drunk • causing traffic accidents and possible death through drink driving • possible sexual disease through drunken, unprotected sex • days lost at work • reduced life expectancy • quality of life • addiction • money spent on criminal justice cases, e.g. drunk driving • waste of police time on public disturbances such as vandalism or fights • local council money spent on clearing up damage

Activity

How much alcohol is safe?

In pairs, visit the Drinkaware website and search for the alcohol unit guidance. Read about how many units of alcohol are contained in different drinks. You can find guidance at this webpage:

www.drinkaware.co.uk/facts/alcoholic-drinks-and-units/what-is-an-alcohol-unit

Are you surprised to read that to stay within the Government's recommended guidelines, a person can only drink six pints of 4 per cent beer, or six medium glasses of 13.5 per cent wine each week?

1 Discuss this information with your partner.
2 Decide what advice you would offer a person who drinks:
   • 2 pints of beer or 2 glasses of wine every night
   • 14 units over the weekend.

Heart disease/stroke

According to the latest figures from the British Heart Foundation (BHF), one person dies from **coronary heart disease** every three minutes.

Obesity, smoking, alcohol consumption and lack of exercise all contribute to the risk of heart disease and stroke. The NHS Long Term Plan was published in January 2019. It recognised the challenges from heart attacks and strokes, and aims to:

- reduce heart attacks and strokes by 150,000 by 2029
- provide exercise and diet-related classes for patients with heart problems, which might prevent up to 14,000 early deaths.

This investment would save the NHS money, as people would not require hospital treatment.

> **Key term**
>
> **Coronary heart disease**
> This illness develops when arteries of the heart become narrower because of a build-up of fatty material (cholesterol).

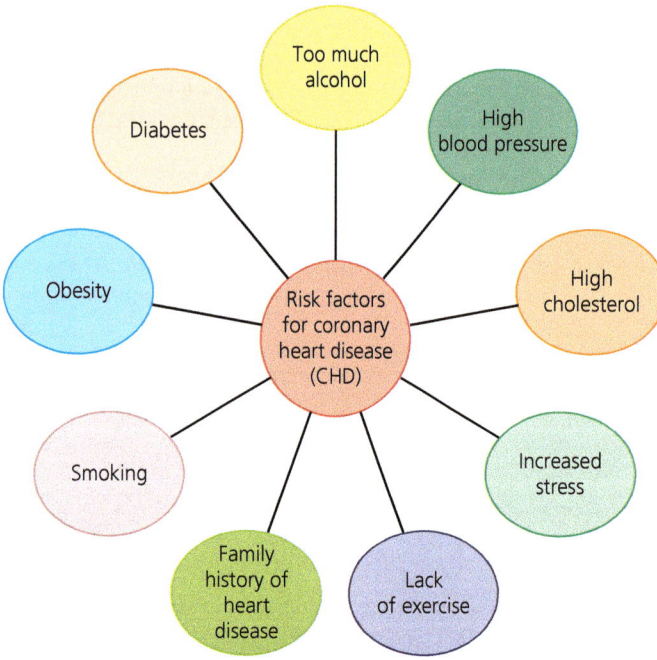

Figure 4.4 The risk factors for coronary heart disease (CHD)

A healthy diet is essential to avoid heart attacks and strokes, so a low-fat, high-fibre diet is recommended, with at least five portions of fresh fruit and vegetables every day. Saturated fat should be avoided as this increases the bad cholesterol in the blood. The following foods should be avoided:

- pastries, such as pies, pasties, sausage rolls
- full-fat sausages
- butter
- lard
- cream
- hard cheese
- cakes and biscuits.

Unsaturated fats should be included in the diet, as they can increase levels of good cholesterol in the blood and help prevent blockages in the arteries. These foods include:

- oily fish
- nuts and seeds
- avocado
- olive, sunflower, rapeseed and vegetable oils.

This change to the diet should result in a healthier BMI for the individual, particularly if they cut down on their alcohol intake at the same time. They may also be able to reduce their blood sugar level if they have diabetes. Exercise each day will also help to keep them fit and healthy.

Figure 4.5 Unsaturated fats have health benefits and can help achieve a healthy BMI

Table 4.5 A summary of the challenges of heart disease/stroke

Challenge	Who is impacted	Impact on individual and society
• To encourage healthy diet and exercise to look after cardiovascular system.	• heart attacks, usually in people aged over 50 • strokes can happen at any age	• NHS costs • early death • days lost at work • reduced life expectancy

Case study: Interpreting Barney's risk factors for heart attack

Barney is 49 years old and works as a lorry driver, travelling all over the country. He finds it difficult to eat healthy foods, as he mainly eats fast food from motorway services. Because he spends most days driving the lorry, he is not very physically active. He is worried, as his father died at 50 years old through coronary heart disease. He has indigestion symptoms and his chest feels uncomfortable after he has eaten his meals. Barney also has diabetes. He weighs and measures himself – his height is 1.83 m and his weight is 91 kg.

1. Work out Barney's BMI. Is he overweight?
2. What other risk factors for coronary heart disease does Barney have?
3. What advice would you give Barney to improve his diet?

Sexual health

Sexually transmitted infections (STIs) are diseases that are spread through unprotected sexual activity (sex without using a condom).

Some STIs have no symptoms, which means that people do not always know they have been infected. However, if STIs are not treated, they can cause serious complications such as infertility, and even death. STIs are dangerous because they are easily spread.

Younger adults are most at risk, as they are more likely to have unsafe sex (without a condom) with different sexual partners. Using a condom and having regular tests will reduce the risk of developing an STI.

The latest figures for STIs show that there were almost half a million cases recorded for 2019. This is a 5 per cent increase from 2018. The most common cases (in order) were for:

- chlamydia for the 15–24 years old group rose by 2 per cent
- gonorrhoea up by 26 per cent across all age groups
- genital warts up by 11 per cent across all age groups
- genital herpes up by 7 per cent across all age groups.

Source: https://assets.publishing.service.gov.uk/government/uploads/system/uploads/attachment_data/file/914249/STI_NCSP_report_2019.pdf

> **Research**
> **STIs**
> In small groups, choose one of the common STIs shown in this list.
> - Research and find out about the symptoms and the treatment for your chosen STI.
> - Produce a PowerPoint on your findings, and present it to the rest of your group. This will be good practice for your health promotion campaign.

Table 4.6 A summary of the challenges of sexual health

Challenge	Who is impacted	Impact on individual and society
• To encourage safer sex.	• everyone who is sexually active	• cost to NHS • infertility • passing on STIs • premature death • working days lost • unwanted pregnancy

Cancer

According to Cancer Research UK, 50 per cent of people diagnosed with cancer survive for ten or more years after diagnosis. This has improved, as 40 years ago survival rates were 24 per cent.

However, there is a huge variation in survival rates, depending on the type of cancer and how soon it is diagnosed. The sooner cancer is diagnosed, the sooner treatment can begin, and the better the chances of survival and a full recovery. For example:

- The survival rate for breast cancer is 76 per cent.
- The rate is 10 per cent for lung cancer.

It is calculated that 70 per cent of lung cancer cases are preventable, because smoking causes most cases and this is a lifestyle choice.

Source: www.cancerresearchuk.org/health-professional/cancer-statistics/survival

The NHS Long Term Plan sets cancer as one of the top priorities, because one in three people will get cancer in their lifetime.

- Better prevention is the key, with earlier diagnosis and innovative treatments.
- People could also make different lifestyle choices to lower their risk of getting cancer, such as eating a healthy diet with plenty of fibre, taking exercise and not drinking too much alcohol.
- Not all cancers are preventable through lifestyle choices, as some are age-related or genetic.

Table 4.7 A summary of the challenges of cancer survival rates

Challenge	Who is impacted	Impact on individual and society
• To encourage people to change to a healthier lifestyle. • To check for lumps and swellings. • To encourage people to go to their GP as soon as symptoms are recognised.	• Cancer can develop at any age but usually affects people over 50.	• NHS costs • early death • quality of life • reduced life expectancy • days lost at work

Physical activity

According to current NHS advice, adults should do at least 30 minutes of moderately intense physical activity/exercise for 5 days each week, if they wish to improve their general health. But any physical activity is better than no physical activity.

Moderately intense exercise includes:

- brisk walking
- riding a bike
- dancing
- hiking
- playing tennis (doubles)
- water aerobics.

Physical inactivity can lead to increased risk of chronic disease and obesity. Exercise can support health in many ways:

- It can help an individual to keep their weight down.
- It can also help to raise self-esteem, as people feel good about themselves when they exercise.
- Stress can be reduced, as the body produces endorphins when exercising.
- Non-exercising overweight and obese people have a higher risk of developing heart disease, hypertension, stroke and **Type 2 diabetes**. Exercise can reduce these diseases by up to 50 per cent, and reduce a person's risk of early death by 30 per cent.
- Physical fitness will improve breathing and heart rate, keep joints flexible and make movement easier.

All these positive aspects of physical activity add up to healthier people who will stay independent for longer and have less need to visit their GP or stay in hospital. An older person who has taken regular exercise throughout their life is more likely to carry out their chosen activity once they have retired.

Figure 4.6 Walking a dog is a good form of exercise

Key terms

Type 2 diabetes This illness can be caused by lifestyle. It usually appears in people over the age of 40. It is, however, becoming more common in children and young people. Type 2 diabetes accounts for between 85 and 95 per cent of all people with diabetes and is treated with a healthy diet and increased physical activity. Medication is often required.

Table 4.8 A summary of the challenges of physical activity

Challenge	Who is impacted	Impact on individual and society
• To encourage physical activity	• everyone, from young children to older adults	• cost to NHS • quality of life • premature death • decreased life expectancy • cost of social care • work days lost

Unit R035 Health promotion campaigns

Mental health

A mental health illness affects how a person thinks, feels and behaves.

Mental health disorders can affect anyone of any age, race, gender or social class. The best way to deal with a mental health challenge is to get professional help as soon as symptoms are recognised.

One in four people will experience a mental health condition in their lifetime. Just like physical disorders, some of these mental disorders are more difficult to treat than others.

- Mental health conditions never used to be mentioned as there was a stigma (feeling of shame) around the issue, but today's society is more honest and open about mental health.
- Many high-profile celebrities have talked openly about their mental health conditions, which has made it easier to discuss the issue and for people to seek help for their mental health.

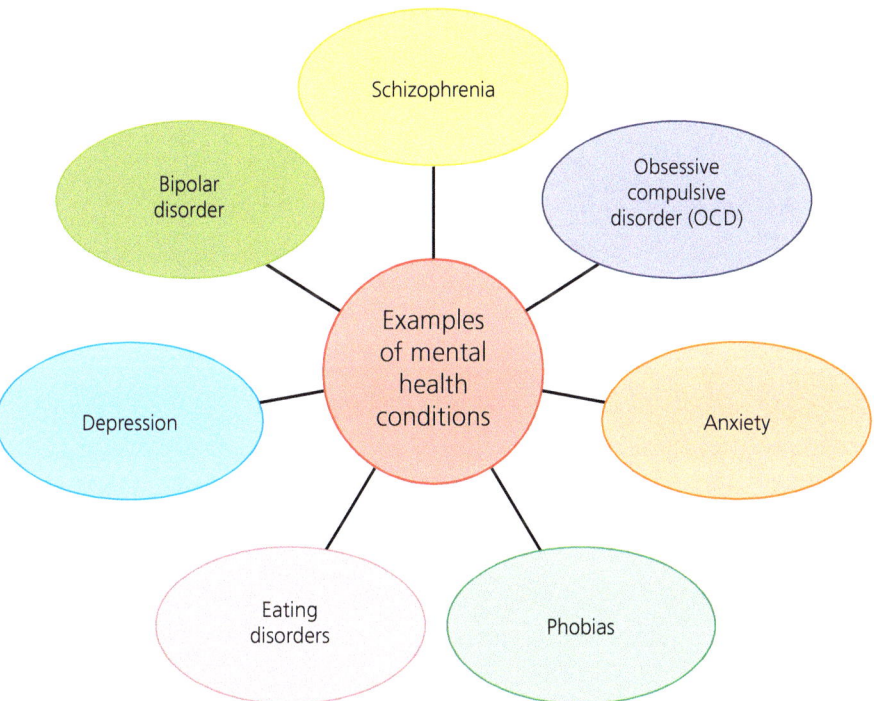

Figure 4.7 Examples of mental health conditions

Table 4.9 A summary of the challenges of mental health

Challenge	Who is impacted	Impact on individual and society
• To encourage looking after mental health. • To encourage people to seek help from their GP as soon as symptoms suspected.	• anyone, from young children to older adults	• absence from school • not being able to learn or concentrate properly • NHS costs • suicide or attempts to take own life • poor quality of life • early death • work days lost • police time and costs in case of attempted suicide, e.g. jumping from a bridge

Smoking cessation

Approximately 78,000 people die every year due to smoking, with many more living with smoking-related illnesses which affect the quality of their lives. Smoking causes 70 per cent of all lung cancers, but it also causes many other cancers (as shown in Figure 4.8).

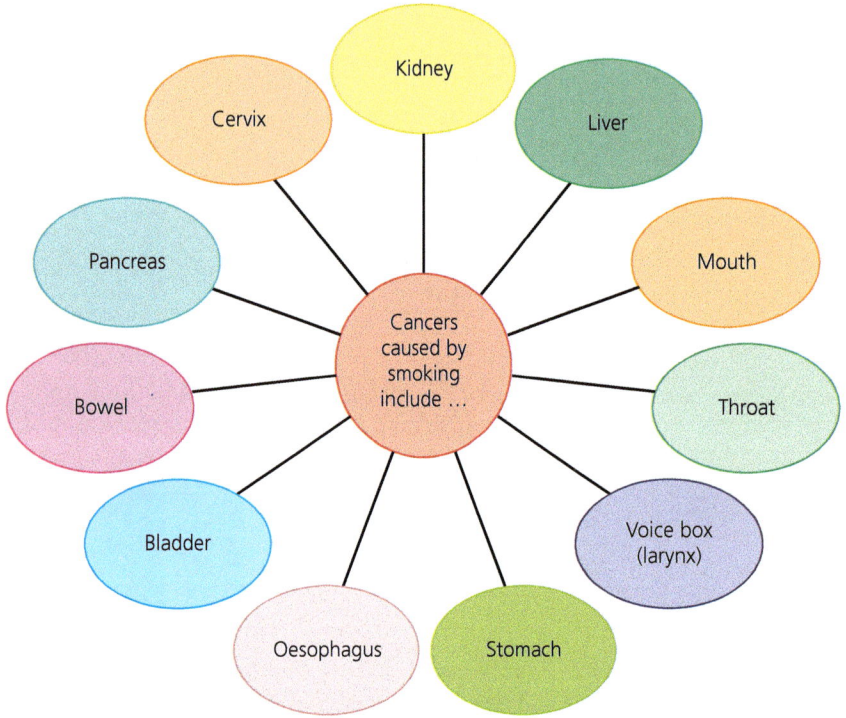

Figure 4.8 Cancers caused by smoking

As well as cancers, smoking can cause other serious health conditions such as:

- heart attack
- stroke
- asthma
- **emphysema**
- **bronchitis**
- **pneumonia**.

Smoking can cause miscarriage or stillbirth in women who smoke during pregnancy.

Passive smoking (breathing in someone else's smoke) increases the risk of cancer and other smoking-related diseases by 25 per cent. It has been illegal to smoke in an enclosed public space since 2007 in England. This means that people can eat in a restaurant, drink in a pub or catch a bus without breathing in someone else's smoke.

> **Key terms**
>
> **Emphysema** A lung disease which causes shortness of breath.
>
> **Bronchitis** Infection of the main airways of the lungs.
>
> **Pneumonia** A lung infection which causes problems with breathing.

Unit R035 Health promotion campaigns

Anyone wishing to give up smoking can join an NHS smoking cessation programme, where they will be advised and helped to give up smoking.

- This is a free service.
- It is staffed by experts who will give professional advice on the best methods of quitting smoking.

Table 4.10 A summary of the challenges of smoking

Challenge	Who is impacted	Impact on individual and society
• To encourage smoking cessation.	• anyone who is subjected to passive smoking • young people • adults • older people	• cost to NHS • work days lost • premature death • lower life expectancy • poor quality of life • passive smoking can kill

Activity

Why do people choose to smoke?

Looking at the evidence about smoking being the biggest killer in the UK and all the other conditions associated with it, why do you think people choose to smoke?

Discuss this question with your partner, and then feed back to group. What was the overall conclusion?

Child dental health

- Children should be encouraged from an early age to look after their teeth by using a toothbrush as soon as they can. Parents can help with this process by brushing the child's teeth as soon as they appear in their gums. They should continue with this help until the child is able to brush their teeth properly by themselves. It is particularly important for the child to go to sleep with clean brushed teeth.
- Parents/carers should take the child with them when they go to the dentist for a dental check-up, so they will be used to seeing and sitting in the dentist's chair. This means that the child will not be afraid of going to the dentist to have their teeth examined.
- Clean teeth mean healthy teeth and less chance of bad breath or decay. Sugary food and drinks are one of the main causes of tooth decay.

Table 4.11 A summary of the challenges of child dental health

Challenge	Who is impacted	Impact on individual and society
• To encourage correct brushing of teeth. • To encourage regular dental check-ups.	• young children • children	• cost to NHS • days off school • loss of teeth

OCR Cambridge National in Health and Social Care

Organisations promoting public health challenges

There are many organisations and charities that support people to meet public health challenges. Most health conditions have a specialist charity which offers advice and support to people suffering from that condition.

Table 4.12 Organisations promoting public health challenges

Organisation	Examples	Funded by	Method of promoting health challenges
Charities	• BHF • Marie Curie • Samaritans • Alzheimer's Society • Mind • Breast Cancer Care	• Generally charities are funded by donations from the public.	• Information and support given to public, e.g. on diet, exercise and care.
NHS	• GP • optician • dentist • pharmacy • hospital • pregnancy services • health visitor • midwife	• Government-funded, although there are some charges in England, e.g. optician, dentist, pharmacy.	• All government departments offer advice, with their websites promoting health campaigns.
Government Health Agencies	• PHE • Department of Health and Social Care	• Government-funded.	• To look after and improve the nation's health and well-being.
World Health Organization (WHO)		• Member countries (194) pay their assessed contributions. • Private donations.	• Promote health and well-being across the world • Help trace disease outbreaks. • Provide extra support when needed.

Test your knowledge

1. Finish this sentence: A person who is very overweight with a lot of body fat is said to be _____ .
2. Name two food categories that contribute most to children's sugar intake.
3. What challenge does the Government face in relation to alcohol consumption?
4. What dietary advice is given to avoid heart attacks?

1.3 Current health promotion campaigns and their benefits

Health promotion campaigns aim to give people information so that:

- they can make better choices about their health
- they feel empowered and able to make their own decisions
- their attitudes and behaviours change
- their health improves and they have a better quality of life.

Table 4.13 explores the benefits of current health promotion campaigns.

Table 4.13 Examples of current health promotion campaigns, their benefits and target audiences

Current health promotion campaign and its brief	Benefits to individuals and society	Target audience
#CoverUpMate – encourages outdoor workers to cover up with clothing or sunscreen when outdoors in the sun. www.england.nhs.uk/south/2016/07/18/coverupmate	• For society – less money spent on skin cancers for NHS. • For the individual – better health and quality of life plus no time away from work for treatment. • The individual is educated, enabling them to make an informed decision about covering up their skin.	• adults • older people • parents for their children
Better Health (Healthier Families) – NHS campaign to ensure parents have support to make healthier choices for their families. www.nhs.uk/healthier-families	• Healthier population with fewer health problems, therefore less need for NHS treatments.	• children and young people • adults • older adults
Count 14 Campaign – to raise awareness of safe alcohol intake of 14 units per week, consumed over the course of the week and not on one occasion. https://healthimprovement.gg/news/article/count-14-has-been-launched	• Fewer alcohol-related issues so fewer health problems for NHS and individuals. Sensible drinking habits established. • Binge drinking discouraged as people are aware of consequences.	• adults • older adults
Be a soaper hero – good hand hygiene for primary school age children. https://nationalschoolspartnership.com/initiatives/soaper-heroes/	• Learn good habits in hand washing early in life. • Fewer germs and diseases spread.	• early years
Catch it. Bin it. Kill it. – to prevent flu infections. www.england.nhs.uk/south/wp-content/uploads/sites/6/2017/09/catch-bin-kill.pdf	• Fewer cases of flu so bed pressure in the NHS over winter is reduced. • Less chance for people to catch flu, so fewer days off work due to sickness.	• children and young people • adults • older adults
Hands. Face. Space. – to prevent spread of COVID-19. www.gov.uk/government/news/new-campaign-to-prevent-spread-of-coronavirus-indoors-this-winter	• Reduces spread through population. • Fewer hospital admissions. • Avoids national lockdowns.	• children and young people • adults • older adults
Drinkaware – information on all aspects of alcohol. www.drinkaware.co.uk	• Alcohol education so people are aware of effect on health and well-being. • Fewer admissions to hospital.	• adults • older adults

OCR Cambridge National in Health and Social Care

Current health promotion campaign and its brief	Benefits to individuals and society	Target audience
Every Mind Matters – tips and advice to look after mental health. Completing a multi-choice questionnaire produces an individualised plan. www.nhs.uk/every-mind-matters	• Helps to prevent mental health issues by encouraging exercises for stress and anxiety. • Less NHS interventions.	• children and young people • adults • older adults
Food Upfront – campaigning for larger takeaways and chain restaurants to provide clear food labelling which includes calorie intake. www.diabetes.org.uk/get_involved/campaigning/food-upfront-campaign	• More information to tackle obesity as people can make healthier choices. • Less obesity-related admission to hospitals.	• children and young people • adults • older adults
Ouch – Your Sexual Health Matters – increasing awareness of STIs, contraception and all sexual matters. www.yoursexualhealthmatters.org.uk	• Increase sex education of young people, therefore fewer STIs. • Fewer cases of STIs at clinics and hospitals.	• young people
Tilly the tooth – how good diet benefits teeth and lots of sugary food does not. www.youtube.com/watch?v=YBf6a4OieZQ	• Less tooth decay and fewer teeth taken out. • Better breath. • Children not scared of dentist. • Less money spent on extractions.	• early years
Stoptober – NHS support to give up smoking. www.blf.org.uk/take-action/campaign-with-us/stoptober	• Reduced costs for the NHS. • Better health and quality of life for individual.	• adults • older adults

Activity

Investigating health promotion campaigns

Divide into pairs, with each pair investigating a different health promotion campaign from Table 4.13.

Read the brief in the first column for your campaign. Search online for the webpages provided, and examine the information on the site so that you can answer these questions:

- Does the information meet the brief?
- What are the positive or negative aspects of the campaign?
- Do you think it would influence the behaviour of the group it was intended for?
- How could it be improved?

Test your knowledge

1. How does 'Be a soaper hero' improve the health of early years children?
2. What does 'Ouch – your sexual health matters' hope to achieve?
3. What was the message of 'Hands, Face, Space' during the COVID-19 pandemic?

Unit R035 Health promotion campaigns

Topic area 2 Factors influencing health and well-being

Getting started

Do you make good choices which will help you stay fit and healthy? Find this link to the NHS website, which gives guidelines for the amount of physical activity children and young people should do per day:

www.nhs.uk/live-well/exercise/physical-activity-guidelines-children-and-young-people/

Read through the information on exercise.

- Do you do enough exercise each week to keep you fit?
- Do you fit exercise into your everyday life, for example, by walking to school or college and back home each day? Does this meet your 60 minutes of aerobic exercise every day?
- Do you take part in sport, dance and gym lessons at school?

Discuss your exercise with your partner, as this is one of your lifestyle choices.

2.1 Factors influencing health and well-being

Lifestyle choices

It is important to realise that lifestyle choices can affect people's lives for many years. Poor choices made about diet, exercise, alcohol, unprotected sex, self-help and smoking can have a negative effect on someone throughout their life. However, positive choices in these areas can lead to positive effects on physical and mental health.

Table 4.14 Positive lifestyle choices and their effects on physical and mental health

Positive lifestyle choice	Positive effect on physical health	Positive effect on mental health
Alcohol Keep to maximum of 14 units of alcohol weekly, spread throughout the week with 2 days without alcohol.	• less likely to develop cancers and stroke/heart attack • fewer hangovers • lower blood pressure and lower cholesterol • better sleep, more energy • stronger immune system • lower blood sugar • brain power improved – able to think faster and clearer	• improved mood • feel more positive • less anxious • better memory
Diet • Eat a healthy diet with plenty of fruit and vegetables, some protein, milk and dairy foods, fibre and carbohydrates. • Eat less processed foods. • Do not eat snacks, sugary drinks or crisps. • Drink six to eight glasses of water a day.	• weight control • less likely to develop diabetes/heart attack/stroke • more energy • better skin tone • look and feel younger • able to be more active • strengthened immune system • better general health	• feel better • good self-esteem • reduce likelihood of depression

OCR Cambridge National in Health and Social Care

Positive lifestyle choice	Positive effect on physical health	Positive effect on mental health
Exercise Take regular daily exercise – at least 30 minutes for adults and 60 minutes for children and young people.	<ul><li>weight control</li><li>less likely to develop diabetes/heart attack/stroke</li><li>boost energy</li><li>look and feel younger</li><li>strengthened immune system</li><li>better general health</li><li>strengthened bones and muscles</li><li>can reduce chronic pain</li><li>improved sleep</li></ul>	<ul><li>feel better</li><li>good self-esteem</li><li>reduced likelihood of depression</li><li>reduced stress</li><li>help relaxation</li><li>help brain health and memory</li><li>reduced anxiety</li></ul>
Protected sex Ensure safe sex by using a condom and not having many different partners.	<ul><li>reduced risks of STIs such as genital warts, genital herpes, chlamydia and HIV/Aids</li><li>reduced risks of pelvic inflammatory disease and cervical cancer among women</li><li>reduced risk of pregnancy</li></ul>	<ul><li>reduced anxiety</li><li>reduced stress</li><li>feel better</li><li>build self-esteem if regular partner</li></ul>
Smoking There are no advantages to smoking. The only way to benefit is to give up smoking completely.	<ul><li>reduced risk of cancer</li><li>reduced risk of cardiovascular disease</li><li>better general health</li><li>reduced risk of many associated health issues, e.g. poor reproductive health</li></ul>	<ul><li>feel better</li><li>good self-esteem</li><li>reduced likelihood of depression</li><li>feel fresher and less smelly</li></ul>
Self-help Psychological therapies can be done in your own time for issues such as stress, anxiety and depression.	<ul><li>increase immunity</li><li>reduce blood pressure</li><li>improved sleep</li></ul>	<ul><li>reduce anxiety</li><li>reduce stress</li><li>feel better</li><li>build self-esteem</li><li>feel in control</li><li>feel empowered</li></ul>

Health

When you think about your own health and that of other people, you need to consider both physical and mental health.

Physical health

Genetics and illness

Even if someone follows all the health advice, they can still find themselves with inherited conditions passed on to them by genes from their parents.

- These can include inherited conditions such as **haemophilia**, **sickle cell anaemia** and **cystic fibrosis**.
- Some cancers can run in families; for example, carrying certain genes increases the risk for breast/ovarian cancer.
- A family history of heart disease can be a strong risk factor in the development of coronary heart disease or **Type 1 diabetes**.

> **Key terms**
>
> **Haemophilia** An inherited disorder where the blood does not clot.
>
> **Sickle cell anaemia** An inherited disorder where the red blood cells become crescent or sickle-shaped. It can cause tiredness, pain, infections which may need hospitalisation, and delayed growth or puberty.
>
> **Cystic fibrosis** A genetic disorder where the lungs and digestive system become clogged with mucus.
>
> **Type 1 diabetes** This illness causes the level of blood glucose (sugar) to become too high. It happens when the body cannot produce enough insulin, which controls blood glucose.

If someone is more likely to have an inherited condition, they can monitor their health regularly and keep to the positive lifestyle choices.

Illness can also affect lifestyle choices. If someone does not feel well, it can be hard to exercise. If they have been in hospital with a serious debilitating illness, for example, COVID-19, they may not have the energy or strength when they first come home to exercise immediately, and will have to build up their stamina.

Mental health

Stress and anxiety

Stress and anxiety are very closely linked and can affect mental, emotional and physical health. This can lead to a variety of physical symptoms such as headaches, digestive problems, low energy or even heart disease.

- Stress and anxiety can come from being under too much pressure or facing big changes or worrying about something or having too much responsibility.
- Stress can lead to burn out, depression or feelings of not being able to cope with anything.
- It can then be difficult for the stressed or anxious person to think about exercising or cooking nutritious meals, as they have little energy and do not feel up to the task.

However, if the person recognises they are stressed or anxious before it reaches the stage where they cannot cope, they can help themselves.

Exercise is recognised as a benefit for physical health but it is also one of the most important ways of beating stress or anxiety. This is because exercise:

- takes the focus away from the cause of stress or anxiety, allowing the person to switch off from their worries
- promotes the release of 'feel good' brain chemicals known as endorphins, which help the individual to feel better about themselves.

However, some mental health conditions cannot be cured by exercise and diet alone, but will need medical intervention.

Figure 4.9 Exercise is good for the body and the mind

Educational and socio-economic factors

Disposable income

This means income that is left over after all bills are paid, which can be saved or spent as the person wishes.

A person with enough disposable income can make choices about their lifestyle, such as:

- pay for gym fees or for a personal trainer to keep fit
- afford high-quality food.

A person with a low-paid job might not have any disposable income. This stops them from making some lifestyle choices, and they might not be able to:

- pay their bills
- heat their home
- afford good quality, filling fresh food so they might turn to fast food instead.

Employment

A well-paid job makes it easier for workers to:

- live in healthier neighbourhoods with less pollution and vandalism, and lower crime rates
- buy more nutritious food.

All of these actions affect health.

Good jobs also tend to provide good benefits such as sick pay and a decent pension. However, someone on a flexible **zero-hours contract** will have little security. They might:

- not have a regular income
- live in a poorer neighbourhood
- find it difficult to feed their family
- have to rely on foodbanks.

> **Key term**
>
> **Zero-hours contract** An employer does not have to provide a minimum number of hours of work for an employee, therefore on some days the employee will have no work and no pay. However, zero-hours workers are entitled to statutory paid annual leave of 5.6 weeks and the national minimum wage in the same way as regular workers.

Literacy

This means being able to read and write. If people cannot read, they miss a lot of health messages on posters in shopping centres, GP surgeries and health centres.

Health literacy is more complicated. This means:

- being able to understand how the body works
- having the knowledge, understanding and skills to evaluate the risks and benefits of health education advice for themselves and their family.

Not having health literacy could mean:

- the family misses vital information, so they cannot take informed decisions about health matters such as vaccination against diseases
- they miss signs of infectious diseases, as they do not know what to look out for.

Qualifications

The better qualified or educated someone is, the better job they can get and therefore the higher wage they can earn.

- This gives them more money to provide for their family.
- They have more choices and opportunities.
- They will be able to understand health statistics and advice produced by health promotion campaigns, and be able to use this information to their advantage.

Culture

Culture refers to the beliefs, values and ways of behaving shared by members of the community or a particular group or society.

Culture can affect people's views of health promotion:

- Health promotion campaigns in the UK have tended to emphasise the need for people of different ethnic origins to adapt to British culture to improve their health.
- This is beginning to change, as both the National Institute for Health and Care Excellence (NICE) and the NHS have produced advice on how to adapt health campaigns so that minority ethnic groups are encouraged to recognise their value.

OCR Cambridge National in Health and Social Care

Access to health services

Access to health services can be affected by a range of factors.

Location

- It is easy to access health services if they are nearby, but some services may be located in a different part of the country.
- There could be a lack of public transport or a long bus/train journey to get there.
- There are also the costs associated with travelling to these locations, and some people may find that they do not have the money in their budget.
- If someone lives in a rural area, they might have to travel into town to access a counselling or well-being group, although they may have access to a GP, clinic or pharmacy in their village.

Opening times

Most health services operate a day service which may be from 8 am to 6 pm.

- This can make it difficult for someone who works during the day to access the service.
- They would have to take time off work and if they are working in a low-paid job, they might not be paid for this time. If they cannot afford to lose this money, this will prevent them from accessing the service.
- If the health service is located far away and there is poor public transport, this can prevent someone from reaching the service during opening hours.

Local resources

- There might be a GP surgery and a pharmacy in rural areas, but some people may have to travel for other health services. In very remote areas, people have to travel to access any healthcare.
- Community healthcare may be available to support older people in the community.
- There could be a rural hub which provides a range of services, linked to online consultations with GPs, clinics, counselling and well-being groups.

Availability

Access to NHS services is usually not immediate, and most treatments have a waiting time. The recommended waiting time for a physical condition is 18 weeks.

Unit R035 Health promotion campaigns

According to the mental health charity MIND, in 2014 the availability of counselling for mental health issues was poor:

- 54 per cent of individuals on the waiting list had to wait over three months for treatment
- 12 per cent had to wait over a year.

Recent news reports have suggested that since the lockdowns imposed in 2020 and 2021 by the Government to stop the spread of COVID-19, more individuals are seeking medical help for mental health issues. Waiting times will probably become even longer.

Investment in mental health services is inadequate and does not meet the demand.

There may be several types of well-being groups in the local council area offering help and support. Some charities may even offer free professional counselling for children and young adults.

Source: www.mind.org.uk/news-campaigns/news/people-with-mental-health-problems-still-waiting-over-a-year-for-talking-treatments

Research
Well-being groups in your area

- In pairs, search your local council's website for health and well-being groups. How many different groups are available?
- Decide which categories they best fit into, such as mental health, health promotion, physical health.
- Share your categories with the rest of the group. Do you agree with each other? Are you surprised at the number of groups offering well-being help?

Test your knowledge

1. What disposable income?
2. Name three ways that physical exercise can improve mental health.
3. Why might it be difficult for an individual to access healthcare services during a normal working day (8am until 6pm).

2.2 Leading a healthy lifestyle

What individuals can do to be healthy

Most health campaigns aim to educate individuals so they can try to change their behaviour, such as giving up smoking or eating a healthier diet. They present facts, and it is then up to the individual to make their own choices. No one can force an individual to change their lifestyle.

The physical, intellectual, emotional and social (PIES) benefits of making healthy lifestyle choices are outlined in Tables 4.15 to 4.19.

Table 4.15 The benefits of making healthy choices on PIES

Making healthy choices	Physical benefits	Intellectual benefits	Emotional benefits	Social benefits
No smoking	• breathe easier • cough less • improved lung capacity • improved blood circulation • more energy • improved immune system • improved smell and taste • improved fertility • fresher breath • delayed wrinkles	• better concentration • improvement to memory	• less stress • less anxiety • less depression • improved quality of life • positive mood	• prevent harm to others through second-hand smoke • smell better to friends and family
Use sun protection	• no burning • no age spots • no thread veins • fewer wrinkles		• better self-esteem due to undamaged skin	
Safe sex	• prevent disease • prevent pregnancy		• peace of mind	• do not pass on STIs to others

Table 4.16 The benefits of healthy eating and drinking on PIES

Healthy eating and drinking	Physical benefits	Intellectual benefits	Emotional benefits	Social benefits
Balanced diet	• strong bones and teeth • more energy • can manage weight • stronger immune system • healthier digestive system, e.g. less indigestion and constipation • more stamina • improved sleep	• improved memory • better academic performance • improved concentration	• better mood/happier • better self-esteem • less stress	• more able to take part in team games • good self-esteem makes an individual want to make more friends • eating healthy family meals together strengthens family ties • pass on good eating habits to next generation
Moderation	• less likely to put on weight • deeper sleep • better skin • healthier digestive system • improved dental health	• improved memory • improved concentration	• better mood • less depression	• more likely to keep friendships • no family issues • no loss of job

Key terms

Age spots Flat brown or black spots on the skin that increase with age.

Thread veins Very slender veins on the face that are visible through the skin. These are caused by over-exposure to the sun.

Unit R035 Health promotion campaigns

Table 4.17 The benefits of good hygiene on PIES

Hygiene	Physical benefits	Intellectual benefits	Emotional benefits	Social benefits
Personal hygiene	• protection from infection and disease • fresh breath • less tooth decay • reduced body odour • clean, germ-free hands • clearer skin • dandruff prevention • feel comfortable	(none)	• feel clean and relaxed • more confident • less depressed	• other people feel more comfortable being nearby • more likely to make friends • less likely to pass on infectious diseases • professional acceptance
Environment	• germs removed from surfaces • less likely to pass on diseases • odours eliminated • pests such as mice and rats discouraged	(none)	• feel better • more confident • environment feels pleasant	• happy to invite others to the home

Table 4.18 The benefits of mental health strategies on PIES

Mental health	Physical benefits	Intellectual benefits	Emotional benefits	Social benefits
Mental stimulation	• reduced tiredness/fatigue • better sleep • more energy	• improved memory • slowed cognitive decline • improved concentration • better focus • better problem solving	• less depression • feel better • reduced boredom • better self-esteem	• more likely to make new friends • sense of purpose
Coping strategies	• reduced tiredness and fatigue • better sleep • more energy	• clear-headed • better focus • better problem solving • better able to cope with challenges	• feel better • feel more in control • better self-esteem • think positively	• more likely to mix with others • sense of purpose
Good sleep	• more energy • reduced tiredness and fatigue • stronger immune system	• improved memory • improved concentration • better problem solving	• feel better • better self-esteem	• sense of purpose

Table 4.19 The benefits of physical activities on PIES

Physical activity	Physical benefits	Intellectual benefits	Emotional benefits	Social benefits
Regular exercise	• weight control • combat health conditions and diseases • more energy • better sleep • well-toned body • strengthened bones and joints	• mind more alert • improved focus • clear-headed • better able to cope with challenges	• improved mood • boosts well-being feeling • less anxiety • less depression	• mix with different people • opportunities for social interaction • raised self-esteem • developed teamwork skills

OCR Cambridge National in Health and Social Care

> **Test your knowledge**
> 1 Ruwan makes the decision not to smoke. What are the social benefits for his family?
> 2 What are the physical benefits of personal hygiene?
> 3 Name the intellectual benefits of a good night's sleep.

2.3 Barriers to leading a healthy lifestyle

What prevents individuals from being healthy

People sometimes think they are too busy to spend time thinking about being healthy. There can be a perception that being healthy takes too much effort, and that cooking nutritious meals from scratch takes too long.

However, being healthy does not take much effort once you change bad habits. The benefits of being healthy and feeling good more than compensate for any initial effort you might have to make.

Advertising/media

The media – newspapers, magazines, television, YouTube, blogs – bombard the public with images which may have a positive or negative influence. Marketing and advertising are powerful tools to influence behaviour. It is the role of advertisers to sell a product by persuading customers that they need it. A good advertisement can affect an individual's decision whether or not to buy.

But when it comes to health, marketing and advertising have been dominated by industries promoting unhealthy habits and behaviours. In the past, smoking and drinking alcohol were promoted as glamorous. For example:

- Cigarettes, spirits and beers used to be advertised at sports grounds.
- This gave the impression that perhaps the sportsmen and women used these products and they were healthy.

High-fat foods are often advertised to encourage children to ask their families to buy them.

- Families are shown sharing pizzas as a reward for a hard day.
- Chocolate bars are handed out as an incentive for going to school.

This makes these types of food desirable to the young (and not so young).

> **Activity**
> **Appealing advertisements**
>
> In pairs, discuss your favourite advertisement when you were a young child.
>
> - Which product was being advertised?
> - Did you pester your family to buy you the product?
> - What was it that appealed to you then? How have your tastes in advertisements changed?
> - What is your current favourite advert? Why?
> - Do adverts affect the foods you eat?
>
> Bring your discussions back to the main group.
>
> - Have you chosen any of the same adverts?
> - How much influence does the group think advertisers have?

Peer pressure

Younger individuals often change their attitudes and values to fit in with their social group's expectations. For example, they were going to choose healthy food at lunchtime, but their friends persuade them otherwise.

Fitting in with a peer group often leads young people to take risks, such as misusing drugs or binge drinking alcohol.

Lack of support

Friends and family

Sometimes, friends and family can dissuade an individual from trying to live a healthier lifestyle by encouraging unhealthy eating and a sedentary way of life. This is because trying to improve often makes others feel uncomfortable, because they know they should be doing the same. They may not want things to change and will put obstacles in the way.

Role models

People who attract a lot of attention from the media can be very influential and become role models. Their behaviour might be copied by younger people, so if they display harmful or disruptive behaviour, this can have negative effects. For example:

- Some celebrities boast on social media about drunken nights out or their number of sexual partners.
- Young people who are impressionable are impressed by these poor role models and feel they want to copy their behaviour.

Figure 4.10 Celebrity posts on social media can influence young people's behaviour

Health professionals

Most individuals access health professionals through their GP. However, many GPs feel they lack the skills to give effective health promotion advice. They say they feel more comfortable managing ill health.

Over a third of obese patients who visited their GP were given advice related to weight loss. But some GPs, although well prepared to give health advice, felt that they had little effect on the patients they did counsel for weight loss. They also lack time to meet this commitment.

Source: www.researchgate.net/publication/51879191_Health_promotion_and_ill-health_prevention_The_role_of_general_practice

Cost

Expense of gym membership

Going to the gym is good for anyone but sometimes the cost is too much for some people. For example, in 2021, monthly membership costs for PureGym were £14.99 for off-peak hours and £24.99 for visits at any time.

However, people can keep fit without spending any money, for example, by:

- walking everywhere instead of using transport
- taking up jogging/running, which does not require expensive equipment.

Healthy food

The cost for healthy food can be up to three times more than for unhealthy food.

- Unhealthy food is much cheaper because the main ingredients are mass-produced and can be kept for much longer as they are non-perishable.
- Foods classed as healthier such as fruit and vegetables are more expensive per calorie than foods high in fat or sugar.
- Sometimes people want food that will fill them up, so although they know a piece of fruit would be healthier, they buy a pack of biscuits for the same price.

Treatment/holistic therapies

There are many different holistic therapies and treatments, from acupuncture to body massage, reflexology to aromatherapy. Many individuals feel that a holistic therapy has had positive effects on their health, such as acupuncture treating migraine headaches.

However, holistic treatments can be expensive, with some costing £60 per hour depending on the treatment and the location of the therapist. This is a barrier for many people who would not be able to afford it on a regular basis.

Test your knowledge

1. How does peer pressure affect younger individuals' decisions?
2. How can family and friends dissuade an individual from following a healthy lifestyle?
3. Why is it unnecessary to go to an expensive gym to keep fit?

Unit R035 Health promotion campaigns

Topic area 3 Plan and create a health promotion campaign

Getting started

In pairs, discuss health campaigns.

- Do you remember any particular health campaign?
- Why do you remember it?
- Did you change your behaviour because of the message it gave?

3.1 How to plan a health promotion campaign

Remember that the evaluation is important to the campaign, and must take place from the beginning of the campaign planning. It is a good idea to keep a diary of everything you do throughout the planning and delivery of your campaign. Although you may be working in a group to plan your health promotion campaign, each person must keep their own individual diary.

Aims of the campaign

What you want to change/improve/educate about

1. First you must decide on the focus of your campaign. Are you going to educate your audience about one of the challenges to public health, such as obesity, alcohol consumption or smoking?
2. When you have decided on the topic, you may need to narrow it down if it is a broad subject. For example:
   - If you choose obesity, you may decide to look at the food that individuals should be eating and use the Eatwell Plate as a basis for your campaign.
   - If you are looking at teeth cleaning, this is a narrower subject and you may be able to cover the whole topic.

Aims related to PIES

Your aims are particularly important and need to be linked to PIES.

1. You must have a main aim which sets out the purpose of the campaign.
2. You then need to have mini aims (objectives) which describe how you are going to meet the main aim. For example:
   - If the aim is to educate Year 4 children about healthy eating, a mini aim may be to introduce them to exotic fruits by tasting them.
   - This would link to the **P** in PIES, as it would improve physical health for the children.
   - **I** in PIES might also be affected, as academic performance could improve.

OCR Cambridge National in Health and Social Care

Timescales

You must be aware of timescales, as you will need to plan every detail when organising your health promotion campaign. It is poor practice to leave preparation until the last minute, because if you do not pay sufficient attention to detail then your campaign may not be successful.

1. Decide on your target audience, and make sure they are available on the date and at the time you want to deliver your health message. You will need to give them a rough timing of the presentation so they know what to expect.
2. Check the availability of resources.
   - You may have to design and produce a PowerPoint presentation.
   - Prepare questionnaires.
   - Decide on your presentation and evaluation methods.
3. Practise the presentation until you are confident about your delivery.
4. Plan the time for your session carefully so that you can deliver your message. Remember to allow time to set up the campaign, and also for filling in and collecting your questionnaires.

Resources needed

1. At the end of this unit, you will find web addresses where you can download resources to help with the delivery of your campaign.
   - A local health promotion team may be willing to help.
   - Avoid spending time producing your own materials when you can access other high-quality resources which are professionally produced.
2. You must also check that you have the right equipment. For example:
   - You may want to use a PowerPoint presentation as the focus for your campaign.
   - If so, you will need to check that a computer is available and will be set up ready for your talk.

Safety considerations

Safety considerations are paramount to any activity.

1. If you are in a different setting from your own centre, you will need to know about fire procedures and the nearest fire exit.
2. You also need to minimise risk. For example, if your activity involves cutting up fruit for Year 4 children, make sure the knife is not left lying around to avoid injuries.
3. You must also show sensitivity to your audience by not drawing attention to anyone or embarrassing them, particularly if you are covering a sensitive subject.
4. It is your responsibility throughout the presentation to protect the rights of the people you are talking to, so you must value their opinions even if they are different to your own.

Unit R035 Health promotion campaigns

- There should be mutual respect and their wishes and feelings should be taken into consideration. For example, if you are giving children exotic fruit to taste, and one child does not want to do that, then they have the right to say no.
- Before the event, you must ask the class teacher if any of the children may be allergic to any of the fruits that you are giving them to taste.

Communication to be used during delivery

You can use various communication methods to deliver health promotion messages. Table 4.20 outlines some of the advantages and disadvantages of the different methods of communication of health promotion campaigns.

Peer group education can be highly effective because of the personal touch.

- Your campaign is designed for a particular group and is therefore individualised for your chosen group.
- They can ask questions, listen to answers and hear other people's ideas.
- This is interpersonal interaction.

You must be well rehearsed and aware of your limitations – if you do not know the answer to a question, be honest and say so. Young children are often very keen to listen to older students from 'the big school'.

Table 4.20 Advantages and disadvantages of different communication methods

Method	Advantages	Disadvantages
Video	<ul><li>suitable for small/medium audience</li><li>can be stopped and started for discussion</li><li>can show reality</li></ul>	<ul><li>requires power supply</li><li>can break down</li><li>small screen limits audience size</li></ul>
Whiteboard	<ul><li>cheap and usually available</li><li>good for highlighting main points</li><li>can be reused</li></ul>	<ul><li>limited audience – up to 30</li><li>must have correct pens or can damage board</li></ul>
Posters	<ul><li>cheap, easy to make</li><li>raise awareness of health issues</li><li>can give contact emails/phone numbers</li></ul>	<ul><li>easily damaged</li><li>impact soon lost</li></ul>
Flipcharts	<ul><li>can be prepared in advance</li><li>easily portable</li><li>nothing to break down</li></ul>	<ul><li>easy to damage paper</li><li>limited to 20 people</li></ul>
PowerPoint presentation	<ul><li>can be prepared in advance</li><li>can be animated</li><li>can be projected onto large screen</li></ul>	<ul><li>can break down</li><li>requires electricity supply</li></ul>
Leaflets, handouts and other written materials	<ul><li>reduce need for note taking</li><li>information can be shared with others later</li><li>people can read later at own pace</li><li>can refer individuals to further help, e.g. websites or phone numbers</li></ul>	<ul><li>easily lost</li><li>not durable</li><li>need literacy skills</li><li>can be thrown away if not read</li></ul>

Appropriateness to individuals

1 Check through your health promotion material carefully to make sure it is suitable for your chosen group. For example, if you are educating young children, some of the information may be too difficult for them to understand and you may need to simplify it.
2 Check the resources available to reinforce the health message you wish to give.

Methods to engage target audience

You can use a variety of methods to engage your target audience, such as an activity. For example, if your health promotion campaign is about exercise:

- Encourage your audience to practise the lunge.
- Find a short film which demonstrates the correct way to perform a lunge.
- Demonstrate how to do the lunge yourself.

A quiz is another good way of engaging the audience, especially if you divide the audience into teams so they compete against one another.

Feedback methods

1 **Questions**: you can ask questions at the end of your talk and see if your audience can answer them.
2 **Questionnaire**: you could prepare a questionnaire to give out to the audience at the beginning of the campaign to measure their knowledge about the subject before you begin. After the campaign, you can check if the audience has gained knowledge by giving out a new copy of the same questionnaire. If you have been successful, more questions will have been answered correctly for the second questionnaire.
3 **Witness testimony**: any observers (such as the class teacher) should be asked to fill in a witness testimony. But you can also ask your audience what they thought of your campaign at the end of their questionnaire.

Test your knowledge

1 Why is it important to check that health promotion materials are suitable for the audience?
2 Why can peer group education be effective?
3 List three advantages of using leaflets in a health promotion campaign.
4 Give two disadvantages of using a PowerPoint presentation.

Synoptic link

Unit R035	Links with Unit R032: Principles of care in health and social care settings
Topic area 3: Plan and deliver a health promotion campaign	**Topic area 3:** Effective communication in health and social care settings

Unit R035 Health promotion campaigns

Topic area 4 Deliver and evaluate a health promotion campaign

Getting started

Within your health promotion group, discuss the following question:

- Are you looking forward to delivering your health promotion campaign?

If the answer is no, is that because you do not like the idea of public speaking? Many people are afraid of public speaking and feel embarrassed about standing up and talking to an audience.

There are many factors you must consider before making a presentation. For example, how can you ensure your communication skills meet the challenge of delivering a health promotion campaign? Think back to R032, especially Topic area 3.

- Decide which verbal and non-verbal skills you would need to consider to deliver a successful campaign.

4.1 How to deliver a health promotion plan

When you have planned your health promotion campaign, you have to deliver it and then evaluate it.

- You should choose a topic that you will feel confident in delivering.
- You need to understand the information you are presenting, so that you can explain the information and answer questions from the audience.

Introduce the campaign
- Tell your audience what you are going to talk to them about. For example, continuing the example of the healthy eating campaign aimed at Year 4 children, explain that you are going to tell them about the benefits of eating fruits and vegetables.
- You should also give your campaign a name.

Welcome
Welcome the audience to your campaign as soon as they arrive in the room.

The campaign group should separate and not all stand together at the front, as it may be intimidating for the Year 4 children. If the group mixes with the children, they will feel relaxed and interested to see new people in their school. Tell the children to take a seat and sit quietly until everyone is in the room.

OCR Cambridge National in Health and Social Care

Settle the individuals/audience

- The class teacher will be with the students, but you should tell the children to settle down as some of them might be excited.
- Tell the audience who you are (everyone in the group must introduce themselves) and which school you come from.
- You should explain what you are going to talk about and why they should listen to you.
- You may need to remind them several times throughout your talk to be quiet and listen.

Delivering content appropriate to the campaign

The depth of the material must be suitable for the age of the audience. For example, if you were delivering information on healthy eating, you would not deliver the message in the same way and in as much detail to children aged 8 years as to those aged 14 years.

Communicate clearly:

- Speak loudly and do not rush your words.
- Take your time and make sure everyone is quiet and listening.
- Encourage participation by asking the audience questions, but ask them to put their hand up so they do not shout out.

If you have activities for the audience to complete during your campaign, it is a good idea to walk around and offer help to those who are struggling. This also helps in your supervision of the audience and keep the children's focus on the session.

Provide support for other campaign group members if they cannot remember something – remember that you are all in it together and need to have a team approach.

Collect feedback

- The group you are delivering the health campaign to may also have asked questions during your delivery session, so you should note whether or not the questions were suitable (you will be able to tell if the group could answer them satisfactorily).
- At the beginning of your campaign, you should have given out witness testimonies to the adults in the room to complete, so you must collect these at the end.
- Collect completed questionnaires from the children in your audience at the end of your talk.

4.2 How to evaluate your own performance

Use feedback

The questionnaires should tell you whether your campaign has been successful. If you examine the pre-presentation questionnaires and compare them to the questionnaires after the presentation, you should be able to see an improvement in how many answers the audiences got right.

Analyse both sets of questionnaires so you will have data to prove that you improved the knowledge of your audience.

You will also have witness testimonies from the adults who were at your presentation. The audience may have given you some comments you could use as well.

Self-reflect

You will have your diary from the start of the project to help you with your reflection.

Look back at all areas of your work, from the planning stage to the end of the campaign. You need to consider what you did well, so look for positive aspects.

Review strengths and weakness

When reviewing your campaign, it might be helpful to ask yourself a series of questions about how you could improve your campaign if you were to do it again.

Your planning

Planning is an important part of any campaign; it can allow the individual to demonstrate their ability to plan and work things out. However, having planned the campaign the individual/group may have to revise their original plan as they realise that it will not be successful because they have overlooked something. For example, they may plan to deliver their campaign on a certain date but the audience may not be available then, so they have to move the delivery date forward, giving them less time to work on the campaign. Working in groups can cause issues as some members of the group may not deliver what they have promised and the other members of the group may feel let down as they have to do extra work to compensate.

Your communication skills

Communication skills are an important part of the delivery of a campaign. If you do not communicate with your audience you risk not passing on the messages you would like them to receive. This would make the campaign and all the effort you have put into it a waste of time. To be successful the presentation must be well rehearsed, and the materials used must be well presented. For example, if you are

OCR Cambridge National in Health and Social Care

using a PowerPoint the audience must be able to read it so there should not be too much information on each of the slides. Any questionnaires given out to the audience must be suitable for the age group so they are able to understand it and respond to the questions asked.

How you engaged individuals

When delivering the campaign it is important to notice if the audience are enjoying your presentation, so you should look for signs of this. For example, signs of engagement might be that they are paying attention or look interested or are asking questions. It is good practice to have a selection of activities that the audience can take part in, so they are not just listening all the time. It is even better if they can extend their knowledge whilst having fun and enjoying the presentation. The audience should know more about the topic at the end of the presentation than they did at the beginning, so questionnaires before and after the event may be useful.

Suggest improvements

There is always room to improve – evaluation is important so that we can do better next time.

During your review of your campaign, you might have thought of minor points that could be improved, but these could be the difference between a good presentation and an excellent one. It does not mean that your presentation has been unsuccessful if you can think of improvements – it is more important that you are aware of your performance.

What would you do differently, and why?

When you evaluate your campaign you must evaluate all your strengths and weaknesses throughout the whole period of your planning, delivery (to include communication skills and audience engagement) and evaluation of your campaign.

Ask yourself: if you were to do the same campaign for another group, which areas could be improved, and why?

- Remember to use feedback from your witness testimonies – they might include suggestions to help you improve.
- The data from the questionnaires should also help you decide if you were successful.

Synoptic link

Unit R035	Links with Unit R032: Principles of care in health and social care settings
Topic area 4: Deliver and evaluate a health promotion campaign	**Topic area 3:** Effective communication in health and social care settings

Unit R035 Health promotion campaigns

Assignment practice

You are a nursery nurse at your local nursery, Busy Badgers. The manager has asked you to plan a health promotion campaign for a small group of parents who want to improve the health and fitness of themselves and their children. The children chosen are nearly four years old. She knows you are interested in keeping healthy and fit. She hopes the information you give the parents will help them and their children to improve their overall health. She wants you to present your findings about your chosen public health challenge to the parents in a handout so they can decide if they would like to take part.

Task 1: Plan a public health challenge

Task 1a: Choose a public health challenge and, from this, a health promotion campaign

Topic area 1 is assessed in this task:

- section 1.1 The importance of a healthy society
- section 1.2 Public health challenges for society.

Your first step is to research the current public health challenges and choose one that you think would be suitable for this group of parents, explaining the reasons for your choice. You must then explain why it is important for this public health challenge to be met.

Top tips

1. When researching and choosing your health challenge topic, remember to consider your audience and decide if the topic would be suitable for them. In this model assignment it is for parents of nursery-age children.
2. When you research and use information from books and websites, make sure it is referenced.
3. Ask your teacher whether your chosen public health challenge is appropriate.
4. Remember, your handout must explain:
   - reasons for your choice of the public health challenge
   - why addressing public health challenges is important to a healthy society.

Task 1b: Choose your health promotion campaign

Topic areas 1 and 2 are addressed in this task:

- Topic area 1, section 1.3 Current health promotion campaign
- Topic area 2, section 2.1 Factors influencing health and well-being
- Topic area 2, section 2.2 Leading a healthy lifestyle
- Topic area 2, section 2.3 Barriers leading to a healthy lifestyle.

The nursery manager and parents agree with your chosen health challenge, as they feel it would be a useful challenge which would have a positive impact on the children, as well as the parents. But before you plan your campaign, the manager asks you to produce a handout which will explain to parents the factors that could influence health and well-being. Also, in this handout you need to explain the barriers to leading a healthy lifestyle that these parents face. PIES benefits should be covered when explaining how to follow the advice of the health promotion campaign.

Top tips

1. When you research and use information from books and websites, make sure it is referenced.
2. In your handout you must include:
   - who the target audience is
   - an explanation of the factors that could influence the health and well-being of the parents
   - an explanation of the barriers to leading a healthy lifestyle for the parents
   - an explanation of the benefits (in terms of PIES) of following the advice of the health promotion campaign.

Task 2: Plan a health promotion campaign

Topic area 3 is assessed in this task: Plan and create a health promotion campaign.

OCR Cambridge National in Health and Social Care

The manager at Busy Badgers has now asked you to plan and create a health promotion campaign for the parents.

Top tips

1. When researching and choosing your health promotion topic, remember to consider your audience and decide if the topic would be suitable for them. In this model assignment, it is for parents of nursery-age children.
2. When you research and use information from books and websites, make sure they are referenced properly.
3. Start a diary or logbook before you start the campaign to record anything that happens.
4. Work out your aims, as this will help you to plan the resources you need.
5. Plan timescales carefully – they are very important as you will need plenty of time to organise resources, etc.
6. Use your own words to explain information; do not complicate the text.
7. Think about the communication skills you covered in Topic area 3 about effective communication.
8. Your health promotion plan must include:
   - aims of the campaign
   - timescales
   - resources needed
   - safety considerations
   - communication
   - appropriateness to individuals
   - methods to be used to engage the target audience
   - how you will gather feedback from your performance.

Task 3: Evaluate your own performance

Topic area 4 is assessed in this task: Deliver and evaluate a health promotion campaign.

As the manager intends to run these health promotion sessions in the future, she has asked you to evaluate your health campaign.

Top tips

1. Use all your feedback materials for your evaluation such as questionnaires, diary/logbook, any feedback form or any comments made by your audience to help you.
2. Self-reflection means giving your own opinion in your own words about what you did.
3. Write about what you did well and what you did not, and how you could improve.
4. Use feedback and self-reflection to evaluate your own performance, considering:
   - strengths and weaknesses of your planning, your communication skills, how you engaged individuals
   - suggestions for improvements: what you would do differently and why.

Read about it

Weblinks

www.ons.gov.uk

Office for National Statistics – this website has statistics about the economy, society and the population at national, regional and local level.

www.bhf.org.uk

British Heart Foundation – this website provides information about all aspects of heart disease and risk factors such as smoking etc as well diet for a healthy heart, exercising etc.

www.drinkaware.co.uk

Drinkaware covers all aspects of alcohol including health effects of alcohol.

Unit R035 Health promotion campaigns

www.nhsconfed.org/calendar-national-campaigns

This website gives detailed information on NHS health and well-being campaigns supported by downloadable resources, such as posters.

www.gov.uk/government/publications/prevention-is-better-than-cure-our-vision-to-help-you-live-well-for-longer

This website gives the Government's 'Prevention is better than cure' vision to help people live well for longer.

www.nhs.uk/conditions/sexually-transmitted-infections-stis

This NHS website gives information and advice on all sexually transmitted infections.

www.twinkl.co.uk/resources/nutrition/food-and-drink-and-eating/fruit-and-vegatable/2

Downloadable resources on many different topics across all school ages from 4 to 18 years. Excellent worksheets for healthy eating. Type 'fruit and vegetables' into the search box on the twinkl page.

Reference books

Fisher, A. et al. (2012) *Applied AS Health and Social Care*. Oxford University Press.

Peteiro, M.F. et al. (2016) *Cambridge Technicals Level 3 Health and Social Care*. Hodder Education.

Glossary

Abstract thinking Being able to solve problems using the imagination.

Adrenaline auto-injector (e.g. EpiPen) An emergency treatment for use if someone has a severe anaphylactic reaction. It is an automatic injector device which contains a dose of adrenaline which is injected into the thigh.

Age spots Flat brown or black spots on the skin that increase with age.

Agility The ability to move the body quickly and easily.

Anaesthetist A doctor who specialises in pain relief and anaesthetics during surgery.

Anaphylactic shock An extreme allergic reaction. Common causes and triggers can be nuts, celery, seafood, and wasp or bee stings.

Anti-discriminatory practices Practices that prevent discrimination from occurring, by treating people equally, fairly and lawfully, and are not affected by their age, gender or culture.

Arthritis A medical condition that affects joints by causing pain, stiffness, swelling and reduced mobility of the joints.

Attention deficit hyperactivity disorder (ADHD) Symptoms include a short attention span, constant fidgeting and impulsive behaviour.

Bacteria Microscopic single-celled organisms which exist everywhere. Many are harmless and some are good for our bodies, but some cause bacterial infection such as salmonella which causes food poisoning. Cholera and tuberculosis (TB) are also caused by bacteria.

Beliefs Ideas that are accepted as true and real by the person that holds them. They could be religious or cultural.

Bereavement Coping with change following the death of someone very close.

Body dysmorphic disorder A mental health condition related to a person's body image, where they are extremely anxious about their physical appearance and see themselves differently from how others see them. For example, they might see one or more parts of their body as too big or too small.

Bronchitis Infection of the main airways of the lungs.

Cardiology A branch of medicine that specialises in diseases of the heart.

Cerebral palsy A lifelong neurological condition that is caused by damage to the brain before, during or soon after birth. This condition affects the body's movements and muscle co-ordination. Symptoms can include jerky uncontrolled movements, and stiff or floppy arms and legs.

Cognitive development The construction of thought processes, including remembering, problem solving and decision making, from childhood through to adulthood.

Confidentiality Limits access or places restrictions on sharing certain types of sensitive information, such as medical records, so that it is kept private and available only to those who need to be aware of it.

Conscious The part of your mind that is responsible for thinking, such as making decisions.

Consultation The process of discussing an issue with another person in order to receive their thoughts, advice or opinion, so that a decision can be made that is acceptable and appropriate for all involved.

Contingency planning A process that takes account of possible future events, i.e. emergencies.

Coronary heart disease This illness develops when arteries of the heart become narrower because of a build-up of fatty material (cholesterol).

Cortisol The body's main stress hormone secreted by the adrenal glands found at the top of the kidneys.

Culture Refers to particular ideas, traditions and customs practiced and shared by a group of people, usually from a particular country, community or society.

Cystic fibrosis A genetic disorder where the lungs and digestive system become clogged with mucus.

Dementia A group of symptoms that affect how a person thinks, remembers, solves problems, uses language, communicates and carries out tasks and activities. They occur when brain cells stop working properly and the brain is damaged by injury, or by disease such as Alzheimer's.

Glossary

Depression A medical condition causing low mood that affects your thoughts and feelings. It can range from mild to severe, but usually lasts for a long time and affects your day-to-day living.

Dexterity The ability to perform an action with the hands skilfully.

Diabetes A condition where the amount of glucose in the blood is too high because the body cannot use it properly.

Disability A physical impairment or weakness that affects an individual's ability to do daily activities.

Disclosure This is when a service user tells you directly, or indirectly through their behaviour, that they have been, or are being, abused.

Diversity The differences individuals and groups have from each other such as appearance, gender, disabilities, cultural or religious background.

Domiciliary care agency An organisation that provides care and support to individuals in their own home.

Empathy The ability to identify with another person's situation and understand how they may be feeling or thinking.

Emphysema A lung disease which causes shortness of breath.

Empowerment Giving someone the authority or control to do something. The way a health or social care service provider encourages a service user to make decisions and to take control of their own life.

Endorphins Chemical substances produced by the brain to reduce pain.

Equality Act 2010 A law intended to prevent discriminatory practice, to ensure service users are treated fairly.

Equality This means treating people fairly and valuing them for who they are. Everyone should be provided with the same rights and opportunities, and this should not be affected by their age, ability, gender, culture or religion.

Fine motor skills Smaller actions using the smaller muscles, such as grasping an object between the thumb and a finger when holding a paintbrush or pencil.

First aid The immediate treatment provided for a service user who has an accident or is suddenly taken ill.

Fungi Organisms that include yeast, moulds and mushrooms. Fungal infections usually affect the skin; examples are athlete's foot, ringworm or candida (thrush).

Gender The socially constructed characteristics of men and women such as roles, expressions and behaviour.

Gender identity A person's sense of their gender and how they feel; this may not be the same as the sex that they were assigned at birth i.e. male, female or non-binary.

Gender stereotypes An oversimplified idea of how people are expected to behave, based on their gender. An example is expecting all boys to only enjoy playing with toy cars, while all girls will only enjoy playing with dolls.

Gross motor skills The larger movements of arms, legs, feet or the entire body using the large muscles, for walking, running, skipping and jumping.

Haemophilia An inherited disorder where the blood does not clot.

Halal Foods that are permitted to be eaten under Islamic dietary laws. An animal can only be eaten if it has been slaughtered in a particular way.

Health and Safety Executive (HSE) The official supervisory body for the health, safety and welfare of people in work settings in the UK.

Holistic care Looking after the whole person, i.e. physically, intellectually, emotionally, socially and spiritually.

Homeostasis How the body adjusts to maintain a constant and steady state. For example, blood sugar levels are kept constant by the supply of insulin from the pancreas.

Hormones Chemical substances produced in the body by the endocrine glands and transported in the blood to other organs in the body. Examples are adrenaline, oestrogen, testosterone.

Hygiene Practices that keep yourself and your surroundings clean in order to prevent illness and the spread of disease.

Infection What happens when germs (pathogens), for example bacteria, viral, fungal or parasitic, invade the body and cause a disease or illness.

Jargon Specialist or technical language, or terms and abbreviations, that are difficult for non-specialists to understand.

Kosher Foods that are permitted to be eaten under Jewish dietary laws, and that can be used as ingredients when preparing food.

Language and cognitive development Learning language and cognitive skills, such as understanding and using words, communicating, thinking, remembering and problem solving.

Law These are passed by Parliament, and state the rights and entitlements of service users. If someone breaks the law, they can be prosecuted by being taken to court.

Learning difficulties A type of difficulty in processing some types of information, such as dyslexia. A person's general intelligence is not affected.

Learning disability A reduced ability to think and make decisions, as well as difficulties with everyday activities.

LGBTQ+ This stands for Lesbian, Gay, Bisexual, Transgender, Queer, Questioning, Intersex, Allies, Asexual and Pansexual.

Life story work An activity that involves reviewing a person's past life events and developing a biography to understand more about the individual and their experiences.

Makaton A form of communication that uses signs and symbols to help adults and children who have difficulties with speech to communicate.

Manual handling Using the correct procedures when physically moving any load by lifting, putting down, pushing or pulling; for example, transferring a client from a chair to a bed.

Mortality Death.

MRSA This is often called a superbug as it is highly resistant to treatment. It usually affects people who are weakened by surgery or illness.

'Need-to-know' basis Information is only shared with those directly involved with the care and support of the service user.

Neural growth Any growth of the nervous system.

Non-binary A person who does not identify as only male or only female; they may identify as both male and female or as neither. The + in the acronym **LGBTQ+** is used to emphasise the diversity of sexualities and gender identities.

Non-verbal communication Messages that are conveyed without words, such as body language and facial expressions including eye contact, body movements and hand gestures.

Obsessive compulsive disorder (OCD) An anxiety disorder characterised by obsessive thoughts and compulsive activities.

Obstetrician A doctor specialising in the care of pregnant women, who assists with births if there are complications.

Oncology A branch of medicine concerned with the diagnosis and treatment of cancer.

Pathogen A bacterium, virus, fungus or parasite that can cause disease. Often more simply known as germs.

Peer group A group of people, usually of the same age, who have similar interests, background and social status. A peer group can influence the behaviour of group members.

Physical disability A condition that affects and limits the way a person moves and their ability to perform physical activities.

Pneumonia A lung infection which causes problems with breathing.

Podiatrist A health professional who provides foot care such as removing corns, hard skin and ingrowing toe nails.

Puberty The process of bodily changes that occur during adolescence, as a child grows into an adult capable of sexual reproduction.

Reflex An involuntary or unconscious response to a stimulus, such as the leg moving when the knee is tapped. In reflexology, the stimulus is provided when pressure is applied to the reflex area on the feet.

Royal College of Speech and Language Therapists (RCSLT) The professional body for speech and language therapists in the UK.

Safeguarding Actions taken to protect service users by ensuring a safe and healthy environment where the risks of danger, harm or abuse are reduced.

Safety measure A particular action, such as putting up a 'Wet floor' sign.

Safety procedure A set process that is followed, such as a fire drill or carrying out risk assessments.

Sciatic nerve A nerve that runs from your lower back through your hips, legs and down to your feet.

Glossary

Sciatica A condition where the sciatic nerve, which runs from the lower back to the feet, is irritated or compressed, causing inflammation, numbness and pain.

Self-awareness The knowledge a person has of their own character and emotions.

Self-esteem How much a person values themselves and the life they live. High self-esteem is associated with people who are happy and confident. A service user with low self-esteem experiences feelings of unhappiness and worthlessness.

Self-worth Confidence and value in your own abilities and qualities.

Sharps Examples include used needles and cannulas (thin tubes that surround a flexible needle that is inserted into a vein to administer medication from a drip). These can cause injury by a needle or sharp edge pricking or cutting the skin.

Sickle cell anaemia An inherited disorder where the red blood cells become crescent or sickle-shaped. It can cause tiredness, pain, infections which may need hospitalisation, and delayed growth or puberty.

Sonographer A health professional who is specially trained to carry out ultrasound scans.

Specialist communication skills Communications with people who have a wide range of needs, i.e. Braille (used by people who are blind or visually impaired and are unable to access materials in print), BSL (used by people who are deaf or hearing impaired), voice-activated software (used by people who have difficulties with their mobility (their ability to move) or in using a keyboard to type due to a physical disability or a learning disability).

Statutory care Services that are provided and paid for by the government such as the NHS.

Stroke A life-threatening medical condition that occurs when the blood supply to part of the brain is cut off by a clot or bleed. Depending on the part of the brain it damages, it can affect how your body works, your communication and how you think and feel.

Subconscious The part of your mind that works without your awareness or control, such as your breathing, your emotions and memories.

Thread veins Very slender veins on the face that are visible through the skin. These are caused by over-exposure to the sun.

Tone The way something is said, such as cheerfully, empathetically, angrily or sarcastically.

Type 1 diabetes This illness causes the level of glucose (sugar) to become too high. It happens when the body cannot produce enough insulin, which controls blood glucose.

Type 2 diabetes This illness can be caused by lifestyle. It usually appears in people over the age of 40. It is, however, becoming more common in children and young people. Type 2 diabetes accounts for between 85 and 95 per cent of all people with diabetes and is treated with a healthy diet and increased physical activity. Medication is often required.

Values Those things in our lives that we value as very important. They can include, for example, our family, our friends, our health, our freedom and our rights.

Valuing diversity Accepting and respecting individual differences such as faith, diet, sexuality, ethnicity and customs.

Verbal communication Using words to speak or talk with others.

Virus Tiny pathogens that need to enter the cells of a living being to be able to multiply. An example is rhinovirus, which causes the common cold. Other examples of viruses include influenza and COVID-19.

Vulnerable A word to describe someone who is less able to protect themselves from harm or exploitation due to, for example, mental health problems, a learning disability or physical impairment such as mobility problems, loss of hearing or sight.

Written communication skills Aspects of written communication, which can include the typeface and font size used for the text, use of grammar, punctuation and spelling, formal or informal styles of writing, and the language used.

Zero-hours contract An employer does not have to provide a minimum number of hours of work for an employee, therefore on some days the employee will have no work and no pay. However, zero-hours workers are entitled to statutory paid annual leave of 5.6 weeks and the national minimum wage in the same way as regular workers.

Index

Note: page numbers in **bold** refer to key word definitions.

abstract thinking **75**, 76
abuse/harm
    accident prevention 57–8
    children's services 112
    domestic abuse 85, 95
    financial abuse 51
    institutional abuse 51
    planning creative activities 160
    protection from 5
    reporting concerns 17, 47, 52, 65
    safeguarding 47–53
access to services 91, 95, 214–15
accident prevention 57, 58, 160
accidents (unexpected life events) 97, 104, 111
active listening 35–6, 44, 45
adapting homes 110
addiction 113, 196–7
adolescence 74–7, 98
adrenaline auto-injectors **58**
advertising 193, 218
advocacy 37–8
age spots 216, **216**
Age UK 115
ageing
increased life expectancy 192
    intellectual 80
    physical 79
    signs of 77
aggression 48
agility 145, **145**
air pollution 94
alcohol 83, 196–7, 209
allergies 58
anaesthetists **31**
anaphylactic shock 58, **58**
antibiotics 190
anti-discriminatory practices 152, **154**
anxiety/fear *see also* stress
    mental health promotion campaigns 211–12
    mind-body healing 131–2
    psychological therapies 210
    as response to life events 87, 89, 97
    services for 109
    social activities 151
aromatherapy 127–8, 138, 139, 141
art activities 149
art therapy 133, 138, 139, 140, 141
arthritis 20, 29, 77, 134, **134**
attachment 74, 88

attention deficit hyperactivity disorder (ADHD) 148, **149**, 150
bacteria 189–90, **189**
bacterial infection prevention 54–6
balanced diet 82, 193–4, 216
BAME (Black, Asian and minority ethnic groups) 93, 213
bankruptcy 104, 108
beliefs 152, **152** *see also* cultural factors; religion
bereavement 88, 100, **100**, 106
bills, paying 90, 212
blind people *see* visual impairments
body dysmorphic disorder 131, **131**
body language 28, 32–5, 164
body mass index (BMI) 108, 194–5, 199
bonding (parent-child) 74
book clubs 153
Braille 28, 38
British Sign Language 39
bronchitis **204**, 205
bullying 87, 101
cancer 83, 191, 201, 204
cardiology 111, **111**
care agencies 121, **121**
Care Certificate standards 17
care homes 112
care plans 18, 19
care settings, types of 3
care standards 18
carers 84, 86, 120, 121
caring attitude 169
cerebral palsy 40, 97, 131, **131**, 148
challenging behaviours 48
charities
    public health 206
    support from 109, 115, 119
cheerfulness 168
childcare 78
children
    child carers 84, 86
    childhood development 71–4
    dental health 205
    safeguarding 51
children's services 112–13
choice
    personalised support through life events 121
    person-centred values 14, 15, 17, 19, 20
    in residential settings 4
cholesterol 199
chromosomes 84
chronic illness 97, 105
circulation 145

Citizens Advice 109
cleanliness 54, 217
clinical commissioning groups (CCGs) 189
cognitive activities 143, 146
cognitive decline 80
cognitive development 73, **73**, 143
cognitive therapies 130–2, 138, 139, 140, 141
commitment (6Cs qualities of a service provider) 17
communicable diseases 189–91, 195–6
communication
    active listening 35–6, 44, 45
    communication skills 27–46, 146, 166, 180
    effective communication 27–46
    impact of poor communication skills 44–5, 166
    importance of effective 42–6
    language development 73
    non-verbal communication skills 32–5, 139, **139**, 166
    planning a health promotion campaign 223
    planning creative activities 162
    play therapy 134
    qualities of a service provider (6Cs) 16
    specialist communication skills 36–41, 45, 166, **168**
    verbal communication 27–31, 139, **139**, 166
    written communication skills 166, **168**
communication profiles/passports 42–4
community bonds 92
compassion 16
competence (6Cs qualities of a service provider) 16
concerns, reporting 17, 47, 52, 65
confidentiality 5, **5**, 17, 30, 34
conscious mind 130, **130**
consultation 7, **7**, 19
contingency plans 162
co-ordinated care 121
coping strategies 217
coronary heart disease 197, **198**
cortisol 140, **140**
costs
    activities 158
    care 191
    healthy lifestyles 220
counsellors 118, 215

Index

courage (6Cs qualities of a service provider) 17
COVID-19 190, 215
creative activities
    benefits of 142-7, 154-7
    delivering and evaluating 166-86
    planning 147-65
Cruse 115
cultural factors
    culture (definition) **152**
    effect on growth and development 92
    eye contact 32-3
    health promotion 213
    informal support structures 114
    planning creative activities 152
cystic fibrosis 210, **210**
day centres 112
DBS (Disclosure and Barring Service) 52-3
deaf people 39, 43 *see also* hearing impairments
debt 89-90, 104, 108, 109
decision-making 15, 17, 78 *see also* choice
dementia **37**, 80, 132, **132**, 149, 151
demonstrations 163, 224
dental health 205
depression 97, 130, **130**, 151, 204, 211
dexterity 145, **145**
diabetes 149, **149**, 191, **202**, 210, **210**
diet *see* food and diet
dieticians 117
dignity 14, 17
disability *see also* hearing impairments; mental illness; mobility issues; visual impairments
    communication profiles/passports 43
    definition **85**
    as life event 85
    person-centred values 15
    physical disability **168**
    planning creative activities 148
    social exclusion 86
disclosures (safeguarding) 47, **47**
discrimination
    anti-discriminatory practices 152, **154**
    Equality Act 2010 15
    person-centred values 17, 18, 20
    racial 93
    sources of 86
disease prevention 189-91, 195-6
disposable income 212
diversity 18, **18**, 152, **153**, 167
divorce/separation 78, 85, 99-100, 106
domestic abuse 85, 95
domiciliary care agencies 121, **121**

door systems 65
drama 134, 145, 151
DSL (Designated Safeguarding Lead) 50, 52
dying 113
Dynavox 40
Eatwell Plate 193-4
economic factors in growth and development 89
education
    access to services 95
    benefits of good education 91
    children's services 112-13
    exclusion from school 101-2, 107
    literacy 73, 76, 95, 213
    qualifications 213
    starting school 101, 107
emails 31
emergency procedures 61-2, 162
emotional effects (PIES framework)
    accidents 97
    adolescence 76
    adulthood 78
    benefits of therapies 140
    childhood development 73
    creative activities 144, 146
    on growth and development 87
    healthy lifestyles 216-17
    informal support structures 119
    lack of safeguarding 49
    not applying person-centred values 22, 23
    older adulthood 81
    planning creative activities 150
emotional neglect 95
empathy 28, 35, 141, **141**, 167, 169
emphysema **204**
employment 89, 102, 212
empowerment 9, **9**, 20
encouraging participation 166-71, 172-3, 181
endorphins 138, **138**, 202, 211
enhanced DBS 53
EpiPens (adrenaline auto-injectors) 58, **58**
equal and fair treatment 6
equality **13**, 152, **153**, 167
Equality Act 2010 **4**, 15
equipment
    safety of 161
    staff training in use of 59, 63
evacuation procedures 61-2
evaluation of activities 178-84
evaluation of health promotion campaigns 225, 227-8
examinations, preparing for 76
exclusion from school 101-2, 107

exercise
    across life stages 83
    benefits of healthy lifestyles 217
    costs of healthy lifestyles 220
    creative activities 148
    health promotion 199, 202, 210
    and mental health 211
expressive therapies 133-4, 138, 139, 140, 141
extended families, support from 114
eye contact 32-5
facial expressions 33
fair treatment 6
fall prevention 50
family income levels 86, 89, 100, 109, 212-13, 220
family security 88
family/friends, support from 114, 119-20, 212, 219
fats 198
fear *see* anxiety/fear; stress
feedback on creative activities 163-5, 175-6, 178-9
feedback on health promotion campaigns 224, 226, 227
finances
    bankruptcy 104, 108
    debt 89-90, 104, 108, 109
    disposable income 212
    health and well-being 212, 220
    income levels 86, 89, 100, 109, 212-13, 220
    life events 104-8
    services for 109
    support from practitioners 120
financial abuse 50
fine motor skills 40, 71-2, **71**, 77, 143, **143**, 145
fire evacuations 61-2
fire safety 63
first aid **57**, 58, 61
five Rs (safeguarding) 52
flu 195-6
food and diet
    balanced diet 82, 193-4, 216
    costs of healthy food 89, 220
    diet and nutrition and development 82
    diet and stroke/heart disease 198
    diet choices 209
    halal 152, **152**
    infection prevention 55
    kosher 152, **152**
    low-income households 89, 220
    nutrition 82
    obesity 82, 108-9, 191, 192-5, 202, 209, 220
    person-centred values 17, 21

planning creative activities 152
safeguarding 50
vitamins and minerals 82
food banks 89
forgetfulness 80
friendliness 168
friendships 74, 78
fungi 189–90, **189**
gardening 142, 144, 149, 150
gender 152–3, **152**
gender identity 93, **152**
gender stereotypes 152, **153**
genetic disorders 98, 105, 210
genetics 84, 210
gesture 28, 33–4
Gingerbread 115
good practice, sharing 19
GPs (General Practitioners) 116, 220
grief 88 see also bereavement
gross motor skills 71, 142, **142**, 145
group work 163
haemophilia 210, **210**
halal 152, **152**
hand washing 55
hand-eye coordination 71, 145
handwriting 73, 76
harm see abuse/harm
hazard prevention 57–8, 160–1
health and safety **5**, 59, 61, 159
Health and Safety at Work Act 58, 159
Health and Safety Executive (HSE) 159, **159**, 160
Health and Safety (First Aid) Regulations 58, 61
health campaigns 189
health centres 111, 116
health literacy 213
health promotion 187–231
health visitors 117
healthcare services
    access to 91, 214–15
    public health 190, 196, 206
    support for life events 111, 116
healthcare settings 3
healthcare workers 118
hearing impairments
    creative activities 144
    and life events 85
    planning creative activities 150, 151
    sign language 28, 39
    volume of voice 30
hearing loop systems 9, 28
heart disease 198–9, **198**
hoists 59
holistic care 112, **112**
holistic therapies/treatments 220
homeostasis 82, **83**
hormones 75, 76, 80, 138, **138**

hospices 113
hospitals 111
housing needs and conditions 94
humour 35
hygiene 53–4, **53**, 217
hypnotherapy 130–1, 140
ID badges 64–5
ill health 84, 97, 105, 111 see also chronic illness; mental illness
imaginative activities 144–5
immune systems 87
imprisonment 102–3, 107
income levels 86, 89, 100, 109, 212–13, 220
independence 14, 18, 110, 120
Independent Living 110
individuality 13, 17
infection prevention 53–6, **53**, 217
infectious disease 190, 195–6
influenza 195–6
informal support 114–15, 119–20
insecure attachment 88
institutional abuse 50
intellectual effects (PIES framework)
    accidents 97
    adolescence 76
    adulthood 78
    benefits of therapies 139
    childhood development 72–3
    creative activities 143, 146
    healthy lifestyles 216–17
    informal support structures 119
    lack of safeguarding 49
    of not applying person-centred values 21, 22
    older adulthood 80
    planning creative activities 149
interpersonal skills 27 see also communication
interpreters 28, 40
jargon **28**, 44
job loss 102
keys, monitoring 65
kosher 152, **152**
language
    creative activities 146
    language development 73, **143**
    languages other than English 29, 43
    non-discriminatory 17
    using appropriate 28–9
law 4, **4**
learning difficulties 110, 149, **149**, 166
learning disabilities 43, 98, **168**
LGBTQ+ **153** see also sexuality
life events, impact of 96–110
life expectancy 192
life stages 70–95
life story work **132**, 133, 149

lifestyle choices 82, 83, 209–10
lifting procedures 60
Lightwriter 40
literacy 73, 76, 95, 213
local authority care 121
lockdown procedures 62
loneliness 100 see also social effects (PIES framework)
low income households 86, 89, 100, 109, 212–13, 220
Makaton 40, 41, 166, **168**
manual handling **5**, 48, 60
marriage/partnerships 78
massage 129–30, 138, 140
medication, safeguarding 50
meditation 132, 139
memory development 73
memory loss 149, 151
menopause 77, 98–9, 105
menstruation 74–5, 98
mental health see also stress
    access to services 215
    benefits of healthy lifestyles 217
    benefits of maintaining service users' rights 9
    growth and development 84
    health promotion 203–4
    lifestyle choices 211–12
    practitioner support 120
    sadness/happiness 87–8
    services for 109
    social activities 151
mental illness see also anxiety/fear
    depression 97, 130, **130**, 151, 204, 211
    life events 84
    public health 203–4
mental stimulation 217
midwives 116
MIND 109, 115, 215
mind-body healing 131–2, 138, 141
mindfulness 132
mobility issues
    creative activities 148, 149
    encouraging decision-making 15
    life events 104–5
    mobility aids 15, 110
    older adulthood 29, 80
    physiotherapists 117
    practitioner support 120
    privacy and dignity 17
    safeguarding 50
money
    bankruptcy 104, 108
    debt 89–90, 104, 108, 109
    disposable income 212
    health and well-being 212, 220
    income levels 86, 89, 100, 109,

Index

212–13, 220
life events 104–8
services for 109
support from practitioners 120
moral impacts of creative activities 146
mortality 192, **192**
moving and handling techniques **5**, 48, 60
MRSA 190, **190**
music 72, 133, 143, 151
'need to know' basis 5, **5**
needs assessments 113, 121
neglect 95
neighbourhoods 93, 94, 114
neural growth **80**
NHS Long Term Plan 201
noise pollution 94
non-binary people 152, **153**
non-verbal communication skills 32–5, 139, **139**, 166
nurses 116
nutrition *see* food and diet
obesity 82, 108–9, 191, 192–5, 202, 209, 220
obsessive compulsive disorder (OCD) 150, **150**
obstetricians 31, **31**
occupational therapists 118
older adulthood 80–1, 103
oncology 111, **111**
overcrowded housing 94
pace of speech 30
pain
co-ordinated care 121
effects of lack of safeguarding 49
effects of not applying person-centred values 23
life events 84, 104, 105
lifestyle choices 210
long-term illness 97
mind-body healing 131–2
physical activities 142–3, 145
therapies 135, 137, 138
panic attacks 87
parenthood 78, 100, 106
partnership working 15, 18
pathogens 189–90, **189** *see also* bacteria
patience 28–9, 168–9
patient records 31, 44
patronising (not being) 44, 45
PECS (Picture Exchange Communication System) 40
peer groups **71**, 76, 77, 98, 223
peer pressure 219
personal care
infection prevention 55
manual handling **5**, 48, 60
safeguarding 48

personal hygiene 54–5, 217
personal information, confidentiality of **5**, 17, 30, 34
personal protective equipment (PPE) 56, 160–1
personal qualities, practitioners' 168–70
personal space 34
person-centred values 13–18, 42, 122
physical abuse 50
physical activities 142–3, 145
physical disability **168** *see also* disability
physical effects (PIES framework)
accidents 97
adolescence 74–7
adulthood 77–8
benefits of therapies 138
childhood development 71–2
creative activities 142–3
healthy lifestyles 216–17
importance of exercise 202
informal support structures 119
lack of safeguarding 49
life events 97–9
not applying person-centred values 21, 23
older adulthood 80
planning creative activities 148
physical health *see also* chronic illness; ill health; pain
growth and development 84
lifestyle choices 210–11
serious illness 84
physical therapies 134–7, 139, 140, 141
physiotherapists 117
PIES effects (physical, intellectual, emotional, social)
adolescence 74–7
adulthood 77–9
benefits of therapies 137–8
childhood development 71–4
definitions 21
healthy lifestyles 215–17
informal support structures 119–20
life events 97–108
older adulthood 80–1
planning a health promotion campaign 221
planning creative activities 148–51
safeguarding 49
unexpected life events 97
planning a health promotion campaign 221–30
planning creative activities 147–65
play therapy 133–4, 138, 139, 140, 141, 149
pneumonia **204**, 205

podiatrists 31, **31**
policies 50
positive thinking techniques 131, 132
poverty 86, 89
PPE (personal protective equipment) 56, 160–1
practitioners, support from 116–19, 120–2
pregnancy 100, 116, 205
pressure sores 50
primary healthcare 111
privacy
communication skills 30
person-centred values 14, 17
safeguarding 48
service users' rights 5
private healthcare 91
pronouns 153
psychological therapies 210 *see also* counsellors
puberty **71**, 74–5, 92, 98, 105
public health 187–231
qualities of a service provider (6Cs) 16
quality of care 20
quality of life 19, 20
questionnaires 165, 175, 224
race 93
rapport 35
record keeping 31, 44
redundancy 102, 107
reflective practice 179–80
reflexes 128, **128**, 140
reflexology 128–9, 138, 140
rehabilitation centres 113
reiki 136–7, 138, 139, 140, 141
Relate 115
relationships
family security 88
life events 78, 85, 99–100, 106
parenthood 78, 100, 106
relationship breakdown 78, 85, 99–100, 106
relaxation techniques 127, 129, 130–1, 149
religion
life events 91, 92
person-centred values 15, 17
planning creative activities 152
as source of support 114
reminiscence therapy 132–3, 139, 140, 141
residential social care settings 4, 6
resources for activities 157, 174
resources for health promotion campaigns 222
respect 15, 17, 44, 169
respite care 112, 113, 120

responsiveness 167
retirement 79, 102, 103, 107
rights
    benefits of maintaining 8–10
    service users' 2–10, 14, 42
    supporting inclusion 167
risk assessments 5, 58, 160
risk minimisation 160
role models 219
role play 134, 163
room layouts 34
Royal College of Speech and Language Therapists (RCSLT) 131, **131**
Run Hide Tell 62
rural areas 91, 121, 214
safe sex 210, 216
safeguarding
    five Rs (safeguarding) 52
    principles of 47–53
    reporting concerns 17, 52, 65
    service users' rights 5, **5**
safety in activities 159, 174
safety in health promotion 222–3
safety measures **57**, 63–7
safety procedures 57–63, **57**
sanitation 190
saturated fats 198
school-based life events 101–2, 107
sciatic nerve 128, **128**
sciatica 138, **138**
security measures 64–5
sedentary lifestyles 219
self-awareness 137, **137**
self-esteem 9, **9**, 76, 134, **134**, 146, 149, 202
self-help 210
self-reflection 179–80, 227
self-worth 146, **146**
sensory activities 144, 150
sensory gardens 150
sensory impairment 85 see also hearing impairments; visual impairments
sensory therapies 127–30, 133, 138, 139, 140, 141
separation/divorce 78, 85, 99–100, 106
serious illness 84
sexual health 200, 210, 216
sexuality 15, 77, 93
sharps 54, **54**
sickle cell anaemia 210, **210**
sight difficulties see visual impairments
sign language
    British Sign Language 39
    communication 28, 39
    Makaton 40, 41, 166, **168**
6Cs 16

sleep 83, 217
smoking 82, 83, 201, 204–5, 210, 216
social care settings 3
social effects (PIES framework)
    accidents 97
    adolescence 77
    adulthood 78
    benefits of therapies 141
    childhood development 74
    creative activities 144, 146
    on growth and development 85
    healthy lifestyles 216–17
    informal support structures 120
    lack of safeguarding 49
    not applying person-centred values 22, 23
    older adulthood 81
    planning creative activities 151
social exclusion 86
social inclusion 50, 86
social media 219
social services 3, 31, 95, 110, 112–13, 118
sonographers 31, **31**
sources of support 108–9, 111–24
spaces, choosing appropriate 34
spaces for activities 159
special educational needs 6, 149 see also disability; learning difficulties; learning disabilities
specialist communication skills 36–41, 45, 166, **168**
speech and language therapy 131, 138, 139
speech-activated software 39–40
standardisation of care 20
starting school 101, 107
statutory care 121, **121**
stress
    effects of not applying person-centred values 23
    impact of poor communication skills 44
    life events 78, 85, 87, 89, 97, 109
    lifestyle choices 211–12
    mind-body healing 131–2
    and physical activity 202
    psychological therapies 210
stroke patients 43, **131**, 198–9
subconscious mind 130, **130**
sugar 193, 206
sun protection 216
supervising activities 172–3
tai chi 136, 138, 139, 140, 141
team working 30–1
teeth, care of 205
telephone calls 31
text-to-speech technology 40

therapies 127–41
thread veins 216, **216**
timescales for planning activities 156–7, 174
timescales in planning health promotion campaigns 222
tone of voice 29, 166, **168**
training
    safeguarding 51
    safety procedures 59–63
translators 40
trip hazards 57–8
trust 10, 35
type 1 diabetes 210, **210**
type 2 diabetes 202, **202**
unexpected life events 96
uniforms, staff 64–5
universal services 112
unsaturated fats 199
utility bills 90, 104
vaccines 190, 196
values 152, **152** see also person-centred values
valuing diversity **18**
verbal communication 27–31, 139, **139**, 166
verbal reasoning skills 72
viruses 189–90, **189**, 195–6
visitors, security measures 65
visual impairments
    Braille 28, 38
    communication profiles/passports 43
    creative activities 144
    life events 85
    planning creative activities 150
visualisation techniques 131, 132
vitamins and minerals 82
vocabulary, appropriate 28, 29, 44, 45
voice-activated software 39–40
vulnerability 47–8, **47**
waste disposal 54
water, importance of clean 190
water pollution 94
wealth 90
weight loss 108–9
well-being
    factors influencing 209–20
    mind-body healing 131–2
wheelchair users 34, 159
willingness, practitioners' 170
witness testimonies 165, 175, 224
World Health Organization (WHO) 206
written communication skills 166, **168**
yoga 135–6, 138, 140
zero-hours contracts 89, 212, **212**

Lincroft Academy
Station Road, Oakley, Bedford MK43 7RE
School No. 8225404 Tel: 01234 822147
e-mail: administration@lincroft.academy
www.lincroft.beds.sch.uk

Lincroft Academy
Station Road, Oakley, Bedford MK43 7RE
School No. 8225404 Tel: 01234 822147
e-mail: administration@lincroft.academy
www.lincroft.beds.sch.uk